TRAINING YOU
TO
TRAIN YOUR DOG

TRAINING YOU

New Revised Edition

TO TRAIN YOUR DOG

by Blanche Saunders

Illustrations by **LOUISE BRANCH**
and **J. KILBURN KING**
Preface by **WALTER LIPPMANN**

Doubleday & Company, Inc.
Garden City, New York

Acknowledgment

I wish to express my appreciation to Louise Branch for her loyal encouragement and for her untiring efforts and skill in obtaining the splendid photographs illustrating the major points to be emphasized, and to Constance Campbell for her aid in revising my manuscript.

I also wish to thank the members of the New York A.S.P.C.A. training classes, the K-9 Obedience Club of Jacksonville, Florida, and the American Kennel Club for their co-operation, and J. Kilburn King for the replacement photographs to bring the book up to date.

Library of Congress Catalog Card Number 65-15553

Preface

by Walter Lippmann:

My reason for writing a few words of introduction to this admirably clear and most engaging book is that my wife and I are the happy owners of two large black poodles, graduates of the schooling which this book teaches, and at this moment of a litter of their six puppies who will soon become eligible to wear the old school tie.

Both poodles came from Mrs. Whitehouse Walker's Carillon Kennels at Bedford Hills, New York, where they were reared and trained by the author, Miss Blanche Saunders. Officially the female is named Carillon Caprice. But with the outer world what it has been in recent years, we did not wish to come home from our work to find a dog who lived up to that name, and was, as the dictionary says, "guided by whim or fancy rather than by judgement or a settled purpose." Our friend and near neighbor in Georgetown, Mrs. Hendrick Eustis, had a charming little flirt of a poodle named Muffin, and Alexander Woollcott, who took all poodles everywhere under his personal authority, ordered us to rename our poodle sweet muffin, that is to say Brioche. . . . The male dog is Champion Carillon Courage, C.D., C.D.X., a fine and fearless fellow, now nearly ten years of age, who likes everyone, believes the best of everyone, and has never heard about an inferiority complex.

What I have discovered from our dogs is that well-trained dogs are much more amusing companions. That is not because I have any interest in exhibiting them in a dog show, or even in having them do tricks. It is because training works on the dog's character, and carries him beyond the stage where he is merely housebroken to one where he is in fact civilized. I am not suggesting that he appreciates art and culture, but only that he has learned how to live, without being frustrated or annoying, with people who have work to do, and a circle of friends, and interests and pleasures.

This training gives something which is over and above the routine of the obedience tests. This is the most important result of the training for the ordinary person who is not a breeder, trainer, or exhibitor, and just wants a good dog. The training educates the dog's character and also, no doubt, the owner's character; the effect is to enable them to get on with each other. I have had untrained dogs, and much as I liked them, I must say that until Courage and Brioche came along I never knew what good companions dogs can be.

The reader may find this personal testimony helpful if, like myself, he has no special gift for dealing with dogs, as Miss Saunders undoubtedly had, but just happens to like dogs, and indeed most animals. I honestly do not know whether by reading this book everyone can train his own dog. I know I could not. For I haven't the time, or, to be really truthful, the perseverance and the patience. But for those who have these virtues, this book makes the matter as clear as it is possible to make it. When they read it, they will be listening to a woman who has practiced with immense success everything she teaches.

To all others, who cannot or will not train their own dogs, the book ought to carry conviction that for dogs, as well as for others, education and discipline are not the accompaniments of tyranny but are necessary to the pursuit of happiness, and contribute something for which shouting and petting, bearing and spoiling, sentimentality and irritability are no substitutes.

Introduction

Every owner wants his dog to obey willingly and happily. With this in mind, no attempt should be made to train the dog for competition in Obedience Trials until the dog has learned the exercises as outlined on the following pages. The praise, the extra commands, and the body motions so essential while teaching are not permitted in the obedience ring.

Owners should avoid using negative terms such as "No!", "Shame on you!", "Bad dog!" to correct the dog in training. A puppy about to get into mischief or even an older dog if he starts to do something he shouldn't, can be warned with "No-oo!" but when a dog has been given an obedience command which the dog disobeys, the command should be repeated. In other words, "Stay!" becomes "STAY!", "Come!" becomes "COME!" This positive approach gets quick results and the dog will obey more cheerfully.

Various factors such as the breed of dog, the age, and the temperament determine the degree of success while training, but mostly it is the ability of the owner to do the training. For best results, follow these basic rules: (1) Keep your dog's attention. (2) Don't let the dog sniff. (3) Give commands before you use the leash. (4) Give adequate praise. Owners can't go wrong if they will give praise after every command and with every tug on the leash. (5) When you use the leash, snap it with authority then give it slack. (6) Without yelling, use a demanding tone of voice when you repeat a command after the dog disobeys. And (7) Remember that the hand motions you used while teaching are the gestures you will use later for signals.

To lighten the chore of raising a puppy and to keep puppy discipline at a minimum, it is suggested that owners secure a wire cage (obtainable at most pet supply houses) in which the puppy can be safely left at intervals. This teaches a puppy to stay quietly by himself. Chewing and spite acts are curtailed. Housebreaking is made easier. At such times when the puppy cannot have supervision, it is nice to know that the puppy is safe from harm and that valuables are safe from the puppy.

Owners who plan to obtain their dog's obedience degrees should study the 1964 American Kennel Club Regulations and Standards for Obedience Trials printed in the Appendix. Permission for this printing has been granted by the American Kennel Club. The varied and miscellaneous items and training equipment used when teaching are not always allowed in the obedience ring. For instance, only certain types of collar may be worn. The dumbbell must be a certain kind and free of everything except paint or varnish. The bar for the Bar Hurdle must be 2 inches in diameter and painted black and white. The Seek Back article must be a glove. All jumps have definite specifications. The new Regulations and Standards, which will not affect the training of a dog, give rules that govern procedure and the judging of Obedience Trials. Exhibitors should be aware that there is a difference between teaching an exercise and the manner in which the exercise is carried out in the obedience ring.

B.S.

Contents

Introduction vii

Part 1: **THE PUPPY**

Choosing a Puppy 3
The Start of Training 8
Why Train a Dog? 11
Dogs and Children 14
The Trainer 17
Feeding and General Care of the Puppy . . 20
Grooming 24
Medical Care 28
The Medicine Chest 31
Worming 32
Car Sickness 33
Breeding the Pet 35
Care of the Brood Bitch 37
Puppy Discipline 41
How the Puppy Learns 42
Paper-breaking 42
Simple Training 45
Housebreaking 46
Curb-breaking 50
Teaching a Puppy to Stay by Himself . . . 52
Breaking the Habit of Barking 54
Teaching a Puppy Not to Chew Things . . 55
Teaching the Dog Not to Jump on People . . 57
Stealing and Refusing Food from Strangers . . 60

ix

Chasing Cars, Cats, and Children 61
The Mean Dog 64
Protection 66
How to Stop a Dog Fight 68
Teaching a Dog to Do Tricks 70
Teaching a Dog to Shake Hands 70
Teaching a Dog to Beg 71
Teaching a Dog to Roll Over 71
Teaching a Dog to Jump through Hoops . . 72
Teaching a Dog to Play "Dead" 73
Additional Tricks 73

Part 2: NOVICE OBEDIENCE TRAINING

Obedience Training 75
The Training Club and Class 76
The Training Class Director 82
How a Dog Learns 85
Know Your Dog's Disposition 86
Color versus Temperament 88
Voice and Signals 89
Do's and Don't's 91
Equipment for Training 93
How to Put on the Training Collar . . . 97
How to Hold the Leash 98
Heeling 100
Right-angle Turn 104
Left-angle Turn 105
Right-about Turn, Left-U-Turn, and Left-about
  Turn 106
Variation in Speed 106
Figure Eight 107
The Sit 107
The Come Fore 111
The Go-to-heel Position 115
The Sit and Stay 117
Teaching the Dog to Sit from a Down Position . 126
Manners during the Training Period . . . 128
Coming When Called (or Recall) 130
The Lie Down 137
The Down and Stay 149
The Stand 154

The Stand for Examination 157

The Drop on Recall 160

The Special or Review Exercise 163

Heel Free 166

Part 3: ADVANCED OBEDIENCE TRAINING

Introduction 171

Holding the Dumbbell (or Rolled Magazine or
Newspaper) 174

Take It 176

Carrying the Dumbbell and Other Articles . . 178

Taking the Dumbbell and Other Articles from the
Ground 181

Retrieving 188

Jumping 191

Retrieving over Hurdles 198

Broad Jump 202

Part 4: MORE ADVANCED TRAINING

Introduction 211

Speaking on Command 212

Stop Speaking 216

The Signal Exercise 216

Scent Discrimination 218

Seeking a Lost Article 227

Group Examination 230

Directed Jumping 231

Trailing and Tracking 239

The Show Ring 250

Conclusion 257

Voice Commands Used in Obedience Training . 260

Hand Signals Used in Obedience Training . . 260

Commands of Instructor or Judge to Handler . 261

APPENDIX 263

Forming a Dog Obedience Training Class . . 263

Obedience Trials Regulations 268

Obedience Trial Sample Judging Chart . . . 291

Sample Work Sheet When Judging 296

TRAINING YOU
TO
TRAIN YOUR DOG

(King photo)

Part 1: THE PUPPY

Don't spoil your dog but train and discipline him, and, above all, love him. The owner who feels that he cannot love his dog and at the same time train him thinks of training in terms of punishment. The fact is that when a person is sincere about his dog and is concerned over his welfare he will want to give him this expert care, because correct training is the best treatment a pet can receive and is a kindness that is often overlooked. Until recent years, all training was done by professionals. It was given exclusively to those dogs that were required to do specialized work and to those that were unmanageable. Now it is an accepted part of every dog's upbringing, essential to his well being. Unfortunately, it is not just the dog that must be trained. The owner needs to be educated even more than the dog. If the dog is schooled professionally, the instruction is still not complete until the master learns how to handle the trained dog. The owner's knowledge and full understanding of the dog's working ability are what make Obedience Training successful.

The purpose of this book is to give the owner the technique and fundamentals of training. It is intended to teach the humane and just method to use in enforcing obedience and to help the unskilled owner become a successful disciplinarian. There are many people who would like to own a dog but feel it would be too great a responsibility. It is hoped that this book will help such persons to decide that owning a dog need not be a problem but a pleasure, and that training, if not always easy, is a challenge to man's ability.

Only the training in general obedience for everyday use and the training necessary for competition in Obedience Trials will be discussed. Obedience Trials are the series of working tests that have been approved by the American and Canadian kennel clubs, in which any purebred dog may compete. When such a dog successfully fulfills all requirements of the trials, he is permitted to have letters after his name that indicate to what extent he has been trained. These letters are C.D. (Companion Dog); C.D.X. (Companion Dog Excellent); U.D. (Utility Dog); and T.D. (Tracking Dog). The 1964 Regulations and Standards for Obedience Trials are published in their entirety in the Appendix.

Obedience Training may best be described as teaching a dog to respond to definite commands or signals. These may be very simple exercises or they may be the more complicated ones given to police dogs, to dogs that lead the blind, and to those that perform other highly specialized work. The following quote from the American Kennel Club rule book will give the significance behind this great movement:

"The purpose of Obedience Trials is to demonstrate the usefulness of the purebred dog as the companion and guardian of man, and not the ability of the dog to acquire facility in the performance of mere tricks."

Training may be done in one of two ways. The dog is either trained to do the right thing by avoiding the wrong, or he is corrected of bad habits that are already a part of his behavior pattern. The owner should use the preventive method whenever possible rather than the corrective, which always calls for the more drastic measures.

When the puppy is young, the training he receives up to the time he is almost a year old consists of teaching him to have good manners and of giving him simple obedience training. After that the training is divided into three parts. The basic training which teaches the fundamental exercises of heeling, sitting, lying down, coming when called, and staying when told is the equivalent of the requirements for the C.D. (Companion Dog) title offered by the American Kennel Club. As the dog's training progresses, the basic exercises become more difficult. In addition, the dog learns to retrieve a dumbbell and is started in jumping. This is the advanced training equal to the C.D.X. (Companion Dog Excellent). The still more advanced training includes scent discrimination, seeking lost articles, and more complicated jumping. For this, a dog wins his U.D. (Utility Dog) title. Apart from dog shows, special Tracking Tests are held where a dog may gain his T.D. (Tracking Dog) title. All obedience titles (except the tracking) are progressive. When a dog acquires the next highest title, the previous ones are dropped. Thus, the C.D. gives way to the C.D.X., the C.D.X. to the U.D., and the U.D. becomes a U.D.T. (Utility Dog Tracker). The exception is that a C.D. dog may pass his Tracking Test before completing the rest of his training. In such a case, the letters would read: C.D., T.D. (Companion Dog,

Tracking Dog). If obedience titles are gained in more than one country a title may then read: Am U.D.T., Can C.D.X., or Am & Can U.D.T.

Choosing a Puppy

The American Kennel Club recognizes 129 different breeds of dogs. To ask the owner of any one breed what kind of dog he likes best would be comparable to asking a mother whether she prefers her own or someone else's child. Choosing a puppy requires individual thought and consideration. It is a case of picking the right kind of dog for the right person.

There have always been and always will be dogs of mixed ancestors. Some make excellent pets and companions and, I must admit, they have a point or two in their favor. Their biggest advantage is availability to the thousands of people with limited means who really love dogs and would otherwise be in no position to have one.

But, on the whole, the purebred dog will bring a great deal more satisfaction. The purebred is appealing in personal appearance; and the fact that the dog is purebred makes him eligible to enter dog shows and, after the owner has made the effort to train him, receive obedience titles. The original investment in a purebred dog makes the owner more conscious of his responsibility and he feels a pride of ownership that he would not otherwise have.

It is not true that crossbred dogs are smarter than purebreds. Mongrels may give the impression of being smart because, through their wanderings, they have taught themselves to do the things we must train our more restricted purebred dogs to do. Don't misunderstand; there are plenty of intelligent mongrel dogs, but, generally speaking, they are not easy to train. Their mixed temperaments follow no special pattern whereas purebreds will run more true to form and behave in a way that is characteristic of their breeds. This gives the trainer the advantage of knowing what to expect from a dog. But purebred or not, every dog deserves to be trained just as every child has the right to an education. Good manners are not exclusively for those dogs in the Social Register.

Each of the 129 pure breeds of dogs falls into one of six groups, depending upon the original purpose for which the dog was bred and what he is being used for today. In Group One, called the Sporting Group, are breeds used to hunt and to retrieve both water and land fowl. Their main interest in life is birds. This is where we find the Pointers, the Setters, the Retrievers, and the Spaniels. Each, in his own right, a king in the sporting world.

Group Two, known as the Hound Group, consists of dogs used to trail fur-bearing game. They have a keen sense of smell and are usually quick moving. A few in this group are Afghan Hounds, Basset Hounds, Beagles, Dachshunds, Greyhounds, Elkhounds, Wolfhounds, and Whippets.

Group Three, the Working Group, is made up of working dogs bred and trained for generations to perform duties of herding, protection, sentry, and man work. It is in this group that the most reliable performers in Obedience Trials will be found. These dogs take their training, for which they have unusual endurance, seriously. Boxers, Collies, Doberman Pinschers, Great Danes, Newfoundlands, Old English Sheepdogs, Huskies, St. Bernards, and Corgis are a few of the working breeds.

Group Four consists of Terriers, originally bred to ferret out underground rodents. Here we find the Airedales, Bedlingtons, Bull Terriers, Cairns, Fox Terriers, Irish Terriers, Kerry Blues, Scotties, Sealyhams, et cetera. The Terriers have an aggressive nature, undoubtedly due to their early training, which makes it more difficult to teach them general obedience.

Group Five is the Toy Group. Though small in size, in many cases Toys are the replica in miniature of their larger editions. A few of the Toy breeds are Chihuahuas, Toy Spaniels, Griffons, Italian Greyhounds, Maltese, Pekingese, Miniature Pinschers, Toy Poodles, Toy Manchester Terriers, and Yorkshire Terriers.

Group Six is called the Non-Sporting Group. This varied assortment of dogs is now used for no one definite purpose but at one time served in a number of ways. The Poodle is one example of the group. Although the Poodle was the original water retrieving Spaniel and has been used to lead the blind and to do essential work in times of war, it is now bred primarily as a pet and for companionship. Boston Terriers, Bulldogs, Chow Chows, Dalmatians, French Bulldogs, Keeshonden, Schipperkes, along with the Poodle—both Standard and Miniature—make up the Non-Sporting Group.

The judging at dog shows today, in the breed classes, is based on these six classifications. In Obedience Trials, all breeds compete against one another.

Before purchasing a puppy there are some things other than what the dog will be used for that one must take into consideration. The size of the dog is important. The individual who lives in an apartment, or one who does a great deal of traveling and wants to have his dog with him, will do best with a medium-sized dog or one that can be carried about. The Great Danes and Newfoundlands should be kept for the country farms and estates where they will have a chance to receive the exercise they need but cannot get in the city. This brings up the question of whether it is wrong to keep a dog in the city. People who work or who are out all day show lack of consideration for a dog if he must be confined long hours at a time. A dog needs exercise. If arrangements can be made for long daily walks and an occasional week-end run in the country, the responsibility of keeping a dog in a metropolitan area will not be so great. And the dog's health and happiness will not be adversely affected by city life.

Another thing to think about before choosing a dog is the kind of coat the dog will have. The long coats need a great deal more grooming and brushing care. Allowance must be made for the extra time this will involve. On the other hand, long hair is a protection against the cold in northern climates and the dog will not need blanketing. Short-haired dogs shed more. Maybe this is because they receive less grooming and brushing or perhaps it is just the coat itself, but, if the shedding of the hair is especially annoying, it is wise to make note of this quality at the time the puppy is purchased. The Poodle, for instance, is one breed that does not shed at all.

Still another point, and one of the most important, is the kind of temperament the puppy will have when he is mature. It is not advisable to pick a breed whose disposition will clash with the owner's and make training difficult. The gentle and kind individual will no more be able to control the "bully" or aggressive type of dog than the braggart would be seen walking down the street with a "shrinking violet" on the other end of the leash. The dog whose purpose in life is companionship should be friendly and tolerant. Under no circumstances should a dog with a vicious or bad temperament be kept as a pet. The place for the belligerent-natured animal is on sentry duty for guarding and protection.

Even though dog fights may be kept more or less under control by training, there are certain breeds that are scrappier than others. If more than one dog is to be kept in the same house, or if the dog must come in contact with others, it is better to buy one without a chip on his shoulder. The joys of owning a dog are limited if one must always be on the alert against dog fights. Oh, very often, two pets will growl and snarl when they are held back by the leash, and then they will have a friendly romp with the former "enemy" if the leash is taken off; but this can be controlled through training methods that will be explained later in the chapter on training.

The smaller the dog the spunkier he is—and the noisier. The reason for the excessive barking, no doubt, is that the small breeds were originally used to warn their masters when anything was wrong. Perhaps, too, they feel that in some way their yapping makes up for what they lack in size. Certain small dogs, then, must be excluded if the question of noise will be of primary importance.

The novice who is about to purchase a puppy would do well to talk with professional trainers, professional handlers, and owners of boarding kennels to get their opinions about the different breeds. These people have knowledge of all dogs. They know their dispositions and outstanding characteristics, and they realize the amount of time that is necessary to give certain dogs proper care. This will give the prospective owner an idea of what he can expect from a puppy. All puppies are appealing when young. It is better to think of them as the adult dogs they very soon will be.

If a person is going to buy a dog, it would be wise for him to attend an all-breed dog show or a specialty show and talk with the breeders and exhibitors. He should watch the dogs in the show ring. This will help the prospective owner to pick out the type of dog he likes best, and then, if he buys from a reliable kennel, he will be certain of the puppy's pedigree and know that he is getting one from a registered litter. The reputation of most pet shops is not above reproach, but it hardly seems fair to condemn them all. A few are reliable, but one should guard against misrepresentation when it comes to dogs' pedigrees and registrations.

Speaking of pedigrees—every dog has a pedigree. It is sometimes believed though that a pedigreed dog and a registered dog mean one and the same thing. A pedigree issued to a purebred dog at the time of purchase does not necessarily mean that the dog is registered or eligible for registration in the American Kennel Club or in the Field Trial Stud Book. All the pedigree does is to list the sire and dam of the dog and their ancestors for four generations. In order for a dog to be registered the sire and dam must already be registered. One should avoid the possibility of disappointment by always asking, at the time of purchase or when breeding to a particular dog, if the dog is registered or is eligible for registration.

Information on the various breeds may be obtained from the American Kennel Club, 51 Madison Avenue, New York City, from various local kennel clubs, and from any group of people united to further the interest of any one breed. Specialty clubs have a breed standard which the secretaries of the clubs are glad to send out on request. More information may be gained from the numerous books and magazines about dogs, by visiting kennels, and by attending dog shows. There is little excuse today for owners to be ignorant about dog affairs with so many sources of information available.

If a person requires perfection, he should not buy a puppy but a grown dog. Regardless of all the promises made by the party who is doing the selling, there can be no guarantee of what a puppy will look like when he grows up. If the real reasons for having a dog are to train him and to groom him for companionship, the buyer is in a position to gamble on a youngster, and he will have more fun in the long run. It is a gamble on both sides, for when a kennel sells a young puppy it also takes a chance on losing a future champion. Perhaps that eight-week-old pup that was sold for $100.00 will win a Best in Show, who knows? It has happened!

There are some people who will buy a new car or a new dress without asking a single question, so I suppose there are people who do the same when they buy a dog. Nonetheless, one should question certain facts even when buying from a reliable kennel. The first is about registration —whether the puppy is registered in the American Kennel Club or in the Field Trial Stud Book as one of a litter, or whether he is registered as an individual. If as one of a litter, either the kennel or the new owner will have to register the puppy again as an individual. At the same time it is wise to ask who will pay for the transfer from one name to the other. The transfer, by the way, will come from the American Kennel Club and may take a month or longer to go through. Information should be obtained about when the puppy was last inoculated and about what inoculations he has received up to the time of purchase. The new owner should inquire about the worming of the puppy—when he was last wormed and what type of worm he had, if any. If the owner is interested in showing the dog, he should ask the kennel owner to be frank as to the dog's show possibilities. There is more satisfaction for the new owner when he is able to say himself what is wrong with his dog instead of being told by someone else. If the buyer is interested in breeding, he should be familiar with the color background of the puppy so he can guard against improper matings. He should also be aware of the possibility of color changes. Many gray dogs, for instance, are born black while other colors will lighten as the dog gets older.

At the time of purchase the buyer should see that the puppy is in good health and in high spirits. It is impossible to get satisfactory results when training a sickly dog. If he feels it is necessary, the buyer should not hesitate to ask permission to have the puppy checked by a veterinarian, especially when buying from an unknown source. One should be wary of diarrhea, of a running nose, or of eyes that discharge pus. A young puppy should not act tired and listless but should be full of fun and play. One that is running a temperature should be watched carefully—perhaps it is only excitement but it *could* be something else.

To the question, then, "What kind of dog should I buy?" one can only answer that there are advantages and disadvantages in all kinds. There are good, bad, smart, dumb, healthy, and unhealthy dogs among all breeds; and it is a matter of favoring the breed with the fewest number of drawbacks.

Every dog, though, has an uncanny memory for his first love. The owner who wants a dog to belong to him should not only take over the responsibility of feeding the dog upon his arrival but should make an effort to keep the dog with him for a few days and establish a pleasant relationship between the dog and himself. This early association will have a lasting effect throughout the dog's lifetime. The dog's memory is so exceptional that he has been known to recognize a person after a period of five years. If the early encounter was a happy and agreeable one, the later meeting is always one of joy. If not, the barrier is hard to break down.

The Start of Training

Dogs do not have the reasoning power that man and some of the higher apes have. Dogs learn through association and through repetition. They perform acts that bring pleasing results and discontinue those that bring displeasing ones. When left to their own resources they act through instinct as well, which is the wisdom of nature and not of reasoning power. Because the dog is loyal to his master and pathetically eager to please he is quick to learn even at an early age, although too much restraint will intimidate a puppy and should be guarded against. A puppy's routine habits can be formed as soon as he is able to walk. At this time he should learn to distinguish between the different tones of voice and to understand the meaning of certain words. For instance, he very soon learns to associate the word "No" with doing something wrong and the expression "Okay" with permission granted. Every puppy, by the way, should learn a quick, short expression, such as "No" or "Stop," so that he can be repressed easily without having to be punished.

Puppies from three to four months old should be taught house manners and be trained to walk on the leash without pulling. They should obey a few simple commands, such as to sit and to lie down when told, to come when called, and to stay in a designated spot. The willful and aggressive type of puppy not only can *but should* be started in his training earlier than most, providing the training is not too strict. Boxers, for example, do well at six months of age if they are handled in a quiet but firm manner and the punishment is not harsh. For the average dog, intensive training for obedience competition begins at ten months, but, again, it depends upon the breed as well as upon the individual dog. Every dog is a puppy at heart until he is a year old, and it is hard for him to settle down to serious work until he has passed this first birthday. Too early and too relentless training of an adolescent puppy may cause him to have a nervous breakdown. The dog becomes overexcited at the least thing, and he may have outbreaks of hysteria. Such a dog should be given a complete vacation for several months, and, when training is resumed, he should be handled kindly and gently and with understanding.

Although Obedience Training in its simplest form may start as early as six months, training clubs and classes usually do not accept dogs for registration until they are eight months or more. Professional trainers prefer an older dog, whereas dogs selected to guide the blind must be one and one-half to two years old before they receive specialized schooling. The training should not be rushed. A gradual improvement over a long period of time will bring the best results. In one exhibition at Madison Square Garden the average age among the twenty-four dogs was six years, and one or two performers were as old as nine.

"Can every dog be trained?" Every dog will improve through training, but, naturally, some learn more quickly than others. The breed of the dog, the age of the dog, his disposition, and the owner's ability as a trainer are factors that determine how successful the training will be.

So often one hears the question, "What breed of dog is said to be the smartest?" All breeds are specialists in their respective fields. The sporting breeds are versatile when it comes to birds, whereas Hounds excel at scenting fur-bearing game. Terriers act instinctively when hunting vermin. If one is referring to Obedience Training, the Poodle is one of the quickest breeds to learn, but he likes to clown. Only momentarily will he take his training seriously and do spectacular work. The next day he will pull a complete boner. The working breeds such as the German Shepherds, the Doberman Pinschers, the Shetland Sheepdogs, et cetera, are easy to train, and are usually dependable. Terriers often present a problem. Sporting dogs are too willing to be distracted by bird or animal scent. However, outstanding wins in Obedience Trials have been made by dogs of all breeds, but no one dog is representative of his breed. Even blind dogs have been trained successfully and have received the C.D. title in competition at dog-show Obedience Trials. A deaf dog can also learn to be obedient. He will respond to signals whereas the blind dog will obey entirely by voice commands.

"Is a dog ever too old to be trained?" Although it doesn't hold true in Obedience Training that one cannot teach an old dog new tricks, the old dog will be slower to catch on, and he will progress less rapidly. An outstanding example of an older dog's ability to learn was a Dalmatian that was started in training at eleven years of age and was one of the first dogs to win all obedience titles. Another was a Sealyham Terrier that was enrolled in the A.S.P.C.A. training classes when ten years old. This Sealyham later became the star of an obedience exhibition at Rockefeller Plaza in New York City during National Dog Week. In the case of a Dachshund that has enjoyed seven years of freedom, it would hardly be worth the effort to give him serious training. Having been unrestrained for such a long time—plus the fact that the breed is noted for its independence and strong objections to being told what to do—he would present a real problem. It is doubtful if the improvement would be worth the effort.

Many times I am asked if viciousness can be overcome through training. A dog that is really vicious (there are not many, but a few) should not be trained but should be destroyed. The trainer would have trouble training the dog, in the first place, and, even if the trainer were successful, the owner would not have peace of mind because the dog would never be trustworthy. If used for breeding, a vicious dog populates the countryside with his offspring, and they too may have bad dispositions. There are so few dogs, though, which warrant being destroyed that the owner should make every attempt to assure himself that the dog's attitude is not one of pretense. Almost always, training will bring about a miraculous change in every dog's behavior.

Very often a person will be the owner of a fighting dog, and he'll wonder if Obedience Training will overcome this problem. Training will not control a dog's inclination to fight to the point where the dog will always be reliable. Obedience Training will teach a dog to respect a person sufficiently so that a command or a word of warning may either avoid a possible fight or stop one that has already started. Nevertheless, a scrappy dog left to himself, even though he has been trained, will still battle with the neighbor's dog.

When one comes to the training of dogs, there are so many things to be considered one hardly knows where to begin. The "clowns," the "bullies," and the scared little "rabbits" all present different problems, while the person who is to do the training is the most important factor of all. Such a person may be as weak as water when it comes to training his own dog, or he may be such a blustering bully that the dog will run for his life. Perhaps the trainer is someone whose school days are so far in the past that it is impossible for him to learn the art of training. At any rate, the success or failure of Obedience Training cannot be credited to any one cause but to many.

Still another question usually brought up is, "Which is better for training—a male or a female dog?" My answer is either. The advantage of training a female is that the owner is able to keep her attention. The male is more interested in other dogs and in what goes on around him. The disadvantage of training a female is that the training will be interrupted and competition at dog shows postponed when she comes into season twice a year. However, there have been an equal number of well-trained dogs of both sexes, so no definite rule applies. When picking a puppy for the purpose of easy training, it is best to choose one that is friendly and happy and keenly interested in what is going on. The most difficult part about training is to get the dog's attention and to hold it throughout the training. The little fellow always watchful of his two-legged master has it all over his less alert brothers and sisters. With attention already centered on the owner, the dog is more anxious to please, and he will accept discipline more graciously.

Why Train a Dog?

Every year, especially around Christmas or on other occasions such as birthdays, graduations, et cetera, puppies find their way into thousands of homes. The new puppy may be the result of much scrimping and saving that has left a rather empty pocketbook. Maybe the puppy was a gift from someone—a long-awaited gift. Maybe the little fellow was picked up off the street, with no place to go. Whatever occasioned his arrival the puppy, although cherished property at the moment, will soon lose his glamor unless one learns how to train and care for him.

When we buy a new car we don't expect it to to run smoothly or to do its job unless we attend to all the little details that keep it in good running order. It is the same with the new puppy. His good points will be brought out only if we take the time to bring them out. But if we do, the puppy will grow more endearing and give pleasure instead of causing regret.

The number of dogs is steadily increasing. A recent report indicates a canine population of 25,000,000 in the United States. Next to the almighty dollar, we might claim the dog to be the greatest common denominator in the world today. Dogs are owned, admired, and loved by everybody. The need for educating this vast army to take its place in domestic life is becoming more and more urgent. Twenty-five million of anything can mean a lot of headaches, and if each of those twenty-five million objects has four legs and a wagging tail, anything can happen.

When a dog is taken into the home, he must be taught to respect the rights and feelings of those with whom he associates. At the same time, we should remind ourselves that we must be considerate of the dog. Training is one way of caring for his welfare. It teaches him manners; it will help to keep him in good physical condition, to have steady nerves, and to become a more congenial and a more amusing pet and companion. Dogs enjoy the experience of training and react spontaneously to intelligent instruction. Here, indeed, is an adventure in discipline, a way to balanced behavior, without stress or strain.

A dog is taught to obey, not for the sake of forcing our will power on him, but to teach him self-discipline. Like children, a dog develops personality. His owner can help him to build character and teach him to be more amiable in his relationship with human associates. Training also adds to the dog's enjoyment of life and to the greater happiness of the family and their friends. When training has become an accepted part of every dog's education and when owners, as well, realize their responsibility, there will be less need of city and state legislation to control our pets. There will be fewer stray dogs roaming the streets, less destruction due to rabies, and more lenient rules to allow pets in public places. A well-trained dog can and should be welcome wherever he goes.

To those of us who like dogs, it is sometimes difficult to understand that there are people who do not like them. If we think about this fact for a moment, we realize that we do not like all dogs either. There are dogs and dogs, just as there are people and people! Those who dislike them as a whole, unfortunately, are often justified in their dislike. But it is not always the dog's fault, for through training he would become more likable. The human master, having taken the dog out of his natural environment, must help the dog to adjust himself to a different way of living or the dog will suffer. The master from the first moment of ownership becomes accountable for the dog and for his behavior. He must see that the dog in no way annoys friends, neighbors, or members of the family. And this requires home training; for animals, like children, reflect home discipline.

Owners frequently allow their pets to behave so badly, one wonders if they know what really good manners a dog can have or how enjoyable a well-mannered dog can be. For example, it is entirely unnecessary to allow a dog to bark when he is left alone, especially at unreasonable hours. A noisy dog will turn even the most sincere dog lovers against our four-footed friends. The dog should not make a mistake in the house when visiting, or chew up valuable property at any time. The postman and delivery boy will have every reason to dislike serving those whose dogs rush out and bark ferociously or attempt to bite them.

Car-chasing dogs are a hazard as well as those which, when taken for a ride, jump back and forth from one seat to another and climb over everyone including the driver.

Guests, as a rule, dislike to be greeted and nearly knocked down by an exuberant dog. Not only is it frightening but the dirty paw marks left on one's clean clothes can be irksome. Above all, a dog should not be the center of attention all the time, nor should he be the chief topic of conversation.

It is annoying to the other members of the family if the dog barks at every little noise such as the doorbell, the telephone, or the sound of approaching footsteps. A dog should not be spoiled. When left alone, or even when the owner is with him, he should not get up on the furniture, nor should he be allowed to steal or to beg for food at mealtime. A begging dog annoys guests and makes serving difficult.

When taken out for exercise, especially in the city, our dogs should be curb-broken and discreet about where they lift their legs. The proper place is certainly not on baskets of fruit or vegetables in the market, or in any little private gardens that they may come upon. They should never be permitted to pull their owners along the street or to dart through doorways ahead of them. Last, but not least, dogs should be kept at home. They will be a nuisance if they stray on to other people's property and fight the neighbors' dogs.

When we consider all these annoying practices, it is not surprising that so many legal restrictions are imposed upon owners and their pets. Undoubtedly there is a growing consciousness of the owner's responsibility, but this responsibility must be extended to include training.

Training, as it is presented here, may not entirely cure every dog of all his bad habits, but it will definitely help to establish good ones and to overcome most of the undesirable ones. It will teach the owner how to keep his pet under control, thereby making more friends for the greatest of all animals—the dog.

The writer by no means wishes to give the reader the impression that Obedience Training is infallible. There are times when a dog would have been better off had he not been trained. When training is improperly done, the harm that can be caused is beyond repair. We sometimes (and all too frequently) hear the remark, "If training is such a good idea, why do so many trained dogs look cowed and unhappy?" This is because the training has been too severe and has been done in a nagging way. The trainer did not recognize the danger line where he should have backed down rather than have forced the issue.

The question of whether or not a dog that is being exhibited in the breed ring should be trained for obedience is debatable. This training has both advantages and disadvantages. The training for close-heel work required in Obedience Trials may cause a dog to crowd the handler in the breed ring, which is not in the dog's favor. Most dogs, however, seem to understand when they are working in obedience competition and when they are not. To help the dog distinguish between the two situations, the training collar should be replaced with a leather one when the dog is being shown in breed. The advantages of having the dog obedience trained are that the dog will stand firmly while he is being examined and that he will move in a straight line and will not pull sideways on the leash. His gait will be free and more natural. The argument that a dog is ruined for the breed ring when he is trained to sit at heel, as is required in Obedience Trials, is a relic of the past. A dog can be trained both to stand on command and to sit at heel, and he is very quick to learn the difference between the two.

The owners of terrier breeds have a point in their favor when they say that training discredits a terrier. A terrier shows himself off to advantage when he is on his toes and ready for adventure. One that has been too strictly trained will often lack this spirit. If a terrier is being shown and trained at the same time, care should be taken that his pep and fire are not dampened.

The breeders and trainers of hunting dogs almost all agree that dogs to be used for hunting should have their obedience training postponed until they are trained for the field. Even though hunting dogs receive a certain amount of obedience work—known as "yard breaking"—prior to the actual field work, this is done only to get the dog under control. Obedience Trials require perfection. Such exactness could easily interfere with a dog's natural hunting instincts, unless he were permitted a great deal of freedom and were allowed to take hunting expeditions by himself.

Depending upon the circumstances, every dog, then, should be trained up to a point, but the training influence that will affect certain factors must be kept in mind throughout the dog's training.

Dogs and Children

The reason that dogs and children get along so well must be that they are so much alike. They think alike, they act alike, and they even train

All youngsters have a great deal to learn

alike. All this creates an understanding between a dog and a child that is beyond the conception of grownups. Unless the dog actually fears children and will have nothing to do with them, which is sometimes true if the dog is shy or has never been around children, he will usually take to a child the moment he enters the house.

I have watched a Boxer, that ordinarily would try the strength of two men, walk along the street with a two-year-old child holding the leash and the leash so slack the dog almost tripped over it. We have all witnessed a dog being mauled by a child to such a degree that, were such treatment attempted by an adult, it would bring disaster. Children will step on a dog's paws, will pull his ears, his tail, and his hair, and all but put the dog's eyes out, and he will take it like a martyr. Dogs have a natural instinct to guard and to protect children. This makes them sense danger in the offing, which will cause an owner sometimes to say he feels perfectly safe as long as "Rover" is around.

When a new baby puts in an appearance, the dog, favored pet of the household, may become jealous. This is to be expected because the dog's feelings will be hurt when he finds himself being pushed into the background and someone else receiving the loving care and attention that he feels is, by right, due him. Owners can so well prevent this from happening if they will only look at things in the right light. At this particular time, the dog should be made a part of the family more than ever. Not that a great deal needs to be done for the dog, because with the new addition there probably will not be much extra time; but the dog should not be ignored. When the owner is fussing over the baby, it will take but a minute to give the dog a pat on the head—and I wouldn't worry about the germs. A kind word spoken to the dog when the owner is talking to the baby, and a tidbit thrown in the dog's direction while the baby is being fed, will make the dog feel important. This extra precaution will be necessary for only a short time, as the dog will soon learn to accept the new member of the family if he is given no cause for jealousy.

I am often asked how old a child should be before he has a dog of his own. As far as that goes, a dog can become a member of the household while the child is still in the crib, but, of course, there is no responsibility involved. Providing the parents take complete charge of the dog and protect him from maltreatment, age does not enter into the question at all. If the child is to have the responsibility for feeding the dog, exercising him, and training him, that is something else again. This should not be undertaken until the child is ten or twelve years old or even older. Youngsters, as well as puppies, have a very short memory. Both forget to do the important things that are essential. They find it hard to concentrate on any one thing for any length of time. Under these circumstances, it is folly to have one attempt to teach the other. Responsibility should not be given to a young child unless the owner sees to it that the child can accept the responsibility. Until such time, the dog's care should be supervised by the parents.

All children should be taught to respect the rights of a puppy or a dog as much as they respect the rights of a playmate. After all, the dog is a playmate too, and, like anyone else, he will take just so much and then he may lose his temper. Children should be taught to play nicely with a dog and not to tease him. They should be made to understand that good companionship does not mean taking advantage of another but does mean creating a mutual enjoyment.

While on the subject of play, remember children should be warned against having a tug of war with a young puppy or with a dog by pulling against something the dog is holding in his mouth. This may cause the puppy's teeth to come in crooked and may pull the dog's mouth out of shape. Tugs of war are also bad for a puppy's disposition. It teaches him the power of his teeth, and it may be the cause of serious biting later on. There are other ways to play, such as throwing a ball or a stick, or running after the puppy in a game of tag, and these things will not bring on a major catastrophe.

Owners frequently feel that if they buy two dogs their problems will be solved. The dogs, they feel, will be company for each other and will get more exercise. This may be true, but usually the owner's problems double. Dogs, on the whole, are companions of people, not of other dogs. The majority will forsake the company of four-footed animals any time they have the chance to associate with humans. The lone dog, once he is trained, is easier to handle in the long run, and he will be just as happy as if he had half a dozen other dogs to play with. Not that I condemn the two-dog owner, but he should save his sympathy for something more deserving than the solitary dog, whose devotion to man makes the company of four-footed friends superfluous.

The Trainer

The person who undertakes to train a dog should first understand what is required of the trainer. He will have to have patience. Training at times is tedious and has its dead levels, but the trainer should not become exasperated or grow lax. He must be able to understand how a

The author and Jester

dog's mind works so he can anticipate the dog's next move, and he must be able to transmit his wishes to the dog. The trainer must know what kind of temperament the dog has. If he is working with a puppy, he will want to watch for certain predispositions in character. Every dog will react differently to the same situation, so the trainer must learn to interpret these reactions for what they are worth. He must know when to be gentle, when to be firm, when to scold, and when to pet. Finally, it is important that he should know at what point he must leave off training. Training is an art and as with all artists, some trainers are better than others. Good trainers are born with the essential qualities necessary in training. The expert has the co-ordination and sense of timing that will distinguish him from the average trainer and will single him out as a "natural."

The owner with the "trainer personality," as we might call it, has the power to impress his authority on the dog through common-sense methods. The proof that one has this personality is a *happy response* from the dog. When such a relationship exists, the trainer can be assured that his efforts will be fruitful and that at the end of the training period the dog will still love him.

During the course of a dog's education the teacher profits as well as the pupil. Let us see what training does for the owner. First, he learns to control his temper. It doesn't do a bit of good to become angry with either the puppy or the dog. He won't understand the anger and the result is upsetting to both dog and trainer. And in the meantime, nothing is accomplished.

The owner learns to be patient in training. He must do the same thing over and over and this calls for calmness and perseverance. Lack of serenity will soon lead to failure. Training also offers mental relaxation and gives physical exercise.

Doctors and other professional people are particularly aware of the therapeutic value of training. It helps to overcome shyness and it teaches one self-control. This is especially true when children are concerned. They learn that dogs have different dispositions, just like their playmates. As a result, they become more understanding of four-footed animals, more tolerant, and more forgiving. They learn the difference between cruelty and justified punishment.

In one training group, a shy little girl was the owner of a very shy dog. Together, the two overcame their self-consciousness and later became happy members of the training class. Another example was a boy who had always taken a "back seat" to a younger and more clever brother. This lad trained his dog and, on graduation day, received not one but two different prizes. His mother said this was the greatest thing that could have happened to Johnny—that it had helped to overcome his inferiority complex, although everything else had failed. A third member of the class was a famous music composer. His wife claimed that from the time her husband had been forced to learn self-control to train his dog he had been a better person to live with and no longer lost his temper when supper was late! Training a dog does have its advantages!

Since the forcefulness with which all corrections are made depends upon the dog's disposition, the trainer must have knowledge of the different breeds. Of course, this can only come with experience, but the trainer must realize that all dogs are not trained alike. One can lay down certain basic rules but they should be flexibly interpreted. The trainer, for example, must be consistent. If a dog is permitted to do something one day he naturally thinks it is all right; he must not be scolded the very next day for doing the same thing.

Last but not least, the trainer must be smarter than the dog if he doesn't want to be outwitted!

Feeding and General Care of the Puppy

Since this is to be a book on training, my only reason for mentioning the feeding and general care of the puppy is the need of having a strong, healthy animal to begin with—one which will make the great personal effort that training requires worth while.

No two kennels and no two people feed and care for their dogs in just the same way, and I shall not attempt to give definite rules to follow, but practical suggestions that may be helpful to the dog owner. The object is the same—to have a strong, healthy puppy with a beautiful coat. Each and every owner, through experience, will find his own method of getting these results.

To have a healthy puppy at birth, one must really start long before the puppy is born by seeing that the mother is well fed and well taken care of while she is in whelp. She must be given such things as calcium and bone meal to aid in building strong bone and good teeth. The majority of persons who have dogs buy them as young puppies. It is recommended, then, that the purchase be made from a reliable kennel where it is known that this proper prenatal care, as well as comprehensive attention after birth, has been given. As stated before, the American Kennel Club, 51 Madison Avenue, New York City, or your own local kennel club will furnish a list of breeders that are usually dependable. It is worth the effort to visit the different breeding establishments and to see for one's self what conditions are like. Only in this way can one know whether or not the puppy has always had the best of care.

From the time a puppy is weaned (which is approximately five to six weeks) to three months of age, four feedings a day are recommended. All meals should be of the same consistency and may be given at 8 A.M., 12 noon, 4 P.M. and 8 P.M. By making all meals the same, stools remain firm.

Milk, which when fed by itself causes stools to be on the soft side, can be added to the puppy's diet.

Up to seven or eight weeks the diet should be bland and concentrated rather than one with roughage. Cooked oatmeal mixed with undiluted evaporated milk, egg yolk, or a whole cooked egg, honey, cooked meat, wheat germ, fat in one form or another, plus vitamins, will keep a puppy in excellent condition until he is able to handle regular dog food.

When the puppy is about two months old, puppy meal can be substituted for the oatmeal, and at three months of age the four feedings may be dropped to three a day—8 A.M., 12 noon, and 6 P.M. With the many excellent brands of scientifically prepared dog food available, feeding is relatively simple. However, owners are advised to read the labels and select meats of the highest quality, government inspected.

At this early age the puppy's appetite grows with lightning speed, and one must keep constantly adjusting the quantity of food given. Owners should not be deceived into thinking a puppy is in good weight just because the puppy has long fur. Ribs and hip bones should be felt to see if they are prominent, in which case the total amount of food should be increased. All young puppies should be on the chubby side, for when they reach maturity they will quickly lose their puppy fat, but the foundation will have been laid for a healthy mature dog.

When about seven or eight months of age, the puppy may become fussy about his eating. In this case, if he is in good condition, the number of meals may be dropped to two a day. The noon feeding may be omitted, but the amount of the afternoon feeding should be increased. If there is no lessening of the puppy's appetite, the noon meal may automatically be discontinued when he is a year old.

Meat, in amounts varying from one-quarter to one pound or more depending on the breed, is the dog's natural food. It should be a part of his diet whether raw, cooked, or mixed with a prepared dog food. The owner who prefers to feed a complete food in the form of meal or of a kibbled broken biscuit should take care that such food is of the best. The good brands all cost about the same. My own preference in feeding is to give a fair amount of raw or cooked meat with two parts of meal and one part of kibbled biscuit. When the meal and biscuit are soaked in a meat or a vegetable soup, the savory flavor appeals to the fussy eater and makes him more keen for his dinner. If a puppy is thin and will eat more food, the amount of each of the ingredients should be increased. But if a puppy leaves some of his food or is getting too fat, the total amount of food should be cut down.

With most dogs, their appetite can be your guide, but if a particular pet makes one wonder if he really is a puppy or a fat little pig, the quantity given must be regulated. The puppy should eat quickly and comfortably without gorging himself, and uneaten food should be taken away after about ten minutes. One should not make the mistake of offering it to the dog later, but should wait until the next mealtime. In this way the puppy will learn that he eats at a certain time and that he must do so immediately.

Over the years I have made a practice of "fasting" all grown dogs in the kennel one day a week. The puppies are fed but are given less than the usual amount. This keeps the dogs' appetites keen and I have no trouble with fussy eaters. Some owners follow this practice with their household pet.

Getting back to the old question of raw versus cooked meat, if a puppy thrives on cooked meat it should, by all means, be given to him. There is a difference of opinion as to whether or not cooking destroys the vitamins, but I have fed both raw and cooked meat with excellent results. Beef is preferable, but lamb or mutton may also be given. Fish, poultry, tripe, cooked livers, kidneys, hearts, and lungs are all excellent foods to give on alternating days. The innards must be beneficial because they are the first thing a dog will eat when he is left to supply his own food. Reliable canned foods may be used in place of meat, and they are handy to have while traveling and for an emergency.

It is advisable to feed the nationally known commercial brands of meal and biscuit, although shredded wheat, whole-wheat bread, or toast may be given occasionally. The formulas for commercial feeds are usually worked out scientifically, and they have the proper protein content as well as the necessary minerals and vitamins. Since the modern dog lives, more or less, under artificial conditions in which he is not free to eat things of his own choosing, these essential food elements may be lacking in his diet and must be supplemented. Mashed carrots or green vegetables are all right but not absolutely necessary. Apples and even citrus fruit are relished and will have no bad effect. Eggs are good, and dogs are particularly fond of hard cooked ones. Recent laboratory tests show that 75 per cent of a raw egg will pass through the intestines undigested and will, at times, cause vomiting. This may be due to the albumen of the egg white, since if only the yolk is given no trouble will result. Cottage cheese and boiled rice are good for dogs, as are thin soups and broths used over meal and biscuit. Don't overlook the fact that a dog may be raised on table scraps, but they must be adequate.

Greasy fried foods and candy should be avoided as well as chicken bones and fish bones. Too much starchy food is not advisable, but, if one is trying to put weight on a puppy or on a dog, a limited amount of boiled potatoes, macaroni, or spaghetti will do no harm and might do some good.

Some owners find that cow's milk agrees with their pets. Others find canned milk is preferred. Some like to feed cooked cereals, others dry cereals or Pablum. Feed whatever the dog will eat and whatever agrees with him. He may have his likes and dislikes the same as we do. What really matters is getting good results.

Nevertheless, every dog requires and is able to assimilate a certain amount of fat. The condition of the coat will improve when fat is included in the diet. This may be given in the form of butter, bacon fat or the fatty trimmings of meat (cooked or raw). I understand dogs do not assimilate the fat of suet, but whether they do or not I wouldn't know.

I do know this, though. One day a Poodle was brought into my shop for her regular clipping. The coat was in a very bad condition, as it was dry, scaly, and had no life to it. I couldn't understand it; I had been clipping this same dog regularly over a period of two years and the coat had always been sleek, shiny and very beautiful. My first question was whether the owner had, by any chance, taken the fat out of Topsy's diet because she had been gaining weight. The owner replied with a smile, "Every little scrap." This was the answer to the poor condition of the coat. When the fat again became part of the dog's diet, the coat was back to normal in four weeks' time.

The owner should keep a careful check on his dog's general condition and weight. The hip bones and ribs are the best guides. They should be well covered with flesh and not too sharply outlined. The owner of an extremely thin dog should consult his veterinarian. The puppy should first be tested for worms and treated accordingly. If this test is negative, the next thing is to make certain he is getting enough food for his size. The average person underestimates a dog's appetite and food requirements. Sometimes a long bushy coat will deceive the owner into thinking that the puppy is in good flesh. Even so, it is probably easier to put weight on a dog than to take it off, and, on the whole, this situation is better for his health. A fat dog will develop all kinds of ailments and his span of life will generally be shortened.

A few years ago a very small Cocker Spaniel was brought to the kennel for boarding. She weighed thirty pounds, which was almost twice the weight she should have been. The dog was immediately put on a strict diet and then weighed every week. For six weeks the scales didn't vary an ounce. Then all of a sudden she started to drop off the excess fat very rapidly, and at the end of the eighth week her weight was down to less than twenty pounds. Pixie, as she was called, was always ready to eat and would willingly have taken many times the amount of food given to her, but I decided it was easier to keep her weight down than to take it off again after it had accumulated. I know how much will power is needed to resist pleading, soulful eyes that ask "second helping, please?"

One last thought on the subject of eating and drinking. Keep a pan of fresh water where the puppy or dog can get it *at all times*. I know this is contrary to what some people think, but when water is always available, animals drink frequently though little at a time. When kept away and given only at intervals, they may overdrink and become sick. The exception to this rule is when a puppy is in ill health and water is given only on the advice of the veterinarian, or when a puppy is being very stubborn about housebreaking at night. For the latter, the water may be taken away during the early part of the evening to prevent the puppy from taking too much liquid before he goes to bed.

A dog that drinks an excessive amount of water should be checked by the veterinarian. An ounce of prevention in this case may, indeed, be a pound of cure. Unusual thirst is often a warning signal that should not be ignored.

Grooming

Next to the feeding, the biggest responsibility of the dog owner is in the grooming—or lack of it—and cleanliness in general. These factors not only improve the dog's looks but are essential to his health. Grooming adds to the dog's comfort. By keeping the coat clean and healthy numerous skin troubles can be avoided. When the dead hair is brushed out and the oil glands are stimulated, shedding is minimized. As a result, the coat will look glossy and shiny, and the dog will do less scratching. A well-cared-for dog is a pleasure to have around, and, at the same time, the dog seems to take pride in his own appearance. Grooming need not be done every day, but it should be done at least two or three times a week.

The basic equipment consists of the proper kind of brush, a comb, and a pair of scissors. For the long-haired dogs, a brush with long stiff bristles which will penetrate to the undercoat is best. The occasional use of a carder will help to loosen the hair where it has become matted. The carder is an oblong-shaped tool with short, bent wire prongs similar to those of the carder that is used on a fur coat. In extreme cases, the dog rake is the only solution. Short-haired dogs require a brush with short, stiff bristles or a hand mitt. For combing out wads of matted hair and for removing some of the undercoat for the purpose of thinning, a steel comb with round teeth is ideal.

Scissors are used for cutting away the hair between the toes, for removing the occasional mats under the stomach and under the ears, and for trimming the feet and feathers to give a tidy appearance. Terrier breeds require stripping two or three times a year. This is usually done by a professional. One breed, the Poodle, needs to have the coat clipped with electric clippers about every two months in order to keep him looking his best. Breeds that are not accustomed to stripping and clipping should be combed and brushed only and *not cut down*. If they are, it will cause the dog great discomfort and will ruin the appearance of his coat.

The owner should have a regular time and place for the daily grooming. When the puppy becomes accustomed to it, he will soon know what to expect and will learn to accept the attention like a veteran. The table or bench should be at a convenient height to avoid strain. For some reason or other, puppies and dogs behave better when they are on a table. If the grooming is started when the puppy is eight to ten weeks of age, the owner will have little trouble making him behave. The lusty yells and fierce struggles will last only a short while, for, once the puppy realizes he cannot have his own way and that he is not being hurt, he will quiet down and later will enjoy being worked on. So many people marvel at the patience of the Poodle breed in accepting hours of clipping and brushing. It is all a matter of training. The clipping is started while the puppy is young and is continued throughout his lifetime. He learns to accept it graciously.

During the grooming procedure, a dog should be checked for fleas, lice, and ticks. A bath, with Pearson's creolin or some other coal-tar product added to the bath water, may be given for the first two parasites. A special preparation must be used for the ticks, as they are hard to get rid of. Taking the ticks off daily by hand is one way. If a dog has parasites, the bath or treatment should be repeated in ten days. It is only through persistent care that fleas, lice, or ticks can be kept under control.

It is hard to believe that any household pet could be in the condition of one dog I saw a few years ago. He was a grown Poodle and his long hair gave no indication of what I was to find when I put the clippers to his coat. When the blade wouldn't cut through the hair, I investigated and found the entire body covered with lice and nits to a depth of one-quarter inch. At first, I couldn't believe my eyes and thought it must be a thick coating of sand. It required three hours of bathing and combing

The puppy should be checked often for fleas, lice, and ticks

to remove the outer layer of lice, and a series of baths at ten-day intervals, for a period of months, to clear the dog entirely of these parasites. A regular check-up would have prevented such heavy infestation, and the more drastic treatment could then have been avoided.

Even a young puppy can be bathed when necessary, but he should be thoroughly dried and kept warm. When bathing all dogs, the ears should be stuffed with lamb's wool or cotton and the eyes protected with a drop of castor oil. If a disinfectant is used in the bath water, special precaution must be taken not to get any in the dog's eyes. A mild soap or a specially prepared dog soap can be used, after which the coat must be thoroughly rinsed. Soap left in the coat will make it feel sticky and appear dull and dusty. When the coat is clean and thoroughly rinsed, it will squeak when rubbed and will look shiny and glossy. In between soap and water baths, a dry cleaner may be used if the dog has short hair, but it is not successful on long-haired breeds. There is a liquid cleaner on the market that now replaces the use of soap and makes rinsing unnecessary. This is proving to be a satisfactory and labor-saving way to bathe a dog.

At the time of grooming, attention should be given to the nails, the ears, and the teeth. These may seem like minor details, but much trouble will be avoided if they are cared for regularly. If the nails are long and pointed, they should first be cut with a nail cutter and then filed. Dogs

All dogs' teeth should be cleaned regularly

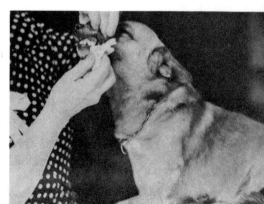

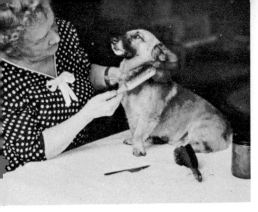

He will enjoy his grooming

object less to having their nails filed than to having them cut off with nippers. Short nails make the paws look neat, and with them there is less danger of tearing or splitting a nail, or of causing injury to the skin should the dog scratch himself. If a nail is cut too short, a drop of Monsol Solution, which may be obtained at any drugstore, will stop the bleeding instantly. The bleeding is not necessarily painful but is usually profuse and, without the proper treatment, is hard to check.

Wax and surplus hair should be taken out of the ears with a pair of medical tweezers and the ears then swabbed out with a piece of cotton dipped in ether or alcohol. The cotton can be wrapped around the forefinger or a swab stick may be used, but, in either case, care should be taken not to go too deep. The dog's head should be held firmly and the stick run down gently with a twisting motion parallel to the side of the head. The ears should be dried, then dusted with a little antiseptic powder. This last precaution may help prevent canker, which is not only painful but sometimes necessitates an operation. Clean ears that give off no odor need a little antiseptic powder—nothing more. Ear trouble is sometimes caused by too much probing. Bismuth Formic Iodide Powder—commonly referred to as "B.F.I."—is an excellent powder to use in the ears.

To keep the teeth white and free of tartar, they should be wiped off

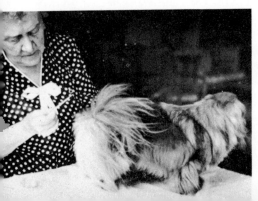

The thermometer is a must in every home where there is a young dog

27

with a mild solution of salt water or with Alcolol, which is an ordinary mouth wash. Tartar which has already accumulated must first be scraped off. There are tools for this purpose, known as tooth scalers, available at kennel-supply shops. Loose and badly decayed teeth should be removed by a veterinarian. This will improve the dog's general health and will prevent an offensive mouth odor.

The eyes should be washed occasionally with a boracic solution or some other eye wash. Long-haired dogs in particular need this attention. The hair irritates the eyes and may cause a discharge which makes the face skin red and swollen.

The anal glands are the two small glands just inside the rectal vent. These glands will sometimes become enlarged, and, in order to avoid infection and to prevent abscesses from forming, they have to be emptied out. Indications that the glands need emptying are: a hard lump on each side of the anus opening; a puffy, swollen appearance around the rectum; and the inability of the dog to do more than drag himself along the floor. To empty the glands, the tail is held in one hand, and, with a Kleenex held in the other hand, a gentle pressure is applied with the thumb and middle finger. The motion is upward and outward. If this is done when the dog is in the bathtub, it will be less disagreeable, as the excrement with its very offensive odor can be washed away quickly. When the glands are distended and are not emptied, they may form an abscess on either side of the dog's tail, in which case, if they do not open by themselves, it may be necessary to have them lanced.

Medical Care

Cleanliness is the first precaution an owner should take to protect a puppy from sickness. Feeding pans and water bowls should be washed daily and kept sterilized. Spoiled or rancid food should be dumped into the garbage pail. Although a young, healthy dog will throw off infection more easily than one that is not in good condition, he should not be exposed to a sick dog or be permitted to use the same dishes or to roam over the ground where the sick dog has been. There is no use in taking a chance.

A preventive serum for distemper should be given to every young puppy and continued at two-week intervals until he is old enough to have his permanent inoculation. Many persons are of the opinion that a puppy should never be taken on the street until he has been permanently inoculated. Viewpoints differ on this matter. There is no rule that will keep the puppy safe from contagious diseases. The bugs may be carried on a person's shoes or clothing, and they may even be contracted out of mid-air. The best the owner can do is to take every precaution, avail himself of the latest scientific care and use common sense in allowing the puppy to build up his own immunity.

Puppy serum may be started when the puppy is six to eight weeks old. The permanent vaccine is given at four to five months, after the second teeth have come in. If the puppy is inoculated while he is teething and has a reaction to the treatment, the second teeth will sometimes come through stained a dark brown and with the enamel eaten away. Also, during the time when a puppy is cutting his teeth, his resistance is low and he needs every bit of reserve strength to carry him through this period. When one sees a dog whose teeth are badly pitted, he can be certain the dog has had distemper and is now immune.

The permanent inoculation usually consists of three shots of vaccine at two- or three-week intervals, with booster shots given a few months later or whenever the puppy is to be exposed to a large number of dogs—as, for example, at a dog show. The veterinarian should advise on this aspect of a dog's care. At the same time, the veterinarian can attend to the inoculation against rabies. Many states now require that a dog receive this treatment, which lasts one year.

The dog's temperature should be taken whenever the owner thinks he is not up to par. A puppy or even a grown dog will often be running a high fever with no visible outward signs of sickness. If the treatment is started early, the dog will have a better chance of getting well. A veterinarian once said to me that if people would only not wait until the last minute to bring their pets for attention, and if they would not attempt to doctor their dogs themselves, there would be more chance of recovery and fewer fatalities. Nothing can replace the home-nursing care the owner is able to lavish on his dog, but it should come after the veterinarian has done his part.

A dog's temperature is taken with a rectal thermometer. The normal temperature of a mature dog is 101 to 102 degrees. A puppy's temperature will average 102 degrees, but excitement may cause it to go up to 103 for a short period. This is not serious, but if the reading is 103 or higher, and if it remains there for any length of time, the veterinarian should be consulted at once. Whenever a person acquires a new puppy or dog, he should run down to the corner drugstore and buy a thermometer to go along with the new pet.

The feces of the dog are another indication of health and condition. If a dog has diarrhea, something is wrong and the owner should find out what it is. Diarrhea may be caused by worms, by the start of distemper, or perhaps by just an upset stomach; but when the stool is not normal the reason should be sought out. The puppy should first be given a physical check-up by the veterinarian. He should be tested for worms. If nothing is organically wrong, certain foods should be eliminated one at a time from the diet to see if there is something the dog is allergic to. It is not natural for a dog to have a consistently loose stool. It is a nuisance to the owner and injurious to the dog. The dog's general health under such conditions will be poor, and he will not act the way he should or be in high spirits.

Most veterinarians are too busy with sick dogs to be bothered with the neurotic owner who runs to him for advice every time the puppy winks an eye. There are, however, indications that the owner would do well to heed, and every veterinarian will appreciate knowing about them in their early stages. One warning signal is persistent vomiting, especially if accompanied by a high temperature. Convulsions may be another sign of danger. There are several different kinds of convulsions, each with one or more causes. It is best, in this case, to let the veterinarian decide. The owner can give temporary treatment by keeping the dog quiet and putting ice on his head. If the fit is of the running variety, a blanket or coat may be thrown over the dog to catch him. Then he can be restrained until he gets over the fit, and he will not injure himself by crashing into objects.

A dog may refuse his dinner occasionally and this should cause no great concern. But if he is normally a good eater and then suddenly refuses all food, his temperature should be taken immediately. This holds particularly true of a dog that has a runny nose, that has eyes that discharge pus, that coughs, or that is tired and listless for no apparent reason.

All animals, and the dog is no exception, can stand cold; but when confined where it is damp, or if permitted to stand around in the cold while soaking wet, they usually develop trouble of one sort or another. A puppy or a dog can stay outside in winter if nature has been given time to provide him with the necessary protective covering. Otherwise, the owner should see to it that the dog has a warm place to sleep, where his own body heat will give him the warmth that he needs. Although the average dog does not need to wear a coat, those that live in a heated apartment and have very short hair can be given some protection, unless they are, of course, running around and getting a lot of exercise. But sitting around in a cold, penetrating wind is of no advantage.

As with people, the dog's hair indicates his general health and condition. Although a dull coat and a dry, scaly skin may be caused by worms or by a lack of something in the diet, it also accompanies every form of sickness and will take months to get back its gloss and sheen, even after the dog is on the road to recovery. If it is a question of skin trouble—that is another matter. There are so many forms of this that an owner would do well to seek the advice of an expert at the first sign of skin disorder. Contagious mange, ringworm, eczema, and dandruff each require different treatment, and early care will prevent spreading.

An owner can gamble if he wants to—everybody does—but when it comes to the health of his dog, he should know exactly what he is getting. The little extra effort put forth at the right time may be the means of preventing unnecessary heartache and prolonged inconvenience.

The Medicine Chest

Although there is no limit to the number of things an owner may keep in the dog's medicine chest, there are a few items that are basically essential. These are:

A *rectal thermometer*—To be used at the first sign of sickness or whenever in doubt.

Enema bag—For use when the stool is hard and chalky. Also, for lowering the dog's temperature during illness and as a douche after worming, or on the advice of a veterinarian during the dog's sickness period.

Milk of Magnesia—To be given both as a laxative and to help cure acidity. It should not be mixed with the dog's dinner but given late at night or early in the morning. Dose is two teaspoonfuls for a small dog and one to two tablespoonfuls to a large dog.

Pepto-Bismol or Bismuth Subnitrate—Tightening agents to help to clear up diarrhea.

Epsom Salts—Useful for soaking an injured or infected paw or other localized swellings.

Skin Ointment—For minor skin irritations.

Boric-Acid Solution or Alcolol—For washing the eyes.

5% Argyrol or 1% Yellow-Oxide Ointment—For an injury to the eye until the veterinarian can be consulted.

Sulphanilimide Powder or B.F.I. Powder—May be used in the ears, on minor skin irritations, or on open wounds.

Zonite or Pearson Creolin—Disinfectants for bathing open wounds.

Monsol Solution—To stop bleeding in case the nails are cut too short.

Aspirin—To aid in lowering a high temperature and to quiet a nervous dog.

Luminal—For extreme nervousness and especially for keeping a dog quiet if he has a convulsion.

Suppositories—To use during housebreaking and whenever traveling.

Cotton and Bandages

Worming

When an owner suspects that his dog has worms, it is not advisable for him to give worm remedies without consulting a veterinarian. There are five types of worms common to dogs and each requires different medicine and treatment. There is the roundworm, the whipworm, the hookworm, the tapeworm, and the less common heartworm.

The roundworm may be easily recognized because it is three to four inches long and has a hard, round, firm body. It is prevalent in puppies and is not difficult to get rid of. These are often called puppy worms. They are clearly seen in the stool, and when there is a heavy infestation, the puppy may even pass them by mouth.

Tapeworm segments look like little grains of rice, and are one-quarter to one-half inches long. They stick to the hair under the tail but may also be seen in the dog's stool. They are a pinkish white when first passed but turn brown as they dry out. The eggs are so hard to find under the microscope that a dog may have tapeworm even though a negative report is given when the stool is tested by a veterinarian. The louse and the flea act as intermediate hosts for this particular worm. If a dog has either of these parasites, he may have tapeworm as well.

Hookworm and whipworm are not easy to see with the naked eye. Both are the size of a very fine hair. The eggs of each, though, are easily recognized under the microscope. Whipworm eggs look exactly like a lemon, even to the color. Hookworm eggs are dark—and oval in shape compared to the roundness of the roundworm eggs. The same medicine may be used for hookworm as for roundworm, but three times the usual dosage must be given in order to get results. The hookworm clings to the intestine and will cause untold damage. The whipworm lives in the so-called "blind gut," which makes it hard to eradicate. An occasional worming is not enough, as the treatment must be given at regular intervals so that the medicine will work its way into the closed passage and rout out the whipworm as well as the whipworm eggs. A dog heavily infested with whipworm must, in many cases, be operated on to get lasting results. The "blind gut," which is the seat of the trouble, is removed. This is equivalent to removing the appendix in a human being.

Heartworm is not common except in certain parts of the country. The South, for instance, has more than other places. To determine whether a dog has this type of worm, the blood, instead of the dog's stool, must be tested under the microscope.

There are many outward signs that may indicate the presence of worms. The coat may be dull, the skin dry and scaly; and the dog may do a lot of scratching. His eyes, instead of appearing bright and full of fire, may have a dull and vacant look. He may drag his rear end along the ground, although this may be a sign that the anal glands need to be emptied. Usually if the dog has worms, he is in thin condition and has a poor appetite, although this is not always the case. With tapeworm, for instance, the dog may be overly fat and he may have a ravenous appetite. Diarrhea, in one form or another, is almost always present. At any rate, except in the case of tapeworm, the surest way to find out if a dog has worms at all is to have the stool tested under the microscope, and the best way to give accurate treatment is on the advice of a veterinarian.

Car Sickness

It is doubtful if anything is more unpleasant than to have a dog get sick every time he is taken out in the car. Not only is it annoying and inconvenient to the owner, but it is upsetting to the dog as well. To avoid car sickness, the puppy should get used to traveling when he is very young. Puppies six to eight weeks of age do not, as a rule, get sick even on their first trip. An older dog may get sick once or twice; but if taken out every day before he is fed, he may get over this tendency in a short time. When a dog becomes uneasy and restless, or if he starts to drool, the car should be stopped and the dog permitted to walk around a bit. He should be given plenty of air while riding and be allowed to sit up where he can see what is going on.

Sometimes car sickness is psychological and can be cured if the dog is permitted to sit quietly in a motionless car or if he is fed there. As a result of such devices he will associate something pleasant with the car. This brings to mind one dog that had only to stand and look at a motor vehicle several feet away for the saliva to start running down each side of his mouth. Usually car sickness is due to nerves, and a sedative or one of the many sea-sick remedies will be helpful. Otherwise, there is little that can be done, except to take the dog out riding as often as possible and to take him on an empty stomach. It is mostly a question of time to

Take him out in the car at an early age

get the dog accustomed to the swaying motion. And when he is, he will enjoy motoring as much as his master does. In this age of motor travel, every dog should be able to ride without getting sick, and the proper age to teach him is under four months.

While on the subject of riding, let us mention the dog's behavior while he is in the car. We are all familiar with those dogs that develop such atrocious manners the moment they climb into the seat that one would almost rather stay home than go through the ordeal of riding with them. The owner who thinks he is doing his dog a favor by permitting him to dangle half way out the window or to hop madly about is inviting trouble. A driver on the road today has a full-time job with traffic without being interfered with by a dog. As a passenger, one should be allowed to relax and enjoy the ride, and this cannot be done if one must associate with a wild hoodlum. For the "hanger-outers," there is always danger of developing eye and ear trouble, and the dog may even be injured should the car stop suddenly and he be thrown to the ground. Quiet and firm handling will soon teach a dog what he can and cannot do in a car. If he is made to act like a gentleman from the very beginning he will be just as happy. It all depends upon what he gets used to doing.

The motorist today does encounter one reason for a dog's bad manners while in a car, and that is the inevitable toll collector. A few years ago such persons were rare but nowadays the toll booth appears all too frequently. I have just recently had half a dozen cases in which the owners came to me in despair because they were afraid their dogs would bite the person who collected the dimes, quarters and fifty-cent pieces. Even though we might feel like letting him do it, it's not a good idea. The dog should be kept on leash and warned to "Watch your manners!" when the car approaches the toll house. At the first attempt to bark or move forward the dog should be rapped sharply across the nose, hard enough to make him draw back by himself. If he repeats his act he should be rapped smartly again. After one or two lessons, if done properly, the dog can be kept under control by merely warning him in advance.

Breeding the Pet

The breeding of dogs runs in a cycle—at least it is certain that if one starts with a puppy one ends up with a grown dog, and, on the other hand, if one starts with a grown dog one usually ends up with puppies.

The adult male presents no problem. If an owner doesn't want to breed his dog, he can refrain from doing so without injuring the dog's health in any way. One who wants his male used at stud will find such use does not ruin the dog for companionship. Very often an owner will feel that if a dog is oversexed it is because he has never been used for breeding. This has nothing to do with it. As a matter of fact, after a dog has once been bred he is more aware of females than ever. There are, in any case, highly-sexed males that must either be castrated to help calm them down or severely disciplined so that fear of punishment will prevent misbehavior.

If a male is to be used for breeding purposes, care should be taken to select the brood bitch whose bloodlines favor his. Lacking this knowledge, it is wise to seek the advice of someone who is familiar with the breed, and who is sufficiently aware of the dog's background to know what points to look for and what faults must be overcome. This will

35

avoid bad breeding, which so often results in inferior specimens of puppies.

At the time of mating, it is customary for the female to be taken to the male for service. By mutual agreement, other arrangements may be made. The owner of the sire receives a stud fee that has previously been agreed upon and is payable at the time of service. The owner of the dam will be the owner of the puppies. If no puppies result from the breeding, the stud fee is not returned but a second service is given when the female comes into heat again. It may be agreed upon that, in lieu of a stud fee, the owner of the sire will receive the pick of the litter at eight weeks of age. In any case, to avoid any misunderstanding the arrangements should be thoroughly understood before the actual mating occurs.

The owner of the female has a big responsibility. It is inexcusable to permit one in season to roam the streets. This is asking for trouble and will bring disastrous results. Males that would ordinarily stay at home are attracted far afield and as a result are often killed by motor cars, cause motorcar accidents, or are injured in fights with other males. Groups of dogs will always gather around a female in season; and if the female gets bred (which she undoubtedly will), there will be no way of knowing who is the sire of the puppies. As a result, the country becomes overrun with a lot of crossbred puppies not eligible for registration.

A female will come in season twice a year, but not necessarily every six months. The full period will last about three weeks, and she may be from eight to sixteen months old when she come in the first time. It is not hard to recognize the symptoms of a female's approaching heat period. The vulva will swell, and there is usually a white discharge before she actually shows color. Male dogs will become keenly interested sometimes a week in advance. After the color begins, it will be still another week before the real danger period—that is, when the female will accept the male and show her willingness by "flagging" her tail. From then on, she must be watched very carefully for ten days or longer.

If the female is to be bred, it is better to wait until the second heat period, unless the bitch is large for her age and unusually strong and husky. A breeder may prefer to have the mating take place on a certain number of days after the first show of color, and he may request more than one service. This may be on two consecutive days or by skipping a day in between. Good results may be had from only one mating, which does not affect the number of puppies. A single mating has resulted in a litter of twelve puppies, but in other cases, where the female was serviced more than once, only one or two puppies were produced.

Even if a female is mated during her period, she will continue to show color and will still accept the male for a number of days. The owner of a female should be considerate enough to keep the dog confined, either at home or in a boarding kennel, during the full three weeks.

When the female is kept in the suburban sections, even though she is in an enclosed yard, the owner can expect the neighborhood "gang" to hang around—unless, of course, he owns an air rifle. This weapon will usually keep the "wolves" away, but it may be the means of breaking up a beautiful friendship with the next door neighbor if he happens to be the owner of one of the attentive dogs.

The city female presents little trouble along this line because almost all city dogs are kept on leash. However, the use of a Dogtex belt will minimize the chances of the female being bred accidentally, and, at the same time, will prevent spots being left on the furniture and on the rugs. Dogtex belts are available at most pet supply shops and they come in different colors.

A female should be bred at least once before she is five years old, if she is going to be bred at all. If she is too old, when bred for the first time, complications may arise in whelping. A female may continue to have puppies as long as she comes in season and remains in good health. She should not be bred during more than two out of every three periods.

A male may be used at stud when he is less than a year old, but not too frequently. He will continue to give service even at the advanced age of twelve or thirteen years.

A female that is not used for breeding can be spayed, but it is preferable to have this done while the puppy is still young and has not yet come in season. The spayed female will not become fat and lazy if the owner watches her diet carefully and sees that she receives plenty of exercise. In fact, spaying is the only solution if a female cannot be given the proper attention when she comes into heat.

Care of the Brood Bitch

The bitch in whelp requires little more than her usual good care and should be given plenty of nourishing food while she is carrying her young. The addition of calcium gluconate, bone meal, and vitamins at this time is beneficial, as it will keep the mother from drawing on her own body for these vital food elements. Limewater added to the milk or the water she drinks will guard against acidity of her milk, which is fatal to nursing puppies.

The brood bitch should receive plenty of exercise. A normal amount of jumping, if she does so from choice, will do no harm. It is not wise to force a mother-to-be to jump against her will. She is the best judge of what she can and cannot do.

With her first litter, the bitch will usually carry the puppies high in back of her ribs, so it is hard to say if she is in whelp or not. If she is, the nipples are usually the first to show a change. They will become red and slightly puffy. The abdomen may not swell until the fifth or sixth week, and the breasts will fill out the seventh or eighth week.

The normal gestation period is sixty-three days, but it may vary by a few days more or less. It is better for the bitch to go over than under this norm because the puppies are then stronger and better developed. A week before the puppies are due, preparation should be made for the whelping. A box in which the bitch can stretch out comfortably in either direction may be put in the bathroom, bedroom, or any other convenient place where it is warm and dry. The bottom of the box should be covered with layer upon layer of newspapers, and the bitch should be encouraged to sleep on these prior to the time the puppies are born. This may discourage her from sneaking off to hide the puppies under the house or in some dark closet. The mother's food during the last week should be on the soft side, and should consist of two or three feedings a day instead of the usual one.

The signs of approaching birth are definite. The bitch will tear up the papers, dig and scratch holes in the ground, refuse to eat, or eat and then regurgitate her food. There will be a drop in the bitch's temperature from the usual 102 degrees to as low as 97 degrees. When all this happens, the owner can be pretty certain the puppies will arrive within twenty-four hours. Nervous panting and general restlessness are natural and no cause for worry. However, if there is evidence for more than one hour of labor involving definite muscular contractions, a veterinarian should be called.

The puppies will arrive anywhere from five minutes to an hour apart and each in his individual sac, unless the sac has broken. In such a case, there is a dry birth. Although many claim that a puppy should make his appearance into this world head first, it is far from unusual for him to come tail end first.

The owner can assist at the actual birth by taking a rough towel and helping to ease the puppy out as the mother labors. This should not be done in a forceful way but just to give some added assistance. When the puppy is delivered, the owner should break and peel back the membrane that surrounds him, and then cut the navel cord so as to leave about one and one-half inches. The towel may be used to wipe away mucus, so that the puppy will start breathing freely, and the mother should be encouraged to lick the newborn puppy—which she will then do very vigorously. The puppy may be guided to the "milk bar" but this is seldom necessary.

Very often a puppy will arrive with no sign of life. If the owner can feel a pulse beat under the forearm, it may just be a matter of starting the puppy breathing. This can be done by artificial respiration. By blowing steadily into the puppy's mouth, the lungs can be sufficiently expanded to supply the necessary oxygen.

During the prolonged whelping period, the mother should occasionally be given a drink of warm milk and, after she has completely finished the ordeal, some solid food made rather soft.

Nature so provides that when a bitch is left to her own resources she will break the cord herself and will dispose of the afterbirth by eating it. In the wild state, this afterbirth served as her only food for the two or three days when she would not leave her new family; it also acted as a laxative. With our modern dogs so well fed and cared for, there is no need of this additional food and, therefore, the afterbirth can be taken away. On the other hand, if the mother should succeed in getting it first (and two to one she will), it will do no harm to give her a dose of castor oil when she has finished whelping to clean her out and to get things back to normal.

Although some breeders will take the puppies away from the mother as soon as they are born, and will keep them away until the last puppy has been delivered, it is doubtful if this is a good practice. It makes the mother worry because it is natural for her to want the puppies near. If she is permitted to keep them she will be more content. It is also better for the puppies if they start nursing immediately and are scrubbed within an inch of their lives as the mother washes and cleans them.

The care of the new family is very simple for three or four weeks. The mother will keep the brood sweet and clean, and if the puppies are warm and getting enough to eat, they will be quiet and sleep most of the time. A constant weak cry is a signal of distress, and the owner should find out what the trouble is. It may be that the milk is acid and the puppies are not able to assimilate their food. Maybe a puppy has a cleft-palate—a slit in the roof of the mouth—and for this reason is not getting enough to eat. In such a case, the puppy should be destroyed, as he will never be properly nourished. A sickly or deformed puppy may be disposed of by holding it under water for a few moments. Or again, perhaps the puppies are cold—or they may be too warm. The nice thing about puppies—even newly born ones—is that they will not hesitate to let everyone know when they are not happy.

The mother should come through the nursing period in a fat and robust condition. She will if she is given all she will eat three or four times a day. If she is not getting enough food, she will draw on her own body to supply the puppies' needs and will look scrawny and thin by the time the puppies are weaned. A thin nursing mother is not inevitable no matter how many puppies she is feeding.

A good diet-and-feeding schedule will consist of the following:

8 A.M.—Milk (as much as she will drink), 1 egg, 1 tablespoonful limewater.
12 Noon—Meat (the amount depends upon the breed of dog), meal and biscuit, calcium, bone meal, cod-liver oil and vitamins.
4 P.M.—Same as 8 A.M.
8 P.M.—Same as at noon.

For the first few days the food should be on the moist side.

There is a proper time for the puppies' tails to be docked and the dewclaws removed. With Poodles this is usually done on the fifth day, but the time will vary with the breed. The length the tail is cut also depends on the breed. Standard Poodles should have tails measuring one and three-eighths inches from the base. Miniatures, one inch. Other breeds call for cutting off one-third of the entire tail. A poorly docked tail will spoil the dog's entire outline, and it is just as easy to cut it the right length as the wrong.

If the litter is not too large and if the dam has plenty of milk, it will not be necessary to give the puppies additional food until they are three or four weeks old. If the litter is a large one, a little warm whole milk or diluted canned milk may be given as soon as the puppies' eyes open—which occurs between the ninth and the fourteenth day. The first drinking lessons will be easy if the puppies are fed with a large spoon. Later they will drink from a shallow and narrow dish. A little raw scraped beef may be given when the puppies are three to four weeks old, and it then won't be long before the puppies become interested in their mother's dinner as well. If the mother at any time regurgitates her own food for the puppies to eat, the owner should not be horrified. It is perfectly natural and is the mother's way of starting to wean the puppies and of teaching them to get going by themselves.

If a female should accidentally get bred, and the sire is unknown, it is sometimes better to take the puppies away before they have a chance to nurse. The mother's milk supply should be dried up by rubbing camphorated oil on her breasts. If the mother has a great deal of milk, a little may be gently squeezed out by hand. But care must be taken, because massaging stimulates the milk glands and will increase the flow more than ever.

There is no truth to the statement that if a female has a litter of mongrel puppies she will never have purebreds again. If the bitch is mated the next time to a purebred of her own breed, the puppies will all be purebreds.

Before going on to puppy discipline, I would like to mention two more points of importance. Young puppies are like small babies. Both need plenty of sleep during the daytime as well as at night. When a puppy wanders off into the corner and drops down exhausted after a hard play, he should not be disturbed. Every owner should respect a puppy's desire to rest and should teach children to respect it as well.

The second point is when a puppy is brought into a home where there is already an older dog, care should be taken that the new and playful member of the household does not annoy or pester the old dog. He may fly at the puppy in self-defense, and as a result the puppy may become frightened and cringe away. Until the new addition learns his place and has been accepted, he should be kept on the leash rather than the old fellow.

The suggestions I have made on general care and feeding are in no way complete. Neither will everybody agree with them—no two persons see eye to eye when it comes to raising dogs. But these are the results of my own experience in raising hundreds of puppies, and I pass them on to my readers with the thought that they may be helpful in answering some of the questions that arise in the minds of every dog owner.

Puppy Discipline

People very often say, "I don't want to buy a puppy and go through all the trouble of puppy raising. I would rather have an older dog that is housebroken and has had some training." Perhaps they are right but such persons lose out in more ways than one. Puppies are lots of fun, and they will provide many hours of entertainment along with their numerous naughty deeds.

Those owners who have had the courage to start with a puppy, and who have survived such things as housebreaking and teaching not to chew up valuable property or to cry when left alone, have already accomplished a great deal. The following pages are intended for those who must still go through this routine training. It is hoped the suggestions will make the task easier.

How the Puppy Learns

In directing the puppy's training as it is presented in the following pages, the owner must keep these five rules in mind:

1. *A puppy learns through associating his deed with pleasing or displeasing results.* He will want to repeat the act that brings a satisfactory reward and quickly discontinue the one that brings discomfort.
2. *The corrective measure should be simultaneous with the act to be most effective.* The puppy must be disciplined the moment he does wrong or he will not remember nor understand why he is being punished.
3. *The correction must be made each time the puppy makes a mistake.* It is confusing if he is permitted to do something once or twice, then later is scolded for doing the very same thing.
4. *The forcefulness with which the corrections are made should be according to the temperament of the puppy.* One must be kind with a shy puppy but firm with one having a willful nature.
5. *By doing the right thing and avoiding the wrong the training will be simplified.* Severe corrections are necessary only when bad habits are already a part of a dog's behavior.

Paper-breaking

A puppy under four months is too young to be housebroken successfully unless he can be taken out of doors every two or three hours. No matter how hard the little fellow tries, he will not be able to hold in for too long a time. When the inevitable mistake occurs and he is punished, he will be more confused than ever.

The only possible thing to do with a newly acquired eight- to ten-weeks-old puppy is to paper-break him and then housebreak him. The owner should pick a small room, such as a bathroom or hallway, and spread several thicknesses of paper over the entire floor. For the next few weeks this is where the puppy should stay most of the time. The idea is to prevent the puppy from making a mistake where there are no papers. If this is done, he will get into the habit of using the papers when necessary. Until the puppy will seek out the papers by himself he should be confined in a small area.

When the puppy has picked out a special corner for use, and when he

A play pen is useful in housebreaking a puppy

returns to it over and over again, a few of the papers can be taken up from around the outside edges. They should be left down in the spot the puppy has chosen for his bathroom.

When an older dog wishes to relieve himself, he will give warning by sniffing the floor. A young puppy, however, will be very quick to squat wherever he happens to be, so he must be watched more carefully. The first time the puppy starts to make a mistake where there are no papers he should be startled by the owner tossing something at his feet. He should then be grabbed up quickly and put on his paper. A puppy that is not housebroken should never be confined in a room unless papers are available.

43

The puppy will soon learn what the paper is for

As the puppy's training progresses and he is given more freedom, the owner should take care to put him on paper immediately after he has had dinner and romped in play. When results are forthcoming the puppy should be praised and made a great fuss over. In fact, every chance the owner has he should let the puppy know he has done the right thing by using the papers.

A puppy that is supposedly paper-broken may suddenly make several mistakes off the paper for no apparent reason; in such a case he should be given a complete refresher course and the entire paper-breaking procedure started from the beginning.

The owner of a small dog will find it convenient to have his dog paper-

44

broken as well as housebroken. This is especially true of an apartment house dog or one that travels about with his owner. It is convenient to have such a dog use a piece of paper in the hotel room or in a train compartment so that there will be no need to take the dog on the street every time he must go outside. This combination of housebreaking and paperbreaking, when the papers are left down at night or when they are used on special occasions, is very desirable and highly recommended. Even an older dog that has never been trained to use papers can be taught, if he is not permitted to go outside until he gets used to the idea of using paper.

Simple Training

Before a puppy can be given further training he must be introduced to the collar and leash. An ordinary leather collar and a fairly long leash are advisable. A harness, however, is not recommended. It will pull the puppy out at the shoulders, and it does not teach a dog to be obedient. Also, the dog is dangled in mid-air like a sack of meal and does not respond to jerks on the leash. For the first few lessons, the puppy should be played with around the house in familiar surroundings. The leash may be fastened to the collar and permitted to drag along the floor until the puppy gets accustomed to feeling something around his neck. Later, when the leash is pulled gently, he will have more assurance and will not be afraid.

When a small puppy is taken on the street for his first adventure into the big world, he should be carried some distance from his usual surroundings and coaxed to walk back. For some reason or other, puppies are better at coming than they are at going. The owner, by patting the floor or his knee and coaxing the puppy to come along, will teach him to have no real fear of the leash—which he might have if he were dragged about in a rough way.

We have all seen puppies, or even grown dogs for that matter, apply all four brakes and refuse to budge. Usually a quick jerk on the leash will start the dog moving. If not, the puppy should be slowly dragged along the floor or the ground until he makes up his mind he would rather walk than slide on his posterior. When he gets up on all four feet and walks along properly, the leash can be loosened and the puppy praised and patted encouragingly.

The simple commands of "Come," "Sit," and "Lie down" should be taught in the house while the puppy is still very young. In fact, the first lesson every young puppy should learn is to come when he is called. When he is young, he will very quickly obey the command if, every time he answers the call, he receives a pleasant reward such as a piece of meat, dog candy, or a word of praise. The owner should never call a puppy and then punish him if he does not come. The next time, the puppy will run in the opposite direction, for which he can hardly be blamed. A dog's willing response to the owner's command to "come" will make him more obedient in every way and help minimize all training problems.

A dog will quickly learn the command "Sit" if his head is held high and a little pressure is applied to his hindquarters. The leash, if it is on, can be used to pull the head up. If not, the collar or the loose skin on the throat can be used as a handle. By repeating "Sit, good boy, sit!" and by patting the puppy as soon as he obeys, he will soon get the idea of what to do. The dog should be made to sit not just in his own home, but also when he is visiting, when he goes shopping with his owner and whenever he rides in an elevator. This will keep him out of the way in crowded places and he will not get stepped on.

The command "Lie down" is taught in more or less the same way as the command "Sit." It is better, in this case, to have the puppy on leash so he cannot dart off. The puppy's front feet should be pulled forward from underneath him and pressure applied to his back to force him down. The command "Down" or "Lie down" is repeated over and over in a low quiet voice until the puppy drops to the floor. When he is lying down, he should not be praised or patted with too much enthusiasm because it will tempt him to get up again. Instead, his head may be stroked or his ear scratched as a sign of approval.

Every dog that has had some preliminary training—that is, is not afraid of the leash and understands what Come, Sit, and Down mean—will learn the subsequent exercises more quickly. Though the owner may not realize it, he has already brought about a certain understanding between the dog and himself.

Housebreaking

When a puppy is four months old and ready for housebreaking, things begin to happen. This is the age when an owner will vow never to have another dog. But with a little precaution and conscientious attention, even the unpleasant task of housebreaking can be made simple.

At this point in the puppy's training, *all papers should be taken up*, unless the owner wishes to combine housebreaking with paper-breaking; if such is the case, the papers are left down at night. An owner will frequently make the mistake of leaving just one piece of paper where the puppy can use it during the day if he doesn't do what he should outside. When a puppy is trained to use papers, he will never learn to be clean in the house as long as he knows the paper will be there when he returns from a trip out-of-doors. I repeat, *all* papers should be taken up and kept up if the puppy is to be completely housebroken. They should be put down only at night if the puppy is to be housebroken during the day and paper-broken at night.

The next rule in housebreaking is: never give the puppy the run of the house. He should be tied or confined for the first few days. When he is given more freedom he should be closely watched. At night, the leash can be fastened to a radiator in the bedroom, or the puppy can be kept in a crate or box or left in a small hallway. Dogs, as a rule, do not like to soil their surroundings; so in order to keep themselves clean when confined, they use control and thus train their muscles to function at definite times. Preventing a mistake is half the battle of housebreaking. I might go further and say that preventing a mistake is half the battle of *all* training.

During mealtime the leash may be fastened to a radiator at the far side of the dining room or in an adjoining room where the owner can see the puppy from where he sits. At other times, the leash may be slipped under the owner's foot or tied to the leg of a chair or table. The puppy should be allowed to run around only if watched, and he should never be permitted out of sight. When he sniffs the floor, the puppy should be warned with a "No! Careful now. Be a good boy!". This may prevent a mishap because it will break the puppy's train of thought and divert him to something else. The puppy should be exercised *the first thing in the morning, the last thing at night, after every meal, and after hard play.* When the puppy is left alone, he should be confined. But the owner should never go away and leave the dog tied, for he might become entangled in the leash and hang himself.

In spite of all precautions, there will be some mistakes. When they occur, the puppy should be held firmly by the collar and taken to the spot and shamed with "Did you do that? Bad boy!" One should never rub the dog's nose in the mess. This method of training is disgusting and will prove to be of no benefit. The puppy should also be given a sharp cuff on his rump, and if he is in the country or where there is a garden, should be put out of doors immediately. I often hear the remark, "I thought a puppy should never be spanked with the bare hand." But the hand may be used if the puppy is held firmly while being spanked. Hand shyness is caused by slapping a dog or by swinging at him as he runs past without following through on correction. Having successfully escaped

"Did you do that? Shame!"

punishment the first time, the puppy will duck away when the hand is again raised. The suggestion that a newspaper be used to punish a dog is not a good one. Those who recommend its use claim the noise will frighten the puppy but he will not be hurt by the paper. By right, the puppy should be hurt—but without being frightened. A puppy that has been whipped by a newspaper will shy away from one even in the reading library. Very likely, the paper idea originated so the owner wouldn't hurt his own hand! It can really sting at times. If a dog is held securely and forced to accept punishment the right way, there will be no reason for him to become hand shy.

It will be to the owner's advantage if he can catch the puppy doing wrong and will discipline him then and there. A dog will not harbor a grudge if punished when caught in the act. If punishment is inflicted after the wrong deed, one must be more careful. A dog's memory, like a child's, is not very long, and he does not always remember that he made a mistake.

The owner should make things as easy as possible for the puppy by feeding him at regular hours and not later than five or six o'clock in the afternoon. And, as mentioned earlier, this last feeding should be of solid rather than liquid food.

Even though a dog is housebroken, he will often show his anger when left alone by lifting his leg and leaving a puddle on the rug. He must be dealt with more severely and made to realize that the owner is thoroughly disgusted and will not tolerate such actions. A hard spanking should be administered and the dog immediately put outside. If he persists in this little game, a switch or a strap may prove more effective and help him to remember his mistakes more clearly. One or two set mousetraps near his favorite spot may work when everything else fails.

A friend had one old dog that convinced me dogs are capable of deliberately thinking up ways to get even. This was a household pet and so the kennel held little attraction—nor did I, dressed in dungarees. To him, dungarees meant being bathed and groomed, and he didn't particularly like either. However, it was a very different story when I appeared in a dress. That brought to mind dog shows and going places, both of which he adored with a passion.

One evening this dog was lying in the living room while his owner was reading. He watched disinterestedly as I, in a dress, came downstairs and went out. After a few moments he got up, stretched himself, and slowly sauntered up the stairs. In a little while he reappeared, gave a deep sigh of contentment, and settled down to resume his nap. The owner thought he had gone for a drink of water. Later, when the maid went into my room, there was a loud cry. The dog had jumped on the bed and had lifted his leg right in the center of the pillow. This was his way of saying "That for you for not taking me with you!" This same performance was repeated every time the dog was left home unless the door of my room was kept closed. For years, in spite of severe punishment, he was never to be completely trusted. He accepted his lickings willingly rather than lose the satisfaction of "getting even" with me.

Another example of spite actions was the behavior of a Miniature Poodle that had been in one of my training classes. One evening I was invited to my "pupil's" home for dinner. During the evening the owner tried without success to make the dog obey a command. At this point I took over, and the dog did what he was told and was very meek and docile about the whole thing. Later that same evening, after his mistress had driven me home, the Poodle quietly strode over to the chair in which I had been sitting and, without hesitating, deliberately lifted his leg against it. The dog was completely housebroken and had never done anything like that before. To my knowledge, he has never done it since.

Curb-breaking

It is not the easiest thing in the world to train a dog to take care of himself in the street and to do what he should on leash. In fact, it can be very discouraging at times. A dog likes to get off by himself where he can hunt around and take his own sweet time, and he normally has a great deal of modesty. Because the leash interferes with this freedom, the dog will not concentrate on the job at hand but will wait until he goes back into the house, where he immediately will make a mistake unless he is tied or confined in a box.

Curb-breaking is something every dog should know. If one is traveling or visiting, or if he lives in restricted areas where dogs are not permitted to run free, it is very convenient and pleasant to have a dog that is trained to take care of himself without fuss or bother.

For the city dog, curb-breaking is, of course, essential. A young puppy will easily learn to perform while on leash, and he will use a paved street with no reserve. Puppies have no inhibitions. But a dog that has always lived in the country and been allowed to roam, especially if he is an older dog, will be slow to make the readjustment and will present more of a problem.

If the puppy is young and has yet to be housebroken, he should be curb-broken at the same time. It works out well when they are done together, and the results are more lasting.

The best way to start curb-breaking is by tieing the puppy's leash, at night, to a radiator or some other object in the bedroom. The following morning the puppy should be taken outdoors for a ten- or fifteen-minute airing. If he does everything, the owner is indeed lucky and should praise the pup generously. Usually, though, the puppy will puddle and nothing else. If the puppy just stands around and does not concentrate on what he is doing, he should be taken back to the house and tied or confined in a small crate. He must not be allowed to run around. If he is taken out later with no results, he should be tied a second time. After the puppy has held in just as long as he can without doing something in the house, he will probably do it outside if given the chance. And when he does, the owner has won the first battle.

Each time the puppy is taken out he should be taken to the same place and walked slowly back and forth with the leash slack. He should be encouraged with "Go on, hurry up. Good boy." For a while, two leashes can be fastened together to give the dog more freedom of movement. The dog may not be so reserved if he can get farther away from people. Also, for one or two days, a glycerine suppository can be used to help get the dog to act quickly. Suppositories are always useful when traveling and should be included in the dog's travel kit at all times.

Curb a puppy at three to four months

Whenever the puppy does what he is supposed to do, he should be praised and taken back inside, and then permitted to play around for a little while. But not for long, because he will be tempted to do something, even though he has already taken care of himself outdoors. From this point on, the same rules apply as for the housebreaking.

51

During the course of curb-breaking, the puppy or dog can learn the difference between the pleasure of going for a walk and of doing his serious duties. When the puppy is ready to relieve himself, the owner should stand or move quietly back and forth in one place and tell the dog to "Hurry up." The leash should be kept slack, for the dog must not be jerked hard when he is sniffing along the ground. When it is time to move on, the leash should be snapped quickly and the dog told to "Come on, now—let's go!" And the owner and dog should then walk off briskly.

As soon as a dog knows why he goes outdoors, he should occasionally be taken to a different place so he will learn to act quickly even in strange surroundings. The puppy or the dog that won't take care of himself unless he has his own special post or plot of grass will be more than handicapped should he ever find himself on the wrong street or in unfamiliar surroundings. And since puppies are always picking up things they shouldn't from the street, this is a very good time, with the puppy on leash, for the owner to teach him to resist temptation. It will avoid many upset stomachs and may even prevent a puppy from being poisoned. Every time the puppy starts to take something in his mouth, the owner should command "No!" very sharply and pull the puppy away. He will learn quickly and, later, the command will serve to warn him from his temptation to raid the gutters.

Teaching a Puppy to Stay by Himself

If a dog is trained to stay by himself, he will not be so tempted to chew up things or to bark in temper and disturb the neighbors. A barking dog is a great annoyance to all within hearing distance, and he is one reason, well justified, why neighbors are frequently on bad terms with one another. They say man can get along without everything except sleep. Whoever made this statement must have been kept awake by a barking dog.

A puppy eight or ten weeks old is certainly less difficult to train than one eight or ten months old. The younger the puppy, the easier the job will be. At first, the puppy should be closed up for short intervals in a crate or some special room that he will think of as belonging to him. His balls and other playthings should be left with him. The puppy's first howls of rage, even though they are annoying, should cause no distress, as they merely indicate temper and will subside when the puppy understands he is not going to have his own way. The training should be started in the daytime. The noise will not seem nearly so penetrating, and if the puppy gets used to being alone during the day, he will accept his night solitude more easily.

If an older dog will not stay alone, you can be fairly certain he has been spoiled and has always had company. Just to go away and leave the dog to bark himself out is not the right kind of training. No one is home to correct the dog at the right time, so he will never get over the habit of barking. The owner should start the training while he is there to carry out the corrections. If the owner is busy in one room, the dog should be shut up in another. The minute he barks, the owner commands, "Quiet!" If the noise continues, a loud rap on the door with, "Quiet. Stop that!" will make him let up at least momentarily. Sometimes a rap on the door without saying anything will be effective. But if the dog is stubborn and persists in raising a rumpus, the owner should go into the room quietly, take the dog firmly by the collar, and shake him or cuff him hard, demanding at the same time that he stop. Every time it is necessary to open the door, the punishment should be more severe. The puppy should get to the point where he would do almost anything rather than see the door open and his owner appear.

A dog is intelligent, and he may soon get wise to the fact that the owner is in the next room and will be quiet while he is there, but will bark the minute he leaves the house. The next step for the owner is to fool the dog into thinking he has gone away. He should go to the outside door and slam it, then sneak back and stand outside the door of the room where the dog is confined and wait for him to bark. At the first sound, the owner calls out, "Stop that!" or he raps sharply on the door without saying anything. It will come as such a surprise the dog will probably be quiet the rest of the day, trying to figure out how the owner got back into the house without his knowing it. If the barking continues in spite of everything, the dog must be taken firmly by the collar and given a severe shaking or held and cuffed hard. By this time, the owner's temper will be about ready to explode, and the dog will fully realize the danger.

One needs a lot of patience when training a dog to stay by himself. Hour after hour will be spent waiting outside of doors to catch the dog by surprise. Kennel owners have their troubles on this as well. Many times in the middle of the night I have sneaked out to quiet a dog that has been left alone in the kennel. I would wait outside the door, then toss a small stone against the window or on the roof of the kennel when he barked.

I remember one night in particular. A new boarder had come in that day and he was feeling very sorry for himself. After several unsuccessful attempts to get to sleep, I crept inside the kennel with a BB gun. I stood in total blackness for fully twenty minutes with the BB gun pointed toward the wooden door of the pen where the dog was kenneled. Perhaps he suspected my presence, for he was quiet for a while and it was a long wait. Finally he decided it was safe to start in again, and then I pulled the trigger. In the dead of night the little pellet sounded like an exploding firecracker when it hit the door. From then on there was perfect silence, and I went back to bed, undisturbed for the rest of the night. When I tiptoed from that kennel you could have heard a pin drop, and yet there were fifty dogs present.

Breaking the Habit of Barking

It is as natural for a dog to bark as it is for him to breathe. This reaction should not be completely suppressed, but it should be controlled. It is commendable for a dog to give warning when a stranger approaches or if something unusual occurs, but when the owner tells the dog that everything is all right, he should stop barking immediately. A shy dog will bark for his own self-assurance more than anything else. He must still be handled firmly even if he is shy, for otherwise the barking will get out of control. It is the cocky little guy, full of his own importance and trying to show off, that must be scolded and dealt with in a much tougher way.

The training should begin when the puppy is young, but even an older dog, when sitting or lying near by, can be taught to keep quiet. The technique is similar for both. The owner places his hands around the dog's muzzle and, holding the jaws together, tells the dog, "No!" in a firm tone of voice. If he continues to bark he should be cuffed on his nose and spoken to more sharply. If the leash is on, it may be used to give the dog a hard jerk or its handle may be flipped across the dog's nose to impress on him that he must heed the command, "Keep Still!" If a dog, especially a puppy, is corrected every time he barks, and if the corrections are severe enough, he will soon learn to respect the owner's warning.

I doubt if I shall ever forget the first night of the series of training classes sponsored by the American Society for the Prevention of Cruelty to Animals, which I conducted in New York City. The class was held in a gymnasium that could comfortably accommodate twenty-five to thirty dogs. But there were fifty dogs present. The bedlam caused by the fifty untrained dogs, handled by untrained owners, was something I can't even describe. No introductions were heard and no speakers understood. I don't remember saying it, but I was told later that when the class was turned over to my care, I made the statement that I had no intention of competing with fifty dogs and ordered every one present to place his hands around his dog's muzzle and hold his mouth shut. The owners were amazed when they realized how easy it was to keep their dogs quiet. This simple act had not occurred to one of them.

When a dog is off leash, he is more inclined to bark every time the doorbell or the telephone rings, or when people enter the room or pass on the street. In any of these cases, the owner should go up to the dog, take him quietly but firmly by the collar, and shake him hard. The dog should be told to "Stop that racket!" and if shaking has no effect, he should be given a good spanking.

Another way that will get results is to sit in the room with a magazine or an old book, or even the dog's leash, handy. When the dog barks, the article is thrown on the floor near the dog, or it is tossed with less force at the dog himself. Several short pieces of chain are especially good for this purpose because of the loud clatter they make when they crash to the floor. Dogs dislike any kind of noise, and if they realize their barking is the cause of it, they will soon learn to be quiet.

Later, the dog should be tested by being left in a room while the owner hides outside the door. An assistant rings the doorbell or knocks on the wall. If the dog is quiet, there is nothing to do. If he barks, the owner should command, "Quiet!" And if the noise keeps up, the owner should go in, take the puppy by the collar, and make the usual firm corrections. Since excessive barking is more easily prevented than cured, the owner should start early to keep his dog from becoming a noisy pest. Also, he can warn the dog ahead of time when he knows someone is coming or some unusual noise will soon be heard.

Teaching a Puppy Not to Chew Things

Without a doubt, every dog has, at one time or another, destroyed something of value. Chewed corners of rugs and cushions, torn wearing apparel, and gnawed legs of chairs and sofas are taken for granted when a new puppy arrives in the house. All puppies go through the stage where they destroy things. It may be when they are cutting their teeth, or when they are just plain bored. The owners can help in many ways to prevent too much damage from being done during the chewing stage. The puppy's toys—a tennis ball or one or two large shin or knuckle bones— should be kept where the puppy can get them any time he feels the urge to chew on something. The owner should avoid giving a bone that will splinter or one so small it might become lodged in the dog's throat. Under no circumstances should a puppy be given anything made of soft rubber. Chewed-up pieces of rubber will cause stoppage of the intestines and may result in the loss of the puppy. The owner should also not make the mistake of giving a dog an old shoe or an old glove to play with. Later, he will be unable to distinguish between the old one and the new and more expensive one, and the owner will be the loser.

Another way to help avoid chewing—just as it was with barking—is to train the little fellow to stay by himself. Often a dog will gnaw on the wrong thing because of anger at being left alone. Shutting the puppy up for short periods during the day will teach him he cannot have company all the time. The owner should peek in at him now and then to see whether he is up to any mischief. If he is behaving, he should be commended. If he is doing something he shouldn't, the owner's appearance will take the puppy by surprise, and he will feel guilty. When he is punished he will hold no grudge, as he was caught in the act of doing wrong. Thereafter, the puppy will be on his guard, for he will not know when the owner will appear again.

If the owner is in the same room, and the dog starts to chew on something he shouldn't, he should quickly pick up a magazine, the leash, or the dog's collar, and, when the puppy is not looking, throw it hard and either hit him or the floor near him as the command "No!" is given. If this is done so it thoroughly startles the dog, he will immediately associate something unpleasant with the chewing of forbidden objects. A few such lessons will teach the puppy what things are and are not safe to chew on. After the correction, the owner should make up to the puppy by calling him and giving him a pat.

If the owner returns home to find the dog has had a very busy and profitable evening, he should take the dog firmly by the collar, lead him over to the damaged articles, and ask in a severe tone of voice, "Did you do that? Shame on you. Bad dog!" A good shaking will be in order, and a hard cuff on the top of his nose or his rump will help to impress on the dog what a terrible thing he has done. In this case, care should be taken, as punishment is being inflicted *after* the damage has been done. As mentioned before, a dog's memory, like a child's, is short, and too much severity will not be understood or well taken.

The older dog that chews out of spite should be held and firmly trounced or whipped. His intentions are deliberate and not through error, and he therefore requires more severe punishment.

Teaching the Dog Not to Jump on People

Jumping up on people is another habit dogs have that will cause as much annoyance as anything else. Most people resent having dirty paw marks left on a fresh suit or dress and dislike being frightened or knocked down by a strange dog that welcomes them too enthusiastically. When the puppy is still three or four months old, he should be pushed down every time he jumps up, and told "No!" in a very displeased tone of voice. The owner must be consistent and be sure to correct the puppy every time. Otherwise, the dog will be confused if allowed to jump up without being corrected and then, another time, is scolded for doing the very same thing.

The older dog already in the habit of jumping on people may be corrected in a number of ways. The advice to step on his back paws is all right if one can be quick enough when the dog is hopping around like a flea. It is doubtful if this is the best method, for he probably does not understand why his feet are being stepped on and, as a result, will shy away and become afraid.

A more satisfactory method is to raise the knee just as the dog jumps. This should be done with enough force to make him lose his balance and topple over backward. If done properly, the dog will not blame the person but himself for the resulting collision. This gesture should be done hard enough to jar the dog thoroughly, or it will make no impression. The knee should be lifted and lowered quickly so that when the dog regains his feet and looks up puzzled, he will find the owner standing there as unconcerned as though nothing had happened. Then a pat and a word of praise will relieve the owner of all blame and responsibility.

Still another method is to grab the dog's front paws and push him over backward. A tumble to the floor will have the same effect as the knee trick because the dog will again associate unpleasantness with the act of jumping on people.

Also, a folded magazine or newspaper can be flipped in the dog's face when he jumps up; or, the owner may drop his hand quickly and rap the dog sharply across the nose, at the same time turning and walking away.

In any case, the correction will only be effective if given with enough severity to leave no doubt in the dog's mind that this is *not* a game.

To prevent the dog from jumping on strangers, a few friends should be asked to help out by making the same corrections. After several persons have treated the dog in like manner, he will expect the same treatment from everybody he jumps on.

One way of teaching a dog not to jump up (King photo)

If the dog is shy or nervous, the training should be done gently at first so that he will not be frightened. If the dog has a precocious nature, one must be severe enough to make an impression. It is extremely important, however, that a word of praise be given after the correction so that the dog will harbor no ill-feeling. Whenever I get a dog that just cannot keep all four feet on the ground, one method I have found very helpful is to command the dog to "Sit" the moment he comes near. He is then patted and praised, but only as long as he remains in the sitting position with all four feet on the ground.

Speaking of jumping up, a dog can be just as happy sleeping on the floor as when he is on the furniture. If an owner wants his dog to get up on chairs or couches, that, of course, is his privilege, but there is a disadvantage in having hair and dirty paw marks left over everything. Then, too, if a dog is permitted on furniture at home, he will do the same when he is visiting. If the owner, even once, makes the mistake of allowing a puppy to get up on something, he will have to be more severe to prevent the next attempt. It is easier to push the little fellow down the first time he takes this liberty and say "No-oo!" as though you could not believe he would do such a thing.

A puppy should have a place of his own that he considers his personal property. A basket, a cushion, or a blanket is suitable. But it should be placed where the dog can see what is going on; he doesn't like to miss anything. The bed should also be protected from drafts. I had one particularly nice corner in my bedroom—so I thought—that I had fixed up with a blanket for the dogs' sleeping quarters. Yet not one dog would remain there for any length of time. I couldn't understand it until I sat down on the blanket one night to play with them. Then I found there was an unusually bad draft due to the window arrangement. When I moved the blanket to another location, the dogs accepted it gratefully. Every owner should check his dog's sleeping quarters after the windows are opened and if necessary offer some kind of protection from drafts.

There is always the dog that will sneak up on the furniture after his owner has left the room and slither back to the floor when he hears his owner returning. A set mouse trap placed in the dog's favorite spot will work like a charm. When the spring is released with a loud snap, the dog will remember that he was the cause of the noise. There is really little danger of catching a dog's paw in the trap, and even if it should happen little damage can be done. It is the same as pinching one's finger, which most of us have done at one time or another. In the case of a small dog with dainty feet, the owner could cover the trap with a piece of cloth, or he can take some of the tightness out of the spring so it will not come together with so much force. In fact, it need not be a mouse trap at all. Anything that will make a noise when the dog jumps up will work just as well. Cellophane that will crackle or a toy that will squawk will get the same results.

The owner of a Poodle came to me one day and told me that a year before I had suggested the idea of the mouse trap to keep her Poodle off the furniture. The owner was afraid it would hurt the dog, so she refused to try it. Finally, in desperation, she did get up nerve enough to test it and found it worked like magic. The thing that bothered her most was the fact that she had suffered needlessly for a whole year trying to keep her dog on the floor.

Stealing and Refusing Food from Strangers

Stealing is one habit that is more easily prevented than cured. The puppy should be stopped from stealing in the first place by following the same technique used in training thus far. The minute he reaches for anything not his, he should be ordered, in a severe tone of voice, "No!" and, if necessary, given a sharp cuff on the nose.

It will always help if the owner can catch a thieving dog in the act. If he can startle him by throwing a magazine or some other article, when the dog isn't looking, he will make the dog understand that taking things without permission is not allowed. (This is another case where the dog will not hold a grudge when caught in the act of doing something wrong.)

Later, the dog should be left alone in a room which offers him the opportunity to steal. Tempting morsels of food should be left in convenient places and the dog observed without knowing he is being watched. The minute he goes near the food, the owner should call out, "Get away from there!"

If the stealing continues, the dog should be spanked, and with increased severity every time he repeats the offense. Bear in mind that a dog caught stealing, chewing, barking, messing in the house, et cetera, will harbor no grudge when punished.

So often an owner will want to know how to stop his dog from foraging in the gutters or taking food from strangers. If the dog starts to pick up something he shouldn't while he is on leash, the correction is simple. Just as the dog lowers his head the owner should jerk hard on the collar and scuff along the ground with his foot. This will teach the dog to keep his nose up. If the dog is not on leash, the owner should have a short piece of chain or some other small article and toss it close to whatever object the dog is smelling. It is a question of timing the correction so the dog will think ill of whatever the gutter has to offer.

Many people are of the opinion that if a dog is taught to refuse food from strangers, he will be protected from being poisoned. This is not necessarily true. Refusal of food is taught to prevent bribery when a dog is left to guard property. A piece of poisoned meat thrown in the yard, even though the dog has been trained to refuse food, may still be picked up by him with disastrous results.

It is a good idea, however, to teach one's dog not to accept food from other people unless the owner gives permission. Irregular feeding will interfere with a dog's diet and may cause him to be upset or to put on too much weight. One or two lessons are usually all that are necessary. The owner should have the dog on leash. A second person should approach the dog with a piece of meat in the left hand and a small switch in the right hand. The switch is held across the right shoulder so as not to be conspicuous. Just as the dog reaches out to accept the food the switch is brought down quickly across his nose, and the food is snatched back so he cannot get it. The owner, in the meantime, makes no correction except to keep the dog under control and to say "No" when the dog reaches forward. He must also praise the dog after he has been stung with the switch. Care should be taken not to injure the dog's eyes during the training. After a few such lessons, the dog may be left by himself while a stranger again tempts him to take something from his hand. The dog, if properly trained, will growl and turn away from the food, but under no circumstances should he attack the person offering the food. The methods used to teach a dog to guard, to attack, and to refuse food are similar. All three are accomplished by varying amounts of teasing. The owner should be on the alert to know when to let up and at what point to stop the teasing, so that the dog will not receive more training than intended and become difficult to handle.

Chasing Cars, Cats, and Children

If the owner has been lax about permitting his dog to run after things, and if he is now trying to cure him of the habit, a course in general Obedience Training is always advisable. A dog trained to obey the basic commands will be less tempted to chase things, because he will be under control and will immediately be conscious of having done wrong when reprimanded for pursuing something he shouldn't.

But, like everything else, the habit, once formed, must be broken. If it is a case of chasing cars, one person should drive the car while another person works with the dog. This latter person should sit inside with a long carriage whip, or, if the owner wishes, he can use a water pistol. When the dog rushes toward the car, the whip should be used severely or the water squirted in the dog's face, and he should be commanded to "Go home!" The dog must associate something unpleasant happening to him whenever he makes the attack. Also, he will be taken by surprise if suddenly the car "chases" him.

If necessary, the car should be stopped while the trainer leaps out and runs after the dog to drive him away with the whip. Several short pieces of chain are very effective for pelting the dog from the rear. In all cases, the corrections must be severe enough to make the dog turn tail and run. The same training may be followed by horseback riders who are annoyed by dogs chasing after their horses. The riders should go after the dog with a riding crop, or have something else handy to throw at them.

One note of precaution. Be aware of the point at which a dog will intensify his attack rather than retreat. If, in spite of severe corrections, the dog at any time counterattacks, the trainer should cease to advance but should stand his ground and verbally warn the dog to "Get out of here!" After the dog has turned away and is no longer facing the trainer, he can be speeded on his way with a little outside help—but not before.

If the owner is by himself and is not prepared when the dog chases a car or a bicycle, he should pick up a clod of dirt or anything else he can grab and *when the dog is not looking* throw it at his heels or hit him on his hindquarters. It must be done hard enough to make the dog turn toward the trainer, after which the dog is called and patted.

It is probably safe to say that more dogs die from motor cars than from any other cause. Dogs are kept on leash so much of the time they have not learned, by experience, to fear or to have respect for a moving car. Some effort should be made to train them to give all moving vehicles a wide berth. This training calls for two people to work together—one to drive the car, the other to handle the dog.

I usually start by walking the dog on leash down the middle of the road. The car approaches slowly from the rear. When the car is only a few feet away, the horn is blasted as loudly as possible, and, at the same time, the dog is jerked off to the side of the road while the car continues on its way. Then I turn and walk back with the dog in the other direction and the lesson is repeated.

It isn't long before the dog will start to look over his shoulder when he hears a car coming and will move off to the side of the road without human command—for which he is praised enthusiastically. He is then tested by having a car approach from the front. If the dog jumps out of the way by himself when he sees the car coming he is again patted and praised. If not, the leash is jerked hard and the dog finds himself unexpectedly in the ditch.

Many people believe that the Guide Dogs used for leading the blind cross busy intersections because the light is green and wait because the light shows red. A Guide Dog has been trained to respect moving objects, and will judge when to cross the street by the flow of traffic. Our pet dog should be given the same chance to prolong his life.

And what about dogs chasing cats? Well, dogs will be dogs and nine times out of ten a dog will chase a cat because it runs from him. When

62

it does, naturally the dog is going to chase it unless he receives some kind of discipline. This is where our three old faithfuls come in: the whip, the throwing chains, or the BB gun. Even if the cat doesn't make things unpleasant for the dog, one of these three will. It is better not to spare the rod in this case, because it takes only one good scratch from a cornered cat to destroy a dog's eyesight. Except in extreme cases, if a cat stands her ground the dog usually retreats. The dog may well remember a previous encounter with the sharp weapons so well concealed within the fur, but it is better for the owner not to take a chance. None of us is always able to resist temptation, and the obedience-trained dog is no exception. He may be more easily discouraged from taking part in such adventures, but he will still chase an occasional cat or two when he has the chance.

This doesn't mean that one cannot train a dog and cat to get along together. One can, even if the dog is the worst kind of cat-hater. One old house pet was at least seven years old when a member of the feline family first took possession of his private domicile, and for some time he never lost a chance to send the intruder to the top of the highest tree. But gradually, through constant association with each other and many scoldings, the cat was accepted. Later, when I recalled the first months of the feud, I stood in amazement when these two friendly enemies ate from the same dish and curled up together before the fire. I decided then and there that one can teach an old dog new tricks.

To an owner reading these pages thus far with hopes of finding the miracle by which his dog can be kept from roaming the streets—let me say now there is no such miracle. There is only training.

Certain breeds of dogs are more inclined to stray than others. Usually a dog will go off with another dog, whereas if by himself, he would remain at home. A dog that is not fed properly or one that is not given a sufficient amount of food will leave the home premises to go on foraging expeditions.

A puppy can be trained to stay within a given area if he learns that all kinds of unpleasant things occur when he goes past the boundary line. The obedience-trained dog has already learned to respect his owner's commands and will respond more willingly to whatever further training in obedience is given. But there is always the "problem" dog with the habit of straying, and he must be cured. He must be made to feel that it is unsafe to leave the premises and that by staying on his own home grounds nothing unpleasant will happen.

If there is more than one opening from the yard, it will take a number of assistants to correct this problem. A person should be stationed outside every exit, armed with empty cardboard cartons or rolled magazines that can be thrown. Evaporated milk cans with pebbles in them also make good weapons. The dog should have no warning of what awaits him, and the moment he starts through any one of the gateways he should be bombarded with whatever is available and told to "Get Back!" The articles should be thrown with a great deal of force at the dog's feet, but not directly at the dog as they are apt to cause injury to his head. I used this kind of correction with success on a dog that belonged to a famous actress. The dog got in the habit of running out after children so persistently that the police in the town began to exert pressure. After a limited amount of training, the dog soon stopped chasing children; but a week later, as one last gesture, she went out at midnight and chased a member of the armed forces. However, it was her last fling and she hasn't done it since.

Yet despite the success of training, in this age of motor vehicles and numerous laws regarding dogs, the owner would do well to spare himself anxiety by fencing in a small area where his dog can be left in safety.

The Mean Dog

There is little the owner can do to change a dog that has inherited a vicious temperament. He can, though, discourage a tendency to develop meanness through teasing. A dog that is teased, even in puppyhood, may grow into a vicious animal and may eventually have to be destroyed.

When a small puppy growls and snaps in rage, we sometimes think his behavior is funny, but if he is teased constantly it may lead to trouble. No dog should have his bones and toys grabbed away, even in fun. Nor should it be necessary for a dog to growl and chase other dogs from his food. Tugs of war should not be encouraged, for this is one form of teasing that will very soon teach the puppy the power of his teeth.

A person is often heard to say, "I can't take anything away from my dog. He won't let me!" If this is the case, the dog has done an excellent job of training his master. The dog's resentment at giving up what he is holding should be frowned upon the first time it happens. The owner should take hold of the object and in a very firm voice say, "Out!" If the dog lets go, the trainer should take it quietly and praise the dog with "Good boy." Then he should wait a moment and give the object back to the dog. If the dog growls and snaps, the owner should not grab at the object or jerk his hand back. Instead, he should hold on to it and demand that the dog stop growling and let go immediately. If necessary, the owner should quietly pry open the dog's mouth and take the article out, or he should whack the dog sharply across the nose to make him let go. Nine times out of ten the dog's behavior is a bluff, and he will be surprised to learn the owner is not afraid. (If you are afraid, never let the dog know.) One advantage, incidentally, of training a dog to retrieve in advanced obedience work is that he is taught, at the same time, to let go of whatever he is carrying.

A dog should also learn to accept things in a gentle manner. If when the puppy is given a bone he takes it quietly, he should be praised. If he grabs for it, the owner must remember not to jerk it back nor to let the dog have it immediately. He must hold it perfectly still while he tells the puppy to behave. If the puppy draws back in surprise and then reaches for it again without snapping, the trainer should let him have it at once.

A dog that refuses to give up an article or to accept one without snatching may be given a slap on the nose. But it must be done the right way: While the trainer still hangs on to the article and after he has told the dog to let go, he can rap the dog sharply on the nose with his free hand, but should not pull back too quickly. In other words, the hand is held there momentarily and then slowly withdrawn. Otherwise, the dog will retaliate by making a counter-grab at the owner.

Some dogs have such bad dispositions they will not permit even their owners to comb and brush them. This attitude might have been avoided if early in the puppy's training he had been placed on the table every day and forced to accept grooming. Puppies soon become accustomed to having their ears looked at and their eyes and teeth cleaned. The owner, at such times, should go over the puppy from head to foot. He should touch him underneath and especially around his tail, and at the slightest growl or the first baring of teeth the puppy should be whacked smartly across his hindquarters and told, "Watch your manners!"

An older dog may have to be muzzled until he gets used to being handled. The owner should take a piece of one and one-half to two-inch gauze bandage and tie it around the dog's nose. With the knot underneath, the two ends are taken around in back of the ears and over the neck and tied there. With this muzzle in place, the dog can no longer open his mouth to snap, and yet it will not interfere with his breathing. When the grooming is tried without the muzzle, the owner should move cautiously and watch for any sign of misbehavior. And the dog should be warned to "Be careful!" A small dog that bites may be lifted up by the collar and the leash, and held in the air momentarily until he stops snapping and growling. He is then slowly lowered to the ground and patted. If he starts again, he should be lifted up a second time. He will soon learn that discomfort is the result of bad manners.

To lift a cross dog from the floor, the owner should hold the leash in his right hand and pull it forward and keep it tight. The dog is then lifted up very quickly with the left hand. If the leash is kept tight as the dog is picked up, he cannot turn his head around to grab the trainer's hand. If the dog is wearing a regular collar, it must fit snugly enough so that he cannot back out of it and escape.

Protection

The number of owners who want their dogs trained to guard and to attack is rather startling. Dogs kept as pets should not be given this training. Their natural instinct to watch over those they love should be sufficient protection in the home, and it is safer when there are children.

If the owner wants his dog to warn the household of the approach of a stranger, that is understandable. But a dog should not be allowed to attack of his own volition. It is amusing and flatters one's vanity if a dog barks when a person comes near or growls when he guards personal property. But if the owner encourages the habit to any extent, it may get out of hand and lead to a difficult situation.

A person who lives alone or in a questionable neighborhood should, by all means, sharpen his dog to the point where he will be on guard. This can be done without making the dog vicious and dangerous to have around. He can be taught simply to be alert and to bark at people or at anything unusual. A dog that is naturally reserved will be easier to train than one that is overly friendly. The shy dog will growl to protect himself and urged to keep on, rather than scolded, he will soon feel he is doing the right thing and will be glad for an excuse to show protection. The shy dog will not make a good attack dog, however, because he will not stand up under fire but rather will turn and run when the pressure becomes too great.

I tell the following story to show how easy it is for people unconsciously to encourage a dog to protect without realizing what they are doing: A two-year-old Standard Poodle, from our own Carillon Kennels, was sold and shipped to another city. The Poodle had a nice disposition but was a little reserved. It wasn't long before we began to hear tales of the dog biting everyone that came to the house. The new owners were afraid they could no longer keep her. Knowing what she was like before she was sent away, I was interested in what could have happened to make the dog act the way she did. I made a trip to the distant city to find out. I discovered that at the time the dog arrived the owners were out of town, and she was left in the care of one of the maids. The Poodle was frightened to find herself in a strange house with people she didn't know. So, whenever she heard a noise, she growled and barked to protect herself. The maid, instead of telling the dog that everything was all right, would reach down and pat her encouragingly and say that she was "a good girl." The Poodle was being given a lesson in guarding every time this occurred. Later, the dog had only to hear the sound of footsteps in the courtyard to rush out and nip the heels of whoever happened to be coming in the house.

This kind of protection was not too serious, but it was unpleasant and had to be stopped. To be broken of the habit, the dog had to associate something unpleasant with the barking and growling, instead of the pat and the reward she had been receiving. The following morning I sat on an enclosed porch with several short pieces of chain handy. The dog was permitted to run around loose. The first time she growled and ran toward the door I threw the chains so hard they hit the side of the door with a crash. The dog didn't see me throw the chains, nor did I say anything. When she looked back in surprise, I called her and patted her when she came. The second lesson took place the same day. This time the growls came from across the room, but the dog didn't rush to the door. The correction was the same, except that the chains were thrown on the floor at her feet. Again I called her and patted her. The third time that someone came toward the house, the dog walked to me without barking or growling and sat down as though to say, "I'll be good," and from then on she was. Thereafter, we received only praise for the way the Poodle behaved.

It isn't every dog that has the temperament to do guard and attack work. A trainer may find only one or two dogs out of several dozen with the disposition that allows them not only to be trained to attack on command, but also to be completely under control in spite of the highly emotional state they are in. For the amateur to attempt such a responsibility is foolhardy. A dog can be ruined for life and the owner may end up with a couple of lawsuits on his hands. When a dog is to be used primarily as a watch dog, he should be sent to a reliable trainer for specialized schooling. If the owner has had no experience along this line, he will do more harm than good if he attempts to do the training himself.

Very often I am asked if it is safe to take a dog as a pet if he has been trained for war work. Most dogs during the last war were used for sentry duty. The dogs were sharpened up to be on the alert and to give warning. These dogs were not really dangerous, because they had not received sufficient intensified training to make them so. Had they been trained to take the initiative, the way the German Shepherds were in Germany during the first World War, they would have been as safe for a child to play with as a loaded revolver. The loaded firearm is a wonderful weapon to have around, but one must be careful it does not go off unexpectedly.

Judging from the number of letters and telephone calls I have been receiving lately, a few owners had better discourage their dogs from showing so much protection in the immediate family, or some of the lawsuits will be husbands against husbands or wives against wives. It almost looks as though the dogs are being acquired to offer protection against one's better half. If I have jumped to this conclusion and an attempt is really being made to train the dog out of bad behavior in this respect, my apologies!

I agree that when a dog growls and barks for no reason, it is very annoying and makes one feel like giving the dog a good boot in the rear, but this would only make him worse than ever. The dog will never change his attitude unless the person he is protecting does the disciplining himself. Too many people are flattered when their dogs show a protective instinct, and they cannot bring themselves to be strict.

To make the dog behave, the leash should be left on and the dog kept close to the person he is guarding. The second party should at least try not to show fear as he approaches the dog, but should take the leash and give it a quick jerk as he commands, "Heel!" and turns and walks away. In the meantime, if the dog shows signs of meanness, he should be reprimanded sharply by the person he is guarding. If both parties will give the dog daily lessons in basic obedience and if the owners will work together, the dog can be made to respect each with equanimity.

How to Stop a Dog Fight

There was a time when dogs were made to fight one another to entertain and amuse the two-legged species of animal. We hope this is a thing of the past. Today, a dog fight will send chills up and down one's spine faster than almost anything else I know. There is something about two dogs tearing at each other's throats that is frightening and nerve racking, to say the least.

Obedience Training will not definitely cure a dog of fighting, but it will help to control the aggressive dog. It may even stop a fight that has already started if the fight isn't too much under way. A trained dog that has learned to respect the owner's voice will heed a word of warning or a command, especially if it is accompanied by a slap on the rear end.

If the dog has a tendency to be scrappy, it will often show up even when the puppy is small. If the dog is trained in basic obedience and made to attend a training class where he will see other dogs, the desire to fight can sometimes be overcome, or, at least, it can be held in check. But the corrections must be severe right from the start. If the dog is on leash when he lunges at another dog, the handle of the leash should be brought down sharply across his nose without hitting his eyes. This is one time when it is permissible to hit a dog. He is over excited and hysterical, and ordinary treatment will have no effect.

Another way that may cure a dog of fighting is to put him in a yard with a dog that is noted for being a winner. If permitted to fight to the finish, the "bully" may be ready and willing to accept defeat. Personally, this is hard to do. I prefer to muzzle both dogs, then put them together. They will sometimes decide of their own accord to be friendly.

Everybody has his own pet theory of how to break up a serious dog fight. We hear of such things as holding burning paper under the dogs' noses, and of dousing the dogs with water. I have never tried the burning paper idea, but I have been on the receiving end of a bucket of water thrown by someone else.

The best way to stop a fight is to choke the most aggressive of the two dogs, or to inflict pain so severe that this dog will let go. A whack across the rear end is sometimes all that is necessary to break up a fight. In the case of females, the back legs can be grabbed and the fleshy part pinched hard to make them release their hold. The hands should be kept away from the dogs' mouths to avoid being bitten. While the dogs are fighting, they will not know or stop to think whether they are biting the owner's hand or the other dog.

Male dog fights are more serious. The owner should administer pain to the most sensitive part of the dog's body, in this case, the testicles. But care should be taken that the dog doesn't turn on the person. After the dogs are apart, they can be kept from each other by the owner holding onto the back legs. It doesn't do any good to try to pull two dogs apart while they have their teeth in each other. It will make them hang on more than ever and skin will become lacerated and torn.

I succeeded in breaking up one terrible fight by choking. In this case, the aggressive dog weighed about seventy-five pounds. By straddling the dog and working my hands forward to his throat, I was able to cut off his wind. When the dog could no longer breathe he let go.

The wise plan is for every owner to train his dog to be obedient, and for the owner to be on the alert when the dog starts jockeying into a fighting position. A dog that is vicious toward people and that has the reputation of being a killer should be destroyed, for even training will not help. It may keep things under control for a while, but the dog will never be trustworthy. If he is used for breeding, the country will become populated with more dogs with bad dispositions.

Teaching a Dog to Do Tricks

Obedience Training should not be confused with tricks or stunts that are taught for entertainment and amusement. The various elements that make up Obedience Training are all practical and useful exercises. They are necessary to the dog's well being and to the owner's convenience. Tricks, on the other hand, such as giving a paw, rolling over, or begging have actually little obedience value, but they are fun to teach, and the dog usually performs with enthusiasm, as though he enjoyed showing off his accomplishments. There are times when tricks and obedience overlap and have such close resemblance it is hard to say where one leaves off and the other begins.

Personally, I have no objections to teaching the obedience-trained dog a few tricks along with his regular obedience. In fact, the trained dog will learn tricks more quickly than his untrained brother or sister, and such learning has a definite place in this world when used to entertain and to instruct young people. It also has tremendous appeal in hospitals, schools, clubs, et cetera.

Teaching a Dog to Shake Hands

Probably the most common and easily taught trick is that of shaking hands. One hand, right or left depending upon whether the owner is right or left handed, should take hold of the dog's collar under his throat to hold his head up. The free hand then taps the underside of one of the dog's paws, and he is commanded to, "Shake hands," "How do you do?", or "Give paw." To get the dog in the habit of lifting his foot immediately when the hand is held out, the dog is thrown slightly off balance by a sideward pull on the collar. This is done just after the command is given. The leg will lift up automatically when the dog tries to catch his balance, and the paw is then taken hold of and the dog praised and rewarded at once. If this exercise is repeated several times during the day, the dog will soon get the idea of what is meant by "Shake Hands" and will lift his paw the moment the hand is lowered toward the floor. When the dog sniffs the hand instead of lifting his paw, he should be cuffed sharply on the nose.

Teaching a Dog to Beg

Begging comes natural to some dogs, but it is hard for others to learn. We are all familiar with the dog who, when told to sit-up, will collapse like a piece of cooked spaghetti. Until the back muscles of such a dog are made strong through constant practice, he will have a difficult time learning to sit up straight. To get impatient with a dog that is not as clever at begging as some other dog is ridiculous and very unfair. All dogs do not have the same sense of balance any more than all people have.

One should start with the dog in a sitting position and with the leash on, so he cannot get away and can receive as much help as possible. If the dog is given a wall or a corner of the room to lean against, he may gain confidence more quickly. Some dogs will permit their front feet to be held while they are lifted to a sitting-up position. Others dislike having their feet touched at all. These latter dogs can be helped up by lifting them gently by the collar or by the leash. They then should be held for a few seconds, after which they are praised and given something as a reward.

A morsel of food held over the dog's head and just out of reach, when he is sitting down, will help to raise his front paws off the floor. It should not be held so high that the dog will stand on his back legs. If he does, the food should be taken away completely, the dog made to sit down again, and the whole procedure started from the beginning. The command may be "Beg," "Sit up," "Up," or any other words that will not later confuse the dog in Obedience Training. When the command is given, a motion is made at the same time. With the hand extended, palm up, the fingers are flipped upward in an exaggerated signal. Later, the dog will obey this signal without the command, and will recognize it to mean that he must beg.

Teaching a Dog to Roll Over

The trick of rolling over is not hard for a dog to learn, and it will afford a great deal of amusement for everyone concerned. Children, especially, enjoy this trick, and it is something they themselves can teach their dog to do. The dog will get the idea of what "Roll Over" means if he already knows how to lie down on command. First, he is made to sit

71

in front of the owner with his collar and leash on. Then he is commanded to "Lie down," and the right hand signals toward the floor. When the dog obeys, he is told "And roll over." While the left hand pushes the dog's head slowly to the floor and holds it there, the right hand takes hold of the underneath paw, and the dog is quickly flipped over to the right.

Until the dog thoroughly understands what it is all about, one should keep in mind that there are two distinct signals and two separate commands. The first is the "Lie Down," with a downward motion of the right hand; and then the "Roll Over," with the same hand making a half circle toward the right. Later, of course, a slight signal or just "Roll over" will do the trick. Praise and special rewards will also help. The leash can be taken off when the dog shows no hesitancy and is quick and willing to obey.

Teaching a Dog to Jump through Hoops

The obedience-trained dog that already knows how to jump over a stick or a hurdle will jump through a hoop in one easy lesson. When the hoop is painted many colors, and when the dog jumps as though he enjoyed it, this trick holds everybody's attention. The dog should be kept on leash the first time even though he is a trained dog. Being familiar with the Sit and Stay, he should be left in the sitting position while the owner goes to the full length of the leash. The hoop is held in the left hand and the leash in the right hand. The command "Over," "Hup," or "Up" may be used, after which the leash is snapped quickly forward to bring the dog through the center of the hoop. After one or two lessons the dog should obey the command instantly, without the leash. A young dog unfamiliar with jumping is taught the same way, but instead of snapping the leash hard, the dog is pulled through the opening very gently as the hoop is held close to the floor. The dog will soon understand what it is all about and will not be afraid. The hoop can be raised higher each time the dog jumps.

In this training there are four different steps. One, the dog is made to sit and stay while the owner moves the hoop into position. Two, the dog is commanded "Hup" or "Over." Three, if the dog does not jump immediately, the leash is jerked hard. Four, the dog is praised or rewarded immediately.

This trick can be varied by holding a hoop in each hand. The dog jumps first through one, then circles around in back of the owner and jumps through the other. The dog should continue to jump as long as the hoops remain in place. Another variation is to hold both hoops parallel to each other, a foot or two apart, to form a broad hurdle. The dog goes through both at the same time. He can also be taught to carry his dumbbell or a basket, or to retrieve through hoops.

Teaching a Dog to Play "Dead"

A dog that knows how to lie down on signal will very quickly learn to play "dead" dog. The owner first points to the floor, and when the dog drops, he is turned onto his side and his muzzle is held flat on the floor while the owner repeats the words "dead dog" several times. When the dog is perfectly relaxed and will stay down by himself, the owner should release him from the "dead" position with a word of praise or an "Okay."

Additional Tricks

The trick of teaching a dog to speak for his dinner or for any other reward is thoroughly covered in the exercise, Speaking on Command, pages 212–16.

Other tricks may include catching food off the end of his nose, jumping over the owner's outstretched arm or leg, or jumping through arms which are held in the form of a hoop. A dog can be taught to "say his prayers," to "take a bow," and to do many other entertaining stunts without interfering with the regular Obedience Training.

It is said that in order to train a dog, the trainer must be smarter than the dog. It is not unusual, though, for the dog to teach the trainer a lesson he will not forget.

One old dog persisted in jumping the fence and taking a walk every evening after his dinner. Hoping to cure him of this habit, I made arrangements to have a second person feed the dog while I hid outside the fence in the tall grass with a whip. After the dog had eaten, he slowly sauntered along in his usual fashion, ready for his daily jaunt down the road. He got to within a foot or so of the fence, then stopped and his nose went up in the air. He gave one loud snort, turned, and walked back toward the house. I was not as smart as the dog. I had not taken into consideration that the wind was blowing my scent directly toward him, and so I had lost an excellent opportunity to make a correction. This lesson taught me not to underestimate a dog's intelligence.

Part 2: NOVICE
OBEDIENCE TRAINING

C.D. (COMPANION DOG)

Obedience Training

Obedience Training, as we know it today, was brought to this country in 1933 by Mrs. Whitehouse Walker, former owner of the Carillon Kennels, breeders of Standard Poodles. Every dog lover in the United States and Canada should be grateful to Mrs. Walker for her efforts in making the modern dog more domesticated—and, therefore, a better pet and more amusing companion in the home, and an animal equipped to fulfill the many services for which the dog is now put to use in the work life of the nation. It was not until 1936, almost three years after Mrs. Walker became interested in the possibility, that the American Kennel Club recognized Obedience Training and accepted it within their jurisdiction. At that time rules and regulations were drawn up governing all trials and the awarding of obedience titles.

Prior to 1933, Obedience Training had long been known and practiced in Europe, where dogs were used in police and army work and acted as guide dogs for the blind. Even in this country, Obedience Tests were not unknown, but they favored the working breeds, and their purpose stressed aggressiveness in line of duty rather than usefulness of dogs as companions and guardians of man. Mrs. Walker wanted to prove that every dog could be trained, and that the owner could do the training.

It is this training that will be outlined here in detail. If an effort is put into the undertaking, and if the lessons as suggested are carefully followed, everyone who reads them will be able to train his or her dog up to a certain point—at least through the basic exercises, which, after

75

The Metropolitan Boxer Club of Greater New York Training Class

all, form the foundation of all specialized training. The war dogs that are used for attack, Red Cross, or messenger work receive basic instruction; so do the police dogs that are used to guard and protect. The circus and the movie dogs, as well as those dogs that are trained to lead the blind, must also know the fundamentals; for without them specialized training is a waste of time.

The Training Club and Class

The enthusiasm with which Obedience Training was accepted in this country soon led to the formation of training clubs and classes for the purpose of schooling both the owner and the dog. Today there are hundreds of organizations that make this education available. The training class plays a very important role in dog obedience. Although skilled

Members of the Poodle Training Club of Greater New York giving an exhibition at Rockefeller Plaza during National Dog Week

instructors are still in the minority, the training class offers the best that are available. Training classes give the dog the chance to work with other dogs. The pet that behaves well at home but is disobedient when in public is no credit to his owner. Training classes stimulate the training and make it more interesting because there is a competitive feeling among the owners. For the problem dog, the advice of a skilled instructor is always helpful. Even a well-trained dog will react differently under various working conditions; so it is to be expected that the novice trainer will have trouble with his pet when there are distractions and excitement such as might occur among any unsupervised group of dogs. A word from a more experienced person will have its advantages. The training classes help to prepare both the handler and the dog for competition at dog shows. The contrast between the actual training and the competition will not then be so great.

If there is an established training class or club nearby, a person should by all means join such a group. If no class is available, perhaps enough enthusiasm can be aroused among dog owners to form a class. A responsible person should be found who can take over the job as instructor. This may be someone who has trained his own dog or has attended other training classes. It may be someone who has worked with war dogs or assisted in a training kennel. Such a person must, however, be a leader and able to take the initiative, since he must handle large groups of people—and that requires diplomacy.

There are several differences between a training class and a training club. Any civic-minded group of people may sponsor training classes, and the participants are not required to be members of the sponsoring organization. Training clubs, on the other hand, consist of a group of people, all members of the club, with elected officers and yearly dues. A training club may become a member of the American Kennel Club, with representation by a delegate and a voice in forming the governing rules and regulations for Obedience Trials.

Organizations that sponsor training classes are the S.P.C.A.'s, the Humane Societies, the Lions Clubs, Scout troop organizations, et cetera. In some cities, the Board of Education holds dog classes under their jurisdiction, and the instructors are paid by the Department of Education. The Department of Recreation, in other places, holds classes as part of their curriculum. Just because dogs are being trained in the classes is no reason why public buildings should not be used for that purpose. In New York City, classes have been and are being held in school gymnasiums, churches, restaurants, and armories. Strict discipline in the running of the classes will leave no cause for complaint.

The cost of enrolling a dog in a training class will run anywhere from $15 to $25 for a nine- to twelve-weeks course. If the classes are sponsored by an organization such as the S.P.C.A. or the Humane Society, the cost is usually low, because such organizations consider the classes a public service. If the classes are run by a local training club, the cost will be higher in order to defray all expenses, such as rent, cost of prizes for graduation, and the other incidentals that go into running any club successfully. If the instructor is paid for his work, this pay comes out of the enrollment fees as well.

I would like to point out one thing that is misleading to the amateur trainer and sometimes has been the cause of disappointment. The diploma that is usually given to a dog that graduates from a training class does not mean that the dog has become a C.D. (Companion Dog). The diploma, which is issued by the training class or the sponsoring organization and signed by the instructor, merely states that the dog successfully completed the training course. Obedience degrees are awarded only by the American Kennel Club, and in order to receive these titles a dog must compete at dog shows under the approved rules and regulations that govern Obedience Trials.

The owner who enrolls his dog in a training class should not expect him to make the same progress he would from the hands of a professional trainer. The owner must remember that *he* is learning as well as the dog. The professional trainer already knows how to handle the

The owners receive diplomas inscribed with the dog's name

different breeds and how to meet the various problems that arise. The amateur, of course, lacks that knowledge, which comes only from experience. When a dog is trained professionally, he requires six to eight weeks for basic training alone; and during this period he is given intensive instruction every day, not for just the one evening a week he receives in a training class. If the owner becomes discouraged at the lack of progress he makes in a training class, he should stop and consider that the chief advantage of the class is that he is learning how to make the dog obey.

Training class or not, home instruction should be carried on regularly. A professional, if he is tops in his field, will train six days a week

and for half-an-hour or more each day. The owner-trainer should put the dog through the training routine for at least ten or fifteen minutes, since it is a wasted effort to attend an obedience class unless the dog receives the home training that is so vital.

The behavior of certain dogs in training class is very often not above reproach. The owner who sees his scared little rabbit suddenly pitched upon by the belligerent bully is given fair cause for complaint. The aggressor may not have seen many other dogs in his life, or his association with them may have been unpleasant; but whatever the cause, it may take a while for him to accept the other dogs as his friends.

The owner, instead of trying to work this kind of dog along with the others, should sit on the sidelines and correct the dog every time he lunges forward to attack. The corrections will have to be severe if the owner wants his dog to get to the point where he will cease to cause trouble. Later, if the dog is permitted to work in the line-up, he should wear a muzzle so that the other members of the class will feel more secure. If the dog doesn't improve over a reasonable period of time, the training director should dismiss him from the class.

The high-strung, nervous type of dog that gets hysterical when he sees another dog should be given an aspirin or some other sedative shortly before he is taken to class—or to a dog show, if he is being exhibited. This will help to calm him down until he becomes more accustomed to the activity. Concentrated association with dogs outside of class will speed up the transformation.

To aid in getting training classes started there is a new *Training You*

to Train Your Dog—Novice Course film available, based on this book. This film may be obtained by writing to Gaines Dog Research Center, 250 Park Avenue, New York City. It can be purchased outright or booked for a showing, providing the organization requesting the film pays the cost of shipping. Other films on advanced training should be in preparation in the near future.

With a capable instructor and with the additional help of training films, books, etc., classes are being formed not only in North America, but all over the world and outstanding results obtained in at least the preliminary training. The advanced work is, of course, always more difficult.

For information regarding the existing training clubs and classes in this country, one should write to the American Kennel Club, 51 Madison Avenue, New York City, and ask for a list of member clubs. Also to Gaines Dog Research Center, 250 Park Avenue, New York City, which has compiled a list including classes run by individuals as well as various organizations. Inquiries made locally among dog owners, trainers, or veterinarians may divulge the existence of a local training class hitherto unknown. New classes are springing up every day, and in almost every part of the country.

There will always be times when it is inconvenient for an owner to attend classes regularly, or he may have no way to transport his dog to and from the class. Under such circumstances, the owner may attend as a visitor and then carry on the training of his dog at home. Or, the dog can be sent to a professional trainer for a period of time, after which the owner should learn how to handle the dog. Unfortunately, people who train for others are not licensed to do so, and, until such time as they are, the best way to select a trainer is through the recommendation of a reliable third party. This may be someone who has had his own dog trained, or it may be from a list of names supplied by the American Kennel Club or a local kennel club. The owner should visit the training kennels and observe how the dogs react to the trainer and decide whether it is the kind of place in which he would like to leave his dog. The charge for Obedience Training is usually made by the week, and the average cost is $65 to $75 which includes board. In the six- or eight-week period, the dog should be well trained in basic obedience and started on advanced training.

The Training Class Director

What makes a good training class director? Before this question can be answered we must point out what makes a good trainer. If the individual is to judge how each and every dog is to be handled, he must be an expert himself. This means plenty of experience. Nothing can take its place. The experience needed is not the kind that is gained from taking one dog through his C.D. or C.D.X. title; on the contrary, it comes from working with dogs of all breeds and under all conditions. When the trainer knows what he can expect from a dog and what the reactions will be, he has the advantage. He automatically anticipates the dog's next move and decides whether to force the issue or to lessen his demands. This knowledge doesn't come because "Towser" acquired his C.D. at an Obedience Trial, and yet many individuals with no more to their credit are setting themselves up as professional trainers and training-class directors. In a field so specialized, we have only scratched the surface.

The good trainer is born with the essential qualities needed in training. He will immediately sense how a dog will reason, and he has the natural ability to co-ordinate his body motions with every move the dog makes. The result is perfect timing. This is why some trainers succeed where others will fail. But the training of dogs is not a mathematical problem with a specific formula. No two dogs are trained in exactly the same way. Temperament and individual characteristics must be considered and the training technique varied to meet the occasion. To know when to be gentle, when to be firm, when to scold, and when to pet is an art. We are not all artists.

Why will a dog so often obey the trainer and not his owner? The answer is simple. The trainer knows what he is doing. The dog knows that he knows and the result is—respect! When the dog's respect is gained through admiration and not through fear, there will be a happy response that is proof in itself of one's "training personality." Therefore, the good trainer is not a bully. A dog can be forced to be obedient but he can't be made to like it. A good trainer will realize that all training is progressive and that each new step becomes easy only when all preceding lessons have been thoroughly learned. He is not afraid to retrace his steps momentarily if it will give the dog more confidence.

Graduation night at a dog obedience training class

Because of his wisdom and understanding, the expert trainer is aware of the disastrous effects caused by constant nagging. He will avoid it at all cost, and, because he is patient, he doesn't become exasperated if the results are slow in coming. He does not expect a miracle. The clever trainer will succeed in making the dog feel entirely responsible for what happens when the dog does wrong. But such a trainer will rightfully take the blame when he is at fault. He is kind, yet firm, and will make obedience fun for the dog.

In addition to all these qualities, the training-class director must be a leader and be able to take the initiative. And what a diplomat he must be! The director must be able to teach others how to accomplish what he is capable of doing, and at the same time he must make the class interesting. The good director will never permit the entire class to be held up for long periods of time while one dog's problem is discussed privately with his owner. Nor will he hold back the entire group for one or two backward dogs. The owners with problems should be requested to arrive early or to stay after class for personal instruction.

A good trainer does not necessarily make a good training-class director. Some people may train at home and give private instruction with success, but when they are faced with a large group they lack the necessary leadership. In a training class, it is not a question of working out a single problem but of solving fifty different problems all at the same time.

The respected director will always start his classes on time and demand attention throughout the training period. He will insist that the training quarters be quiet except for the customary commands. Social gatherings should take place elsewhere, as the classroom is not the place for idle chatter. The instructor's responsibility does not end with the calling out of the commands. By word he must create a mental picture of every exercise, and he must repeat each step over and over until the owners grasp the idea. Most training classes are made up of adults whose school days are a thing of the past and they are not as quick to learn the technique of training.

It is wise for the training-class director to divide the beginners' class into two parts. This will allow a rest period at which time the different groups may watch the other owners and see how they train. A lot can be gained from watching, if only to learn what not to do.

The good director will never dismiss his class without introducing some new exercises or a variation of the class routine to encourage home-training. This will deflate the egotist who thinks his dog is so good that homework is not necessary.

The administrative aspect of the training class should not fall upon the shoulders of the director. He has enough to worry about. It should be given to someone who is made responsible for seeing that the entire training program is taken seriously and run in a business-like way. At the beginning of the course, the director should announce the requirements for graduation and should abide by the rules regardless of hurt feelings. The dog that is permitted to slide through with inferior work is being done an injustice because he will not be able to do the more difficult advanced training.

There are two types of training classes. One is the kind in which members are permitted to join at any time and to come whenever they feel like it; the other, in which a specific number of lessons make up the course, the members are required to be present a definite number of times. There is no question but that the latter is the better system. We were not permitted to enroll in school when the term was half over, nor was the matter of attendance left to our own discretion. A training class, with its curriculum, is a school for dogs.

The showing of training films, demonstrations with trained and with untrained dogs, and, finally, graduation night with outside judges officiating and the awarding of diplomas inscribed with the dogs' names single out the training classes of the country as an essential part of Obedience Training—but the success of the training class hinges on the training-class director.

How a Dog Learns

In Obedience Training, a dog learns, just as the puppy does, through associating his act with pleasing or displeasing *results*. These associations, linked up with the trainer's commands and signals, are what cause a dog to obey. When the commands and signals are repeated sufficiently often for the dog's behavior to become a habit, we have what is known as *obedience*.

Training is an art in which the technique will vary with the individual, but basically the principles remain the same. The voice first commands obedience and is then immediately followed by the application of force with the leash; after this, a word of praise or a good pat will make the dog forget the correction and put him back in good spirits. There must be co-ordination between the trainer and the dog and accurate timing of the entire action. When this method of training is followed, a dog will learn to be obedient without associating unpleasantness with the training.

Lately, we hear a lot about the psychoanalysis of dogs. Since a dog's behavior is the subject under question, I suppose this term can be applied here, but there is very little mystery involved. The reason a dog behaves the way he does can almost always be traced to a sensual relationship. Dogs do not reason to the extent that humans do, and they act through an instinct that secures their own self-preservation. A good dog trainer, then, is in reality a psychiatrist, since he delves into the cause of whatever association makes a dog act the way he does.

Know Your Dog's Disposition

From the start it is important that the owner should realize that training will not change a dog's natural temperament. In other words, a dog that is by nature shy and retiring will never make a good attack dog, and neither will a vicious dog ever be completely trustworthy. Training does bring about a better understanding between the dog and the master because dogs, like people, vary in disposition and must be handled in different ways. Training makes this sympathetic relationship possible. If a person is going to buy a dog just for training, he should, naturally, select

These classes are of great value to both owners and dogs

one with the right temperament. The dog should not be too sensitive nor too clownish, and he should be anxious to please. It is to be supposed that a quiet, friendly dog with steady nerves and a keen interest in what goes on will be more responsive than the dog that is stubborn, sulky, vicious, shy, or what have you. For the moment, however, let us assume that one already owns a dog. Let's study him a bit and see how he should be approached.

Is he shy? Shyness may be acquired or it may be inherited, but, whatever the cause, the dog must be handled gently and his confidence won through exaggerated encouragement and praise. Every little effort on the dog's part must be recognized. On the other hand, the owner must not baby the dog too much. At times it will be necessary to force him to do something against his will for his own good. Training will definitely give a shy dog confidence, and over a period of time the dog will show remarkable improvement.

Is the dog lively, aggressive and determined? In this case quiet handling with firmness and, if necessary, severity is required. The owner must be definite in the way he gives the commands and signals to leave no doubt in the dog's mind as to what is expected of him. Praise should be given sparingly while the owner prepares for a battle, for he most certainly will have one.

Is the dog lazy, slow, and lackadaisical? The object then will be to get more pep into him. The best way to accomplish this is through sudden bursts of speed in all one's actions. This should be accompanied by considerable praise and petting, and the dog should be talked to in a "come on, come on, hurry up" tone of voice. Corrections coming from a second person rather than from the owner will have a more lasting effect on the slow-moving type of dog.

Maybe the dog likes to clown. Here again one must be firm and give very little praise. This type of dog thinks everything is a game and the slightest thing will set him off in play again. Under no circumstance must his antics bring laughter or applause. The dog must be taught when he can clown and when clowning is not permitted.

One of the most difficult types of dog to train is the one that has a suspicious nature. He regards every movement with distrust, and he remembers every correction that has ever been made. The trainer of this kind of dog must be clever and resourceful enough to invent new ways of doing things; otherwise the dog will outwit him.

There is also the type of dog that is overanxious and must be steadied down by the trainer using a slower training tempo. Voice commands play an important role here, as they enable the trainer to keep one jump ahead of the dog.

And of course there are those dogs that want to fight every dog they see, and those that are mean enough to turn on their own masters. One cannot reason with these last two and, to get results, the owner must be a lot tougher than the dog.

It is an accepted theory that the personality of the owner will be reflected in his dog. It is true that, over a period of time, a dog will take on certain characteristics of his master. The nervous, energetic individual will often find himself with a restless and overactive dog. The phlegmatic person ends up with the placid, slow-moving dog. An orderly person will almost always have an orderly dog; a careless person will have the opposite. Perhaps this is why we like certain breeds and dislike others. There is no harm in a dog's readjusting himself to his environment as long as his character does not suffer. Frequently we hear the remark that an obedience-trained dog will lack spirit and act unhappy about the training. Unfortunately this is sometimes true. Training that has been too severe or of a nagging nature will make a dog sulky and indifferent. Although the lazy type of dog may give the impression of lacking vivacity, this is the dog's natural temperament and cannot be blamed on the training.

Successful training is the result of knowing what one can expect from a dog on the basis of his temperament. When the training is done properly, it will in no way make a dog less spirited—rather, it will help to overcome his shyness, develop his personality, and bring out his best qualities.

Color Versus Temperament

Does color influence a dog's temperament and how much does it affect his training potentialities? Gervase Markham wrote in the late 1400's (I think) on color in the water dog, obviously the prototype of the Poodle. Blaine's *Rural Sports*, edited 1848, quotes Markham: "First, for the colour of the best water dogge, all be it some (which are anxious in all things) will ascribe more excellencie to one colour than to another as the blacke to be the best and hardest, the lyver-hued swiftest in swimming and the pyed or spotted dog quickest of scent, yet in truth it is nothinge so, for all colours may be excellent good dogs, and any may be most notable curres, according to their ordering and fraying. . . ."

It is doubtful if much research has been done on this subject. From my own personal experience, both with numerous all-breed training classes and in the breeding and handling of Poodles, I am inclined to believe that color does affect temperament and has some relation to a dog's ability to be trained.

It is an oft repeated statement among humans that the color of the hair and the pigment of the skin produce certain recognizable characteristics. Red-haired people are noted for their quick emotional response; the dark skinned people of Latin origin, for their excitable nature; the blonde Scandinavians for their calm and self-possession. If this be true, there is no reason why color of coat and pigmentation should not affect dogs as well, but one must first determine the dominant color in a breed to know what the color influence may be.

For instance, in the breeding of cattle, it has been found that black is dominant over red. In horse breeding, bay dominates black. Among dogs there is no set rule because color dominants vary with breeds. In Poodles, black appears to be the strong color, but in Dachshunds red takes precedence over black and tan; in Boxers, brindle over fawn.

One cannot single out color as being completely responsible for a dog's temperament. The breed of the dog must be considered, his age, the environment in which he has lived since puppyhood and the most important thing of all, the genetic factors that affect the mentality and emotional make-up of a dog. Commercialized breeding, for one thing, is often the ruination of a breed's natural temperament. An example of this is what happened to the German Shepherd during the twenties. It took the breed almost thirty years to recover from the harm done by dog dealers who cared more for money than they did for dogs. Carelessness among such so-called dog breeders is all too common, and because ill-advised matings are so liable to produce puppies of poor disposition, they should be guarded against today more than ever.

No matter what the color of his own coat may be, every dog is carrying a color heritage from his ancestors, that plays an important part. That is why a dog, even though his own coat may be brown in color may have inherited genes of another color, which affects his own temperament and which he in turn will pass on to his progeny.

Albinism in humans is usually linked with weaknesses of one form or another. We have evidence of this in dogs too, because defective hearing and vision are sometimes found in Dalmatians, white Bull Terriers, and the occasional white Great Danes and Boxers. This must be true in other animals as well for the old-time horse breeders will tell you to avoid the horse with a great deal of white as they consider this a sign of lack of stamina. This prejudice is expressed in the old English rhyme which goes: "One white foot—buy him, Two white feet—try him, Three white feet—look well about him, Four white feet—go without him."*

There is no doubt but that certain colors are linked with certain characteristics and the subject of color versus temperament should be an interesting one to dog breeders and trainers the world over.

Voice and Signals

There are three tones of voice used when training dogs. The coaxing tone is for the beginner who is just learning. The trainer coaxes the dog along step by step as he reassures him and gives him confidence. Once the lesson has been learned, the ordinary voice is used to give the command so the dog will know what he is expected to do. This is called the

*From *Popular Dogs*, August, 1951.

All breeds can learn

commanding voice. When the dog refuses to obey even though he knows what he should do, the trainer *demands* obedience in no uncertain terms. These very same tones of voice are used every day with children, and we all know how quickly the demanding tone will get results when the child doesn't choose to have good hearing. It works the same way with a dog.

Men usually get quick response in their training because they handle quietly and give their commands with authority and in a low tone-of-voice. The dogs know better than to take advantage and, instead, soon have great respect for the men of the household. Women with definite, positive personalities make just as good trainers as men. For these same reasons a dog will obey a professional trainer when he will not obey his owner. The trainer knows what he is doing. The dog knows that he knows, and the result is—respect! One can't get away from it. It's a matter of how a certain thing is said or done and not just the words or motions, although the dog will learn to associate certain commands with a specific action. Take, for instance, a young puppy that steals. The first time the puppy takes something he shouldn't the trainer raps the puppy's muzzle sharply and says "No" in a very reproachful tone of voice. Another time, when the puppy sniffs the table, he will remember his previous lesson if the trainer just quietly says "No-o-o" without taking action.

Since all corrections are made with the hands, motion means more to a dog than voice. As the training progresses, voice and signals become of equal importance, providing the voice has the right intonation of authority. Whiny and hysterical commands will always get poor results. When hand signals are given, the trainer should not be careless but should make each motion clear and distinct; otherwise the dog will become confused.

Even though an owner plans to use the voice or the signals one at a time, it is to his advantage to give the two together at first. Then he may alternate them until the dog responds to either. Once the leash has been taken off, the most effective means by which the trainer will be able to control his dog when he is at a distance is by using his voice. Similarly, a dog not within hearing range will respond to a given signal if he understands what it means.

During one of our many exhibitions at Yankee Stadium prior to a big-league baseball game, one of the twenty-odd dogs that took part, although beautifully trained to come when he was called, had never learned to respond to the equivalent signal. The distances at which the dogs were required to work in such a vast place made it difficult for them to hear the voice commands, especially when the laughter and applause from 70,000 baseball fans added to the din. Several attempts were made to make this dog hear the command to do the Recall over the three hurdles that had been placed in a row with an overall distance of 150 to 200 feet. Finally, the owner, in desperation, moved up past the first hurdle until the dog caught the sound of her voice and started over. In the meantime the owner tried to get back into position but the dog was too fast and they collided. I believe this person has the reputation of being the first woman to slide into second base at Yankee Stadium! Needless to say, the dog soon after learned to recognize the signal to come when called even when he was far away.

Do's and Don't's

To get the best results and to accomplish the most in training, certain do's and don't's must be followed. The most helpful of these are:

(1) Play with the dog. This may be before and after each training period and between the exercises, but when working be earnest and let

the dog know it is serious business. Never laugh at the dog's antics nor tease him in a joking way.

(2) Do not overtrain. A dog's mind tires easily. At first, five to ten minutes a day is all that is necessary. Gradually increase the training periods to twenty minutes or half an hour and, if possible, train more frequently rather than for a long period of time. Have a regular hour for training and do not train immediately after a dog has eaten a hearty meal. In hot weather, be considerate of the dog by working him during the coolest part of the day.

(3) Be consistent. So as not to confuse the dog, always use the same words and give the same signals. Never say "Jester, come," then "Jester, come over here," and then "Jester, here." Repeat the same command or signal until the dog obeys either one. Since dogs learn more quickly through what they see than through what they hear, signals constitute about 75 per cent of the dog's training and the voice about 25 per cent.

(4) Be patient. The dog can absorb just so much at a time, so training must be taken slowly. The trainer must not move on to a new lesson until all preceding ones are thoroughly understood.

(5) Vary the work. The dog must not get bored. He should look forward to his training with eagerness and not act like a puppet on the end of a leash.

(6) Be firm. Even if it is necessary to stay half an hour longer at a particular exercise, the lesson should not end with the dog having his own way. The dog must do what he has been commanded even though his performance is not perfect.

(7) If the owner feels himself losing his temper, that particular training session should be discontinued. Nothing will be accomplished.

(8) Don't expect a miracle. A dog will learn certain exercises in two or three weeks time, but it may take months to steady him, that is, to establish him in his performances. A gradual improvement over a long period will give the best results.

(9) Keep the hands off the dog as much as possible. Use the training collar for all corrections. Constant grabbing will cause the dog to shy away.

(10) If a dog fails to perform a given exercise, go back to the beginning and start over again. A good trainer is never afraid to review the work.

(11) Do not make a practice of rewarding a dog with food. A tidbit is all right to overcome certain training problems, but the dog should learn to work because he is asked to, and his reward should be a word of praise and a loving pat.

(12) Remember that kindness will accomplish much more than harshness and cruelty. A dog has a wonderful memory, and he won't forget one's attitude toward him.

(13) Use the dog's name as little as possible. Stress the words that make up the commands for each exercise. When a dog's name is repeated too frequently, he becomes uncertain and makes more mistakes than ever.

(14) At first one person should do the training. The dog should be taken far away from other dogs, children, or things that will distract him. He should be taken to the same place every time he is trained. Later, to make the dog steady under all conditions, his places of work should vary, and other members of the family should handle the dog as well. No pet is considered a well trained dog until he respects and obeys every member of the household.

(15) A dog should have his own vocabulary. "No," "down," "come," "all right," "good boy," "bad dog," and many other words should have a definite meaning.

(16) The dog should never think the trainer is to blame for correcting him. The dog should be handled in such a way that he will feel responsible for what happened and that any unpleasantness was the result of his not paying attention.

(17) Never punish a dog by striking him in temper. By the tone of voice and the sharp jerk on the collar he can be made to understand he has done something displeasing.

(18) Do not punish a dog unless he knows what he is being punished for. The dog has no way of letting the trainer know that things have not been made clear to him.

(19) Use the correct tone of voice at all times.

(20) The trainer should see that the dog is in a happy frame of mind at the close of each training period. If the dog is given something pleasant to remember, he will anxiously await the next lesson.

(21) In training, use a plain rolled leather collar for the puppy; a rolled or nylon slip collar for the small dog; a plain chain slip collar for the older, stronger dog.

Equipment for Training

The only essential items used to train a dog in Novice Obedience are the training collar and the leash. The other articles listed below are not necessary for teaching good manners, but they are required for the more advanced training. Through their use even the amateur will have more

How to make the collar

fun training his dog, and the dog will get more enjoyment out of his work.

Training Collar: A rolled leather one for the puppy. A rolled or nylon slip for the small dog; but for best results, when training the older, heavy-set dog, the collar should be made of metal links and is called a chain slip collar. There are heavy link chains for the large dogs and light ones for the small, willful-type dog. Owners sometimes have the idea that when a lightweight chain is used on the large dog, it will not hurt the dog. It is really just the opposite. The thin chain will cut more deeply into the neck since there is less surface upon which to bear down.

When the collar is on and pulled tight, it should be long enough to allow two or three inches of overlap, provided the length will allow the collar to slip over the dog's head easily. It is better to have the chain too short than too long. The long chain will get in the trainer's way and will require exaggerated motions to get the same results.

One may ask why a chain collar is used and not a leather one. The metal slides more easily and, in addition, the constant rattle of the chain will help to keep the dog's attention. A leather slip collar may be used on long-coated dogs to avoid wearing the hair down, but the training results will be slow. In certain cases a spike collar will be necessary, but one should not make a practice of using it all the time. A spike collar has prongs which pierce the neck on all sides. If it is used consistently it will cause a dog to work in a dejected fashion, since the dog obeys because he is afraid and not because he is anxious to please his trainer.

There are arguments for and against the practice of leaving the training collar on all the time. From the trainer's point of view, the obstreperous type of animal is kept more under control when the dog knows the training collar is there ready for use. On the other hand, the lazy or less enthusiastic animal that enjoys showing off only now and then may be pepped up if the collar is put on just prior to his working periods. For the hunting breeds or for those dogs that roam a great deal, there is a danger-element when the collar is left on. It is always possible for something to catch in the ring and choke the dog. Then, too, a dog that travels around a lot and has his nose constantly to the ground may lose his collar by having it slide over his head. If a dog is permitted much freedom, it would be advisable to have him wear a plain leather collar rather than the collar used for training purposes.

Leash: The leash should be made of flat pliable leather, ½ to ¾ of an inch wide, depending upon the size of the dog. It should be about a foot longer than the trainer is tall and should have a strong snap that will not open by accident. Under no circumstances should a 3-foot leash be used for routine training. Nor is a chain or a round leather leash practical. The chain will cut the trainer's hands and the round leash will slip through them.

Jumping Stick: The jumping stick is a piece of ½- or ¾-inch doweling, 30 to 36 inches long. It must be large enough so the dog can see it, and strong enough so that it will not break if the dog steps on it. A sawed off broom handle or a cane may be substituted.

Long Line: The long line may be a clothes line or a special leash, 20 to 50 feet long, with a snap fastened on one end.

Rolled Magazine: A small rolled magazine taped at each end with adhesive or bicycle tape. The size of the magazine will depend upon the size of the dog's mouth.

Dumbbell: A wooden dumbbell with size in proportion to the dog. The raised center makes it easy for the dog to pick it up.

*chain collar; leash; dumb-
bell; rolled magazine; jumping stick; long line*

The solid hurd

The bar hurdle

The broad jump

Jumping Hurdle: A high jump 5 feet wide and adjustable to any height up to 3 feet, 6 inches. The boards of the high jump form a solid wall. (See illustration, page 96.)

Jumping Bar: The bar jump is similar to the high jump except that it has a single bar instead of being made of solid boards. (See illustration, page 96.)

Broad Jump: The broad jump consists of four separate hurdles. They are constructed on an angle, so that when viewed from one end they appear like one long solid jump. The four hurdles are built to telescope for convenient handling. (See illustration, page 96.)

Scent-discrimination Articles: Six each, identical articles made of wood, leather, and metal, for the Scent-discrimination exercise. These may be clothespins, spoons, wallets, blocks of wood, et cetera. Or they may be an assortment of articles sold especially for this purpose.

Seek-back Articles: A glove or a wallet or a similar article, not too conspicuous nor white in color.

Automatic fishing reel and line or a long clothesline and a pulley: These will be used to train the dog to "go" in the Directed Jumping.

Tracking Harness: The harness is the shape of an ordinary harness. When made of webbing material it will not cut into the dog's body while he is tracking.

Before going on to the technical part of training, I would like to suggest to the women trainers that they wear comfortable shoes and practical clothes. A dress or skirt that blankets the dog's head at every step will interfere with his training and make him duck away. Spike heels haunt the best of us. If the shoes have low rubber heels, this will permit the leash to slide under the instep when the dog is made to lie down and at the same time prevent the trainer from taking a nasty fall. There is little attraction between wooden floors and leather-soled shoes. Just where women get the idea they can train with a pocketbook the size of a suitcase slung over their arm, I do not know; but I never fail to have at least two or three such individuals in each new training class. *Both* hands are necessary while training, and this goes for men as well as for women trainers.

How to Put on the Training Collar

There is a *right* way and a *wrong* way to put on the collar. The right way is to place it on the dog's neck so that when he is sitting on the trainer's left side, the leash is fastened to the end of the chain which passes *over* and not *under* his neck. (See illustration, page 98.) This allows the collar to loosen automatically when the leash is made slack. If the owner is not certain that he has the collar on the right way, he should slip it off, turn it over, and put it on again. If the leash is fastened to the end of the chain passing *under* the dog's neck, it is wrong. Another test is to put the collar around the left wrist and pull it tight. If the collar is on correctly, it will loosen when given slack; if not, it will

(1) correct   *(2) incorrect*

HOW TO PUT ON THE TRAINING COLLAR

remain tight. The trainer should make certain that the collar is on correctly each time because it is very easy to put it on the wrong way.

How to Hold the Leash

With the dog still on the trainer's *left* side, the leash should be taken in the *right* hand with the loop around the palm. It is then grasped a little more than halfway down with the left hand and transferred, at this point, to the right hand. The right hand is held in front of the trainer, waist high and close to the body. From now on both hands are used; the right hand (the guiding hand) holds the leash. The left hand is comfortably placed on the leash a short distance above the dog's collar and is the means by which the dog is controlled. The left hand lets the leash out when necessary and takes it in when there is too much slack. The left hand is also used for making correction and for patting the dog encouragingly. Even though this may at first seem awkward, the trainer will have more control over the dog if he will get in the habit of holding

(1)

(2)

(3)

This is incorrect

THE CORRECT WAY TO TAKE HOLD OF THE LEASH

the leash this way. Later, after the dog has had some training, the leash may be carried completely in the left hand if the trainer wishes, as this will sometimes make the dog more alert during his heeling exercises.

Heeling

Heeling means that the dog must walk on the trainer's left side with his head close to the trainer's left knee.

A dog is taught to heel on the left for more than one reason. The original purpose was to keep the right hand free when the dog was used in police work. The prisoner walked at the officer's left side. The dog walked between them and at the prisoner's right in case he should attempt to draw a gun, in which case the dog would attack. For the dog owners of today, since most people are right-handed, there is less inter ference from the dog with him on the left side and out of the way. Right-handed people have more control over the dog during the training period if the leash is held in the right hand and the dog is trained to walk on the left. However, there is no reason why a dog cannot be trained to heel on the right side if the owner wishes; nor, why a dog cannot be retrained to walk on either side. But for the purpose of this book I will discuss how a dog is trained to heel on the left.

Before the trainer begins to teach the heeling exercises, he must get the dog's attention and keep it throughout the training period. The trainer must acquire a certain freedom of the leash—a oneness between the dog and himself. The best way to do this is for the trainer to play with the dog while he alternately lets the leash out and takes it in again. The dog should be patted, praised, and talked to; and when his attention strays, he should be given a sharp slap on the rump or jerked with the leash to make him watch the trainer. When the dog keeps the leash slack of his own accord, and when he responds to the slightest tug of the leash, the trainer commands, "Jester, heel!" and pulls the dog around to his left side with his left hand. When the dog steps out of line, the command is repeated and he is again pulled back. He must be made to understand that the command "Heel!" means to stay on the left, close to the trainer, even though the trainer may be standing still.

Next, a quarter turn is made to the left, and the dog is again told to heel as he is motioned back into place. Then a step is taken to the right and the same thing is repeated. *If the dog's attention is on the trainer,* he will stay close to the trainer's side no matter where he moves. Now with the dog in the proper heel position on the left side, the leash should be held (as discussed previously) in both hands. The trainer commands,

Correct leash while heeling   *Incorrect leash while heeling*

"Jester, heel!" and steps forward briskly after the word heel. The left hand gives the leash a sharp jerk forward in the direction of travel (not up in the air) immediately *after* the command, but it is then slackened immediately. It doesn't make much difference which foot the trainer uses to step forward when the command is used because the dog is obeying the command and not the action. But, since more accurate work will be required in the Utility Class, and since the right foot moves first whenever the dog is made to stay in a given position, it is a good idea to get in the habit of moving the left foot first at the start of heeling.

When the dog catches up with the trainer, he should be patted and praised and told, "That's it. Good boy." When he goes too far ahead, the trainer should *slow up*, not try and keep up with the dog. At the same time he should give the leash a sharp backward jerk as he demands "Heel!" in a more severe tone of voice, or he should stop moving entirely and motion the dog back into position. Only when the dog is again in the proper place should the training proceed. Dogs that are unmanageable will be brought more quickly under control if the trainer will turn and go in the opposite direction every time the dog lunges ahead. A series of fast about-turns, one after the other, will get results quicker with an unmanageable dog than anything else I know.

If the dog does the opposite and lags behind, both the trainer and dog should speed up. The leash should be snapped in a series of short, fast jerks and the dog talked to in a "come on, come on, hurry up!" tone of voice every time he lags. When working with a long-legged dog the trainer may take long steps; but when training a short-legged dog he should adjust his own stride to that of the dog's so he will not "walk away" from his dog.

The point to remember when teaching a dog to heel is to keep a slack leash except when making a correction. A dog will never learn to walk without pulling if he is kept on a tight leash and if he is dragged instead of snapped back into place. The leash should be tightened momentarily and then kept loose. The motion is not an exaggerated one. Otherwise, the dog will learn to fear the trainer. The trainer should get the idea across to the dog that the most comfortable place is close to his side, but the dog won't agree if he is dragged about with the left hand. Later in the training, the right hand makes the corrections, by snapping the leash, and the left hand is used almost exclusively for patting the dog. At this point the right hand is carried off to the right side and the leash is snapped through the left hand so the dog cannot see the motion. If the dog is not afraid of his trainer, he will not heel wide nor lag behind unless he is just lazy.

When it is impossible to get the dog's attention with an ordinary snap of the leash (and there are plenty of such times), the trainer should make the correction by using a series of snaps. Just one jerk on the collar may not be enough to make the dog look in the trainer's direction, and, therefore, the dog may have to receive a number of such jerks one after the other and each more severe than the last. Several quick about-turns will also help to get the dog's attention. When the trainer gets the dog to look at him, the training can proceed as usual.

A good heeling practice is for the trainer to circle continuously to the right, then to reverse the direction and circle continuously to the left. A zigzag course should be done across the training yard with a three-quarter turn first to the right and then to the left. The trainer will get the dog to heel more accurately if he keeps changing his directions, as the dog will be kept more on the alert if the heeling is not always done in a straight line.

Some dogs, while heeling, will grab at the trainer's arm or hand in play. At such times the trainer, instead of jerking his arm away, should hold it still and by voice command order the dog to let go. The end of the leash should be brought down immediately across the dog's nose, but when the dog draws back he is praised at once. One or two such lessons will convince the dog that heeling is serious work and that the trainer means business.

102

Small dog—small steps   **Coax a stubborn one**

Once the trainer has started to teach his dog to heel, the training should be carried out even when the dog is walking along the street. When it is a question of the dog relieving himself, the trainer should walk slowly, or stand quietly and give the dog more freedom of leash. Otherwise, a normal pace should be retained, and the dog made to heel without sniffing the ground and stopping at every hydrant or post he comes to.

If the dog tries to attack every other dog he sees, the owner should never stand still and permit uncontrolled barking. He should turn away immediately in the opposite direction and snap the dog hard as he does so. The dog may be corrected by flipping the end of the leash sharply across his nose. At these times the dog is all keyed up and the ordinary command or correction will make no impression—but a whack on the nose will give him something else to think about other than fighting. In extreme cases, a small switch may be carried in the right hand to use when the dog growls or lunges forward.

The hysterical type of dog will growl and jump around and climb all over the trainer when he finds himself restrained by the leash the first time he is made to heel. The dog may even lunge at the trainer and try to bite. A sharp cuff on the nose, which is the usual correction, will only make him worse than ever. Instead, he will have to be handled severely and firmly in another way. He should be lifted up momentarily by the leash and held at arm's length with his front feet in the air. When his

103

anger subsides, he should be lowered quietly to the ground and then patted. If he still misbehaves, he should be lifted up a second time. In some cases, especially with a large dog, the trainer will do well to turn slowly in a circle while he is holding the dog in the air. The centrifugal force will prevent the dog from getting close enough to bite or paw the trainer. When the dog realizes the trainer is not afraid and that biting brings the discomfort of being choked, he will avoid further attacks.

The mistakes the trainer is apt to make when he is teaching a dog to heel are: (1) the leash is held so tight there is no room to give the proper snap, (2) the leash is held too loose which calls for too much motion, (3) the leash is held improperly so that valuable time is lost when making corrections, (4) the timing is off with no pauses between commands, corrections, and praise, and (5) the trainer has not gauged the right degree of severity.

The mistakes the dog makes are: (1) lagging behind, (2) heeling wide, (3) interfering with the handler, and (4) sniffing the ground. To overcome the first two, the trainer should do everything in his power to entice the dog to stay close, without giving the impression that he is responsible for the corrections. All unpleasantness, when possible, should come from a second person. By keeping something in his pocket like food or the dog's toy, the owner may trick the dog into close heeling. For interference while heeling, the only corrections are quick turns and banging the lifted knee into the dog with a great deal of force. In the case of the problem dog that sniffs the ground while heeling—and if the dog is on leash—the trainer should kick hard along the ground between the dog's nose and the spot he is smelling. If the dog sniffs only when the leash has been taken off, he can be corrected by having a second person toss a throwing chain at the spot that has proved so fascinating to the dog.

When training a dog to heel, the trainer should never take his eyes from his dog. If he does, he will lose many opportunities to bring in a correction at the crucial moment.

Right-angle Turn

The right-angle turn is a ninety-degree-angle turn to the right. The trainer pivots on his left foot and steps out with the right foot. The turn is made when the dog is not looking, and the leash is jerked sharply to the right *after* the trainer makes the turn and has warned the dog by saying, "Heel!" When the dog is snapped up short, he will blame himself for the discomfort caused because he was not paying attention. When the dog catches up to the trainer, he should immediately be patted and praised and told, "That's better. Good boy!" It is always best to do not just one right turn but half a dozen or so, one after the other, to impress the dog with the importance of this new routine.

Left-angle Turn

The left-angle turn is a ninety-degree-angle turn to the left. This time the right foot is used to pivot and the trainer steps out with the

Right turn—Jerk is made on leash when dog least expects it

Left turn—The right knee is lifted against the dog's neck and chest

left. This turn is also made when the dog is not looking, or when the dog is a little ahead of the trainer. In this case, as the trainer turns on the left foot he lifts the right knee and strikes against the dog's neck and chest. If the trainer is working with a small dog, he should bump against him with his ankle or the inside of his foot. In other words, the leash holds the dog back while the trainer steps into the dog unexpectedly and commands "Jester, heel!"—using a tone of voice that implies, "Shame on you for bumping into me! Watch where you are going!" Again, it is good practice to do several turns without a break.

105

Right-about Turn, Left-U-Turn, and Left-about Turn

There are three different about-turns. The right-about turn is made by both the trainer and the dog turning to the right and going in the opposite direction. The dog is kept on the *outside*. The trainer takes a small step backward with his right foot as he pivots around and steps forward with the left foot. He gives the leash a jerk after *he* makes the turn. The dog is caught up short and looks around to find the trainer going in the opposite direction.

The left-U-turn is made by both trainer and dog turning to the left to go in the opposite direction. The dog, this time, is kept on the *inside* and pushed around to the left. The turn is made on the left foot. The corrections are the same as for the left-angle turn. The leash holds the dog back and the trainer steps into the dog as though by accident.

The left-about turn is made by the owner turning to the left and the dog turning to the right. The leash is passed in back of the trainer from the right hand to the left hand then back to the right hand again. The jerk on the leash comes after the trainer has made the turn and is already headed in the opposite direction. This turn is the most difficult to teach a person to execute. The owner is too conscious of his dog. It will not be so hard if he will only forget for the moment that he even owns a dog and perform the left-about turn by himself. The dog will then take care of himself. The left-about turn is no longer required in Obedience Trials, but it does help to train the dog to work more accurately.

All turns—the right-angle turn, the left-angle turn, the right-about turn, the left-U-turn, and the left-about turn—should be made in a military manner. This will keep the dog at attention and on guard for sudden changes of direction. If at any time the dog walks *behind* the trainer, or if he cuts in on the trainer's right side, a quick but careful kick backward with the right foot or a cuff on the nose with the right hand is the correction.

Variation in Speed

The trainer should alternate a normal walk with a slow walk and a slow-running pace. He should go from one into the other, making sudden stops after each. The dog should remain close to the trainer's side with the leash slack, no matter how quickly or slowly the trainer moves.

Figure Eight

To train the dog to do the Figure Eight, two objects are placed six to eight feet apart and the trainer and the dog circle around them. Posts or trees will serve. If the dog attempts to pass on the wrong side at any time, the leash is pulled tight and the dog is held in that position until he corrects himself. When he does, he should be praised for doing so. Circling will help to train the dog for the Figure Eight required in Obedience Trials at dog shows, and will teach him to stay close to the owner when passing people, other dogs, and all stationary objects on the street.

When the circling is done to the right with the dog kept on the outside, the trainer should take small steps so he will not get too far ahead. When the circling is done to the left with the dog on the inside, the trainer should take long steps to make it unnecessary for the dog to change his pace.

The Sit

Whenever the trainer comes to a halt, the leash is pulled tight in the right hand and the dog is made to sit down. To keep the dog under control, the leash—which has been held in the left hand just above the dog's collar while heeling—is transferred to the right hand just before the trainer stops and before the dog is given the command to sit. This will shorten the leash so the dog cannot swing away from the trainer. The right hand pulls the leash up and backward, and, at the same time, the left hand pushes down on the dog's hindquarters just over the hipbones. The dog is commanded, "Sit!" The trainer takes a short step backward with his left foot and bends his right knee slightly. His body remains erect from the waist up and he continues to face straight ahead. The right hand adjusts the position of the leash by moving it from side to side, or forward or backward, while the left hand keeps the dog close to the trainer.

The dog should sit squarely on both hips, with his head near the trainer's left knee—not too far back, not too far ahead. Also, he should not sit at an angle. There is only one correct sitting position, and the handler should insist upon it every time the dog sits down.

The trainer should avoid trying to get close to the dog by stepping backward or to the side but rather must coax the dog to come close to him. Otherwise, the dog will shy away from the trainer's feet. If the dog is inclined to use the trainer as a leaning post, this should be dis-

TEACHING THE DOG TO SIT

Leash is pulled up with right hand

Left hand pushes down on dog's hindquarters

The Sit must be square and close to the trainer

couraged by knocking hard against the dog two or three times with the left leg.

To get the dog to the point where he will sit more quickly, the leash should be jerked with more of a snap and the dog slapped down to a sitting position. Every time the dog starts to get up without permission he should be told again to sit and snapped down harder than ever—until he will remain where he is. This exercise is repeated until the dog understands what the word "sit" means and will obey the command instantly.

It is surprising how quickly a dog will learn to sit down without being pushed to a sitting position. The first time the dog is slow to obey, though, the owner should not hesitate to slap him down without warning. A dog will accept harsh corrections with a philosophic attitude if the trainer is generous with his praise.

The average dog will, when he sits down, swing his rear end away from the trainer or go so far ahead he must turn and face the trainer at an angle. To overcome the first mistake, the left hand is used to sting the dog on the outside hip. The trainer must not wait until the dog is already sitting but should whack him before he gets all the way to the ground. To prevent the dog from going too far ahead, the left hand should hold the leash tight over the spot where the trainer's hip pocket would be, and, at the same time, the left leg should be stretched across in front of the dog to keep him from going ahead or from swinging to the side. When the dog sits down as he should, the leash is made slack and the left foot is brought back into place at the side of the dog. A second method is for the trainer to heel the dog close to a wall so the dog will knock up against the wall every time he sits incorrectly.

It is impossible to snap a heavy breed to a sitting position with any force, especially if the dog weighs 160 pounds and the trainer weighs 95 pounds. The trainer, then, will do better if he or she uses both hands on the leash and pulls steadily until the dog finally sits down. At this time the pressure on the collar is released and the dog immediately praised. The dog that is stubborn and will not sit down under any circumstances can be persuaded to do so by pulling the leash tight to hold the dog's head high and then whacking him hard across the rear end with the end of the leash. This heavy type of dog requires more severe handling than most, as nothing else will make an impression.

Then, too, there is the dog that will growl and show his teeth when he is made to sit, and the one that will snap and attempt to bite. The first type should be kept under control by the trainer pulling the leash forward and holding it tight across his left knee; at the same time, he should slap the dog sharply across the rear end to make him sit. If the leash is held tight enough, the dog will not be able to turn his head back to grab the trainer's hand. And, of course, the voice should be more demanding than ever. The dog that snaps and tries to bite is brought under control by holding him momentarily in the air to cut off his wind. When the dog quiets down, the training can go on as usual.

Let us take a moment and mention the things the trainer is apt to forget or do incorrectly when he is teaching the dog the Sit. If the dog is just learning, the leash should not be too long; otherwise, the dog will get out of position before he sits down. The trainer should not neglect to transfer the leash from the left to the right hand a moment before he halts so he will be ready to enforce the correct sitting position. When the dog is slow to sit, the trainer must remember to sting the dog on the rear end with his left hand or with the end of the leash.

If the Sit is wide and crooked, the sting should come on the outside hip—not after the dog is already sitting, but just as he lowers his rear end to the ground. An owner is often at fault when his dog sits too wide if he has taken a step to the side and into the dog every time he halts. The dog is afraid of getting stepped on and naturally moves farther away. The same is true when the dog sits too far to the rear. The trainer, instead of making the dog come up close, may have moved backward to

A DOG QUICKLY LEARNS TO SIT

get nearer the dog. If the dog has already formed the habit of sitting too far back, an assistant should walk along quietly behind the dog with one or two short pieces of chain or with a light bamboo rod in his hand. When the dog starts to sit down a chain is tossed lightly at his tail end, or the rod is used to tap the dog to make him move up of his own accord.

The dog should always be on leash when these corrections are made, and the timing as well as the way in which the dog is corrected are what are important. Correction must be done gently so as not to frighten the dog and yet in such a way that it will get results. To correct the dog that goes too far ahead and faces his trainer at an angle, the leash should pass in back of the trainer's body and be held tight with the right hand while the dog is smacked hard with the left hand on the off hip. When the dog does the opposite by sitting in back of the trainer with his tail end too far to the right, the trainer should take up the slack in the leash when the dog halts and, at the same time, kick backward with the right foot to catch the dog just as he sits down. This will make the dog square himself around and sit straight. The corrections, however, should not be so severe as to cause the dog to swing too far in the opposite direction.

During the dog's first few lessons, especially in the heeling and sitting routine, the trainer should never take his eyes off his dog. By watching the dog carefully, the trainer can usually anticipate what the dog is going to do and, if he chooses, prevent it. One very successful way to teach a dog to heel and to sit is to walk the dog between two people. The person on the dog's right gives the commands. The person on the left makes the corrections. Both give generous praise.

The Come Fore

While a dog is being trained to heel and to sit, it is a good time for the dog to learn to sit and face the trainer. This is known as the Come Fore. Since almost every exercise concludes with the dog in the sitting front position, he must be taught to sit squarely and close to his handler. While the trainer walks with the dog at heel position, and with both hands holding the leash as when heeling, the command "Come fore!" is given. At the same time, the trainer walks backward two or three paces *without changing the position of his hands on the leash.* The dog will turn around to follow the trainer when he hears the word "come" and when the trainer steps back from the dog. After the dog swings around and faces the trainer, and while the dog is still moving, the slack in the

111

Heel

Come Fore

Sit

112

Heel

e left hand is held
in back of the body

"Good boy"

leash is taken up by both hands and the dog is commanded, "Sit!" For this, the hands are held against the body and low down. It may be necessary to reach over the dog's back and push him down to the sitting position, but the leash must be kept tight at the same time. The trainer should stand with his feet placed apart to block the dog from going past him.

The leash moved from side to side or forward and backward controls the correct sitting position, which should be squarely in front and as close as possible to the handler. If the dog sits too far away, the trainer should pat his tummy and take a step backward to coax the dog to come closer. If this doesn't work, the dog should be pulled in slowly on a tight leash and held there until he sits properly. Those dogs that sit crooked (a very common fault) can quickly be squared around by jabbing them lightly with the fingers on whichever hip is out of line. This correction must not be made unless the leash is held tightly in both hands so the dog cannot jump away.

When the dog is first learning the "come-fore" exercise, the trainer should pivot back to heel position each time after the dog is made to sit in front. The trainer does more heeling, then the Come Fore, and finally a pivot back to heel position. By stressing this one particular part of the training, the trainer will find that the dog will more quickly understand what is expected of him and the commands "Come fore" and "Come front" will have real significance.

Invariably, the dog that neglects to sit in front of the trainer when he is called but goes directly to heel position was not trained with care to do the Come Fore. Neither was the dog that sits carelessly at the completion of each exercise. There are so few times when a dog is not required to sit in front of the trainer that the value of the Come-fore exercise cannot be stressed enough. Even the household hoodlum can be made to keep all four feet on the ground if the owner has taught him to sit in front of him and insists that he obey even when over excited.

There are very few owners who do the Come-fore exercise with any degree of smoothness when they try it for the first time. They make the exercise, which is so simple, as difficult as possible. Their first mistake is to take the left hand off the leash or to change its position on the leash. The result is that the trainer immediately loses control of the dog. The directions are that the trainer should walk backward without changing the position of his hands until the dog turns around, after which the left hand slides up the leash and joins the right hand at the trainer's waist.

Invariably, even though this exercise has been thoroughly explained and has been demonstrated over and over, some owners will insist upon

114

turning around themselves instead of letting the dog do the turning. All the trainer has to do is walk backward—simple, isn't it?

Another mistake is keeping the leash so tight the dog is dragged around instead of being able to go around by himself. The leash must be kept slack, for the jerk on the dog's collar when he goes too far is as important here as anywhere else. All too frequently, an attempt is made to square the dog around into place with the foot, without at the same time holding the leash tight to keep the dog from jumping away.

Last, but not least, those trainers who hover over their dogs instead of standing up straight are enough to give anyone who just watches them —including · the training instructor—a backache. The owner should practice the Come Fore during the heeling and sitting exercises until it comes naturally to him and requires little effort.

The Go-to-heel Position

As stated in the previous paragraph, all through the dog's training, except for the heeling and the "stays," the dog must sit facing his trainer. But no exercise is considered complete until the dog is back in the original heel position. This is known as the "finish" in Obedience Trials. The dog, having been taught in his very first lesson the meaning of the word "heel," already has a general idea of what is expected when he hears the command, but he must learn to go to that position by himself.

The first lessons should be as easy as possible. This is accomplished through a series of progressive steps: (1) By the owner first walking forward to turn the dog. (2) By pulling the dog to a standing position and then walking forward to make him turn around. (3) By taking one step backward with the left foot and guiding the dog around with the left hand held under the dog's chin. The left foot is then brought forward while the owner pats his left leg to coax the dog to sit close. Each step is repeated several times without interruption because the dog is learning a new exercise.

After the dog gets the idea of turning around, and does it with the leash slack, the trainer moves on to the next step. With the dog in the Come-fore position, and the leash held in both hands and rather low down, the command "Heel" is given. The left foot immediately takes a step backward from the dog and both hands, which are holding the leash, drop to the left side with a snap. The purpose of this is to teach the dog to start moving immediately when he hears the word "heel"—which he will do if the jerk on the collar is hard enough. When the dog gets up on all four feet, the trainer moves forward a step or two, halts, and the dog is made to sit down at once. Even though the trainer did most of the work the dog should be praised generously.

115

To train the dog to follow through far enough so he can make a complete turn, he is urged on by a series of short jerks with the left hand as far back as the trainer can reach. When the dog has continued to the point where he can make a full turn, the left hand lets go of the leash and immediately pats the trainer's knee to coax the dog to come up close. Then the dog should sit squarely and not do a sloppy finish.

If the dog is stubborn, the trainer may have to walk backward three or four steps before he can get the dog on his feet, but the jerks on the collar should be harder than ever to make a greater impression. If the trainer is getting the right response, the dog should move by himself the moment the left hand starts to slide down the leash toward the trainer's left side.

The heel position and the Come-fore exercise should be practiced together, doing first one and then the other. Fewer steps should be taken and less assistance given each time. The leash should be kept slack except when it is used to make corrections or when the dog is assisted into place. At such times, the leash is jerked hard and then loosened at once. No dog will learn the Go-to-Heel by himself if he is dragged or pivoted around on his tail.

In Obedience Trials, a dog is required to obey either a command or a signal, but not both together. During the instruction for the finish, the dog for the first time is given a definite signal for an exercise, and the trainer should encourage the dog to respond. The trainer starts by giving the command and this is followed by the correction (or the signal) and then the praise. The procedure is then reversed. The signal is given first, then the command, and then the correction again (if necessary). It will be to the trainer's as well as the dog's advantage if this pattern is followed throughout the entire training whenever commands and signals are used.

When the command "Heel," or a shrug of the shoulder, or a slight motion with the left hand is sufficient to cause the dog to immediately move into the proper heel position on the trainer's left side, the training may be considered successful. Every owner should strive for this perfection.

A second method used in the finish is to have the dog go to the trainer's right and pass in back of the trainer to heel position on the left side. Some owners use this method, but I prefer the former because when the dog is on leash his passing in back makes it necessary to change the leash from one hand to another to avoid having it entwine itself around the trainer. And it is sometimes difficult to change the leash when both arms are full of bundles.

To teach the dog by this method, the right hand instead of the left is used to give both the jerk and the signal. The command is given as usual, and when the dog passes in back, the trainer pats his left side and coaxes him into place. The dog should immediately sit down.

Until the dog will go to heel position by himself with the leash completely slack, there is no use in trying it with the leash off. A good performance *on* leash means a good performance *off* leash.

The trainer's mistakes will be failure to snap the leash hard at the start and neglecting to follow through with the left hand so the dog will have room to make a full turn. With certain breeds that are stubborn, it will take the full power of both hands, in a downward stroke, to jerk the dog forward and to get him on his feet; some of the heavier dogs may even have to be assisted around by the trainer "booting" them lightly in the rear with the right foot.

The Sit and Stay

The next important lesson is to teach the dog to stay on command. With the dog sitting on the trainer's left side, and with the leash in the right hand as usual, the left hand is placed around the dog's muzzle, and the trainer steps forward with the *right* foot. He turns and faces the dog. The command is "Sit and stay" with the emphasis on the "stay." Notice that the dog's name is not used here. The trainer should avoid saying the name whenever the dog is to stay by himself. The left hand held in front of the dog's muzzle, palm back, is the signal to stay and should be used whenever the dog is left in the sitting, the lying down, or the standing position.

If the dog starts to move, and the chances are he will, the leash is snapped upward and the dog is pushed down again to the sitting position. The command is repeated more forcefully. The trainer waits a few moments, and if the dog doesn't break he pivots back to heel position *without circling the dog*. This is done so the dog will not be tempted to get up, as he might be if the trainer were to pass in back of him. The dog is then told to stay and the trainer leaves him a second time.

If the dog, after he has been told to stay, follows the trainer when he steps forward, the trainer, as he moves his right foot, should drop his left hand quickly and bounce the palm of his hand off the dog's nose. Another correction is for the trainer, as he steps forward, to hold the leash short in his left hand and jerk the dog backward.

When the dog gets the idea of remaining in the sitting position, the trainer *slowly* backs away from him to almost the full length of the leash. The leash is played out a little at a time so it will not pull the dog and

**The left hand held in front of the dog's muzzle, palm back, is the
signal to stay** (King photo)

make him move. To be ready to make the correction when necessary,
the leash is transferred to the left hand, which is held waist high and
close to the body, and the right hand reaches out and takes hold of the
leash at arm's length. Later, when the trainer circles the dog, the hands
are reversed. The leash should have just enough slack to give a good jerk,
at which time the trainer snaps the leash up and away from himself so
the dog is thrown back on his haunches. The leash may also be flipped
up sharply to whack the dog under the chin. The command, naturally,

118

becomes more demanding. *A dog that continues to break from the Sit-stay position is not being corrected with enough severity.*

The trainer next, instead of stepping back to heel position, circles to the right and goes around in back of the dog. To keep the dog from turning his body when the trainer circles him, the dog's muzzle is held gently in the left hand and his head is twisted slightly toward the left. Later, when the leash is held straight up from the dog's head, this action will keep the dog from turning around. In the beginning, the dog must be made to stay in the sitting position without twisting and turning about even if the trainer must hold him with both hands and knees to keep him there. During this part of the dog's training, every motion the trainer makes should be slow *except* when he corrects the dog, and then he should act with lightning speed.

When the trainer is able to stand at the full length of the leash, he should walk back and forth in a semicircle to create a little activity and to get the dog accustomed to a certain amount of confusion. If the dog doesn't break, the trainer should return to heel position, wait a moment, give a second command to "stay!" and leave the dog again. This cycle is run through several times without praising the dog—so he will not move before he is told.

The trainer not only faces the dog during this exercise but he stands in back of him as well. At first, he stands close to the dog so he can correct him when he pivots around. Later, the trainer moves back to the full length of the leash. The dog should be permitted to turn his head—which he will do if his attention is where it should be—but he must never break the Sit by turning his body.

The Sit-stay is next done with the leash lying on the ground but still attached to the dog's collar. If the dog moves, the trainer can quickly step on the leash with his foot or reach down and grab it up to snap the dog back to a sitting position. Instead of just dropping the leash, the trainer should make a practice of leaning over and placing it on the ground. When he does this he should quietly say, "Stay!" After waiting a moment, he should lean down, pick the leash up, and again tell the dog to stay. The dog should remain no matter what the trainer does. If the dog lies down, he should be jerked up hard with the leash so he will understand from the start that he is not permitted to assume this position. If the dog is made to sit squarely on both hips, he will not be so tempted to lie down.

The trainer can usually tell when a dog is going to break if he will watch his dog closely. When the dog moves, or when, by his actions, he indicates uncertainty, the trainer repeats the command, "Stay!" At

119

1. The instructor is ready to make a correction

2. The dog is watched closely

3. The instructor circles the dog

4. The instructor always stops at heel position

5. Foot steps on leash

6. Off leash

121

all other times one command and one command only should be used. In other words, if the dog is sitting quietly the owner should not keep repeating, "Stay! Stay! Stay!" or the command will have no meaning.

The first time the leash is taken off, the trainer should remain close to the dog. It is better to be certain at one yard than doubtful at two. The distance can be increased when the dog gets used to the idea of staying alone.

A dog hates to be ignored, so he should be tested by the trainer walking to a chair or a bench and sitting down, lighting a cigarette, or reading. If the dog breaks, this is the chance the trainer has been waiting for, and the correction should be hard enough to make an impression.

The trainer then goes out of sight, but the first time he disappears he should stay for only a few moments. If the dog follows or goes to look for him, the trainer should quietly go up to the dog, hook his finger in the ring of the dog's collar, and take him back where he was left. And in a severe tone of voice, accompanied by a sharp jerk on the collar, he should demand that the dog stay. The trainer disappears again. Even if the dog doesn't move until the trainer returns to heel position, the trainer should wait a long time before praising him. When the owner has been out of sight, the dog's joy at seeing him again will know no bounds, and he will be more excited than ever. But he must not be allowed to move until permission is given. The length of time for the Sit-stay should be increased until the owner can remain out of sight for ten or fifteen minutes.

As the training progresses, the trainer should tempt the dog by running past him, throwing balls along the ground, making noises, et cetera. This will prepare for the unexpected that always happens at Obedience Trials. Work first with the leash fastened to the dog's collar and lying on the ground, later with the leash off entirely. When the dog breaks under these conditions, he should be taken quietly back to where he had been left and told to stay in no uncertain terms. *Do not correct the dog from a distance.*

A dog that creeps forward on the Sit-stay should be broken of the habit at once. The trainer should hold the leash rather short and, just as the dog moves forward, should lift his knee quickly and strike the dog under his chin or against his chest. This will make the dog draw back of his own accord. Another way is to whack the dog hard under the chin with the right hand. This should be repeated as many times as necessary and should be done more severely each time until the dog will remain in the spot where he is left.

When a dog is being trained to stay, the trainer should draw an imaginary circle around the dog and see that he remains inside the boundary. If he doesn't, the dog should be given whatever correction is necessary to keep him there.

The dog that breaks consistently should be corrected by a second person who stands in back of the dog and holds the leash. There should be just enough slack to give the dog a hard jerk when he moves. It may even be necessary to have two leashes on the dog, one for the owner and one for the person who is helping the trainer. In both cases, the corrections must be firm in order to get results.

There are all kinds of problems on the Sit-stay. There is the dog that squeaks and whines consistently. There is the dog that lies down or stands up when he thinks his owner doesn't see him. And there is the dog that just won't stay at all. It sometimes is effective for a second person to stand near and make corrections as well as the owner. The dog can either be yelled at or have a chain tossed on the ground to startle him into consciousness of the fact that he has done or is doing something wrong. When the owner is out of sight and the dog breaks the Sit by either lying down or leaving the spot completely, there are two things that may be tried. The assistant may correct the dog, or he may signal to the owner in some way so the owner, without being seen by the dog, can command him from a distance to sit and stay.

In one particularly stubborn case, the dog was trained in the hallway of the house and the second person, in this case myself, hid on the second floor, leaned over the balcony, and quietly dropped a chain in back of the dog every time he whined or lay down. This kind of a correction, of course, should be done gently and not be given the dog until he has had a lot of training. Otherwise, he will become frightened and will never stay by himself.

The trainer should be most insistent when it comes to doing the Sit-stay exercise. A dog that is permitted to be careless in this particular part of his training will be unsteady throughout. He will break whenever he is made to stay and will anticipate parts of every other exercise. An occasional error is to be expected, but a dog that is consistently disobedient when it comes to staying must receive strict discipline if the training is to have any value.

The trainer, when teaching a dog to sit and stay, usually makes the following mistakes. He does not jerk the leash hard enough when he corrects the dog, or he waits too long before he makes the correction. If the dog looks away, the trainer will make the error of calling the dog by name to get his attention. This will almost always cause a dog to move. After the dog has been trained to come, the trainer will frequently forget

All training classes begin with utter confusion

But soon both dogs and owners get the idea

This is real obedience

The dogs are tested for steadiness

to alternate the Sit-stay with the Come exercise. As a result, the dog will anticipate the Come and inadvertently be breaking on the Sit-stay. Very often the owner will neglect to give the proper Sit-stay signal. When the trainer leaves the dog from the heel position, the signal is made with the left hand, palm back. When the dog is left from the Come-fore position, the right hand is extended, the palm toward the dog's muzzle. When the trainer steps back from the dog, the fingers are flipped up under the dog's chin as a signal to stay. Owner after owner will confuse his dog by giving the command to sit and, at the same time, hold his hand palm downward—which is the signal to lie down.

Teaching the Dog to Sit from a Down Position

During the time a dog is learning to sit and stay he will often lie down by himself. To make the correction, the trainer must actually train the dog how to sit from the down position. Later, when the dog is made to lie down on purpose, this training will be useful.

The dog must learn to go to a sitting position immediately on either command or signal. The most practical way is for the trainer to hold the leash in the left hand, waist high and close to his body, but not to the full length of the leash. The right hand reaches out and takes hold of the leash half way down. The trainer commands, "Sit!" Immediately after the command, the leash is jerked up. If the dog doesn't respond to the pull on the leash, or if he is slow to obey, the trainer taps the dog's paws with his right foot or moves in to the dog as though he were going to step on him.

The signal for this exercise is the right hand extended, palm upward, while the fingers flip up in a quick motion. Since this is the same motion that was used to correct the dog on the Sit-stay, he should respond immediately whenever he sees it. I can only repeat that a dog will not obey when the leash is off unless he obeys when the leash is on. The trainer should take every advantage to train the dog so he will get an instant response to either the command or the signal while the dog is still on the leash. The order in which the exercise is carried out is also very important. The command is given first. It is immediately followed by the jerk on the leash or the hand signal, and then by tapping the dog's paw with the foot. In other words, all three things are not done at the same time, but with a slight pause between each part of the exercise.

When this method is used, the dog will learn to obey either the command or the signal. In any case, if the dog has received fair warning

126

TEACHING A DOG TO SIT

Hand is reversed, palm up

The foot brushes into the dog's paws

This is the signal to sit

and still chooses to ignore the directions, the trainer should not hesitate to pounce on the dog's paw to make him get up at once.

To make the dog sit when he is at a distance from the trainer, the signal or the command is given, and a second person makes the corrections by either pulling up on the leash or by tapping the dog's paw with his foot. Each time the dog is given assistance the correction should be more severe.

Manners during the Training Period

The heeling, sitting, and sit-stay exercises will usually complete a dog's first lesson. Perhaps the owner worked at only some heeling, or the heeling and sitting, but whatever was done the training must not end with the lesson itself. Not that the trainer should nag the dog constantly to obey his commands; but he should put the dog's training into use throughout the day whenever it is necessary. The dog should be made to enter and leave the training yard in the correct heeling position. He should be made to sit when he rides in elevators and to lie down and be quiet when visiting. When he is taken on the street, the dog should be made to walk along without pulling on the leash. Here, I would mention the dog that lunges at other dogs barking ferociously. Such behavior is inexcusable and totally unnecessary, especially when the dog is in training. One that misbehaves in this manner should be jerked severely and told to, "Stop at once!" If this makes no impression, the end of the leash or a switch should be flipped sharply across the dog's nose as he lunges forward. This is one time it is permissible to hit the dog, because in the excitement of wanting to fight he will be hysterical, and drastic treatment is the only thing that will make an impression.

I would like to point out that the well mannered dog will permit his master to pass first through a doorway or gateway. When approaching either the dog should be made to sit and wait for the door or the gate to be opened. He should then be made to stay for a moment before quietly passing through in the heeling position. There is an excellent cure for the dog whose one aim is to tear through every open door he sees. With the dog on leash, the door should be opened just enough to permit the little dear to get his head through the opening. It is then closed quickly but carefully in such a way as to catch the dog just behind the ears. He should be held for a moment while he struggles to free himself, after which the door is opened wide and he is told to get back to heel position. Nine times out of ten the dog will be only too glad to obey and thereafter will wait for his master to go first.

128

Then, there is the dog that will rush up and down stairs and cause his owner to take a nasty fall. To overcome this bad habit, the trainer should approach the steps slowly with his dog on a slack leash. The end of the leash is held in the right hand with about six or eight inches left dangling. Just as the dog lunges ahead, the trainer should snap out the command, "Heel!" and, at the same time, should bring the leash down sharply across the dog's nose. It will help if the trainer turns and goes in the opposite direction each time the dog darts ahead. This is based on the same principle used when training the unruly dog to walk on the street without pulling, and it will have the same effect.

After a dog has been in training a short while, the time may come when the trainer feels that he is making no progress. It may appear that the dog is going backward in his training instead of forward. This slump is to be expected. Training may be fun and exciting for the dog at first, but after a few lessons he may become bored and take the attitude, "This training business isn't what I thought it was going to be." At the same time the owner must be on guard that he himself is not to blame for the dog's attitude. This is the critical time in a dog's training when the trainer can either make or break a dog's spirit, and the trainer should never hesitate to back down if, as a result, the dog will be kept happy. If it is a question of the dog trying to get out of work the owner must be firmer than ever, for his authority is being put to the test and it must be decided whether he or the dog will be the boss. Firmness and the patience to "hold out" until the dog gives in first will make the training run along more smoothly. It won't be necessary to get tough; just quietly and definitely win each battle so the dog will acknowledge defeat and will recognize the master as being the victor.

The owner should not become so enthusiastic over Obedience Training that he trains his dog all day long. Some dogs are never given a moment's peace. If they walk around the room once too many times they are told to, "Down and stay!" When they wander into the hall from the living room they are told to, "Willie, come!" Even a friendly tail wag will bring the command "Sit!" Except for the regular training periods dogs should be allowed to relax and to be natural, providing, of course, they are being well mannered. Dogs that are being trained constantly will react in precisely the same way as people who are always being nagged. More harm than good will be done.

The two-dog owner should be advised to train his dogs individually until each is thoroughly familiar with the work. Later, when the dogs practice together, it will not be so confusing and they will be kept under control.

Every owner should take time out occasionally to play with his dog. The dog that is played with will develop an attachment to his owner and at the same time be much happier in his Obedience Training.

Coming When Called (or Recall)

As stated earlier in the chapter on puppy training, the first thing a young dog should be taught is to come when he is called. This is not hard to teach when a puppy is small if the owner has the patience and the perseverance and if he will make an effort to start the puppy off in the right way. The puppy's love and admiration for the owner will make him anxious to please, and when he is urged to come he will respond in a natural way. The wise owner will take advantage of this reaction.

The older dog that has never learned what "Come!" means must be trained to obey as part of his regular Obedience Training. The dog has already learned to sit and stay. He also knows how to sit in front of the trainer; so the next thing is to teach the dog to answer to the command, "Come!"

The dog is left in the Sit-stay position and the trainer steps back to the full length of the leash. The leash may be held in either hand, but I prefer the left. The trainer should wait to see that the dog does not break, then walk slowly backward two or three steps and command the dog to "Come!" The leash is given one quick snap at the start and then is made slack. The motion is similar to that of cracking a whip. The trainer stands erect and with both hands in front of his body. As the trainer steps back, he pats his stomach (or his chest if the dog is large) to coax the dog to come forward. At the same time he talks to the dog cajolingly. The leash is gathered up in both hands when the dog comes in, and he is made to sit in the Come-fore position.

The trainer should avoid leaning over to pat his knee or his thigh. This will make a dog crawl in with his head down rather than come in a gay fashion with his head high in the air. If the trainer will stand with his feet placed apart, he will block the dog from going to the side. By gathering the leash up in both hands he will be able to control the dog sufficiently to make him sit squarely. When the dog has been brought in, he is praised, then told to stay, and the trainer moves back to repeat the exercise. This cycle is repeated until the dog will come with the leash completely slack and receives little assistance from the trainer.

If the dog won't move when he is called, the leash is snapped hard in a series of jerks, and the trainer runs backward several steps while he repeats, "Come. Come. Come!" I like to teach a dog to come by putting

"Come" on leash

"Come" off leash

THE RECALL

the exercise into use when the dog least expects it. For instance, when I am teaching a dog to heel, I will step back quickly to get as far away from the dog as possible and then give the command in a loud tone of voice. At the moment the dog reaches the end of the leash, I jerk it hard and he is caught up short. He associates this un-pleasantness with his failure to come when he was called. I do the same thing when the dog is looking elsewhere and is inattentive. After each correction, the dog is patted and praised, or given some special tidbit. There is magic charm in pieces of cooked liver and chicken. This is one time in a dog's training when I highly approve of giving food if it will keep the dog happy. The majority of owners forget that when they teach a dog to come, they must avoid offending him. This they will never do if the dog is jerked too severely or reprimanded in a careless way for not coming. The dog should feel that his trainer is the most wonderful person in the world; he should not be like the little boy who knows he has done something wrong and is afraid to go home because of what awaits him.

As the trainer carries out the procedure for teaching the dog to come when called, he should move his own body as little as possible and rely upon his voice and the accompanying jerk on the leash to get results. Here again, the timing is what is important. The trainer should quietly give the command, "Come." Next he should pause a moment, then snap the leash hard. The moment the dog is on his feet, the trainer should start talking in a cajoling way to encourage the dog to continue coming forward. If the dog starts immediately when he hears the com-mand, the leash should not be jerked, but the voice should still be used to urge the dog on. Both hands should be held in front of the body and the leash gathered up in a hand over hand motion to encourage the dog to sit straight. This is as good a time as any to teach the dog to respond to the signal as well as to the command. In one respect every correction is a signal, and if care is taken to make the motions distinct, and if the action is timed as it should be, the dog will be gaining perfection in his work.

And now for the problem dog that darts off to either one side or the other instead of coming directly to the trainer. The chances are if the dog had been trained to do the Come Fore properly, the owner would not have this trouble. But since he does, the best way to get the dog over it is for the trainer to walk backward very slowly while the dog is made to follow along quietly close to and in front of him. Every once in a while the trainer should stop and the dog be told to sit. For this pur-pose the leash is held in the left hand, but the right hand should reach out and take hold of the leash above the dog's head. Whenever the dog darts off to one side or the other, he should be checked immediately and brought back in line by a short, hard jerk of the leash.

The dog is then called from the sitting position. But first, while the dog is still three or four feet away, the trainer snaps out the command, "Sit!" At the same time both hands reach out from the body to keep the dog at a distance. The command is familiar so the dog should obey the order to sit, even if he won't do anything else. This way, the dog is kept under control before he has a chance to lunge off to the side.

The same training is used for the dog that comes tearing in and all but knocks his owner to the ground. The dog is kept at a distance from the owner by using both hands on the leash, which is held at arm's length, and the dog is made to sit by voice command.

The trainer should attempt to achieve perfection while he still has the dog on leash and under control, and he should not be too anxious to trust the dog by himself. Every mistake the dog makes while the leash is on he is going to make when the leash is taken off.

Does your dog run away? Don't run after him. If you lean down and coax him, you *might* persuade him to change his mind. Show me a dog that won't wait for the leash to be taken off, then scamper away and defy everybody to catch him. The mistake is in running after such a dog. It is a big temptation, but the dog will only run farther away than ever. If the owner will kneel down and coax the dog to come close, or if he will sit quietly on the ground and talk to the dog in a squeaky voice, the dog's curiosity may get the better of him. He will want to know what the trainer is doing. If the dog comes near enough so the trainer can touch him, the trainer should reach out and scratch the dog's ear or pat his head, quietly slip his finger through the ring on the collar, and put the dog on leash. The trainer should never correct the dog harshly when he has come of his own accord, nor after the dog has been caught. Neither should the trainer grab at the dog in passing. If he does, the next time the dog won't come at all.

Another way to capture a dog that says, "Catch me . . . if you can!" is for the trainer to start walking away from the dog and to snap out the command, "Heel!" in a tone of voice that implies—"If you know what is good for you, you had better obey!" The left hand signals the dog into heel position at the same time. If this doesn't work, the trainer should raise his hand in the down signal and demand that the dog lie down— providing he has already received this training. When he does lie down, the trainer circles around him to heel position exactly as though he were doing the Down-stay exercise. A dog that has been well trained in heel

Never run after a dog

Coax him to come instead

work and knows how to lie down on command should obey in spite of his occasional desire to play the fool.

To correct the dog that runs away, the long line is used. The regular leash is taken off and the line fastened to the dog's collar. The coiled rope is thrown in back of the trainer as he walks with the dog at heel. When they reach the other end of the training yard they do an about-turn. The dog is told to sit and stay, and the trainer retraces his steps in a line parallel to the outstretched rope and halts near the end. If, when the dog is told to come, he runs off elsewhere, the trainer should step on the line quickly and snap the dog back with a jerk.

Still another method is to tie the end of the line to a stationary object such as a tree or a post, without the dog realizing he is tied. The trainer walks with the dog at heel, does an about-turn, halts, then leaves him. Should the dog dart off by himself, he will be jerked back by the line, and, if the trainer manages to say, "Come" just before the dog is stopped short, the dog will again associate the correction with failure to come when he is called. When the dog finds he has nothing to gain by running away, he should come without the use of the line.

In addition to the problem dog that responds to the "Come" by tearing off in the opposite direction, there is the dog that won't come at all, and the one that comes but so slowly it is hard to believe he is really moving. There is also the dog that is easily distracted and does not "hear" the command; and the dog that runs to somebody else for protection while he makes it clear to everybody that he thinks his trainer is a cad and a bully. In all these cases, the idea behind the training is that the dog must associate something unpleasant with everyone except his trainer. He should be given no sympathy but should be reprimanded severely by outsiders. If several people will throw a small cardboard box at the dog when he ignores his owner's command to come, the dog's association with those people will be an unhappy one. It will result in the dog fleeing to his trainer for the protection he seeks.

In a training class a dog can be made to come when called if the members will form a circle (without their own dogs), each with a leash or box in his hand. The owner and the dog remain within the circle. When the dog makes a dash for freedom, each person in turn should toss whichever object he has onto the ground to drive the dog back. The owner leans down and coaxes the dog to come to him and rewards him generously.

When the owner has no one to assist him in this exercise, he can tie a ten- or twelve-foot piece of rope to the dog's collar and let it drag along the ground. The dog should be permitted to run around and play. The trainer unexpectedly should give the dog the command to come and at the same time step on the end of the rope. As the dog does not see the action, he will not associate the trainer with the correction. Unfortunately, the dog will probably get wise to the fact the rope is there and will not run around as much as he would otherwise. The length of the rope is gradually shortened until only a few feet remain and then it is taken off completely. If the owner has managed to get in even one or two good corrections while the rope was on, perhaps the dog will have learned his lesson.

The trainer can sometimes make a dog come by picking up a clod of dirt, or a stick, or by using his leash rolled up in a ball. *When the dog is not looking*, the trainer should throw it at the dog or on the ground near him. This will startle the dog; and when he looks around in a bewildered way, the trainer should call him and offer protection. As one carries out the Recall exercise, the distances are increased so the dog will come from any part of the training yard. The dog should be called when he is at play and when his attention is on other things. Leave no doubt in the dog's mind that the command, "Come!" means "COME!"

The dog that comes before he is called is, in reality, breaking on the Sit-stay. The dog should be left at one end of the training yard while the trainer faces him in the exact position he would were he going to call the dog. But, after waiting a few moments, the trainer should instead return to heel position. This is done a number of times. Then, if the trainer will alternate the Sit-stay with the Come, the dog will learn not to anticipate.

The dog that finishes before he is told is handled the same way. A number of recalls are done, one after the other, without permitting the dog to complete the exercise. After this the dog can be allowed to do a complete Recall, which includes going to heel position.

From watching the dogs in the training classes and in the Obedience Trials, and from correspondence which has been received over a number of years, I would say that the slowness with which dogs move when they are called presents the biggest problem. Frequently a dog will start out in his training with a pep and vigor that is a joy to watch, only to turn into a "slow freight." A general slowing down is to be expected since the dog is being brought under control. But the trainer should take care that the dog's enthusiasm is not dampened too much.

It is especially difficult to get speed out of the slow-moving breeds. So the trainer should take every advantage he can. If, for instance, he will give the dog a pleasant reward, the dog may learn to expect it and will not be bored with the usual routine. It may be necessary to trick the dog into coming, such as by the owner jumping in the car and driving away while the dog runs for his life to catch up.

Although the dog's name should not be used too frequently while he is learning a new lesson, especially when he is away from the trainer, it is good practice to use the name in this exercise. The command would then be, "Jester, come!" Almost every dog will move instinctively when his name is called, and this fact may be the means of making the dog peppier than usual.

The Drop on Recall is probably more to blame than anything else for a slow response. This cannot be completely avoided, but when teaching the exercise the trainer should take care not to be too arduous.

There are two other suggestions I might make to help speed up the Recall. The first is to have a second person stand close in back of the dog. After the owner calls the dog he claps his hands loudly. On the word "Come!" the person standing in back of the dog taps the dog's hindquarters to get him off to a flying start. The owner's applause keeps the dog from thinking ill of the correction. The second suggestion is that after the owner calls his dog he turns and runs from the dog, clapping his hands cheerfully. Later he merely pivots, making a complete turn, again giving loud applause. He then calls, clapping his hands without pivoting. The reason for so many slow Recalls is lack of praise while the dog is learning. During those first few lessons it isn't "Jester, come!" it is "Jester, come! GOOD BOY!" The praise and the clapping of the hands can be dropped after the owner gets the response he is after.

The Lie Down

A well mannered dog is one that will lie down on command and obey immediately. Many a dog's life has been saved and an accident frequently avoided when, under unexpected circumstances, a dog was required to act quickly in this respect.

The Down position is the most natural position in the world for the dog to assume. As a puppy, he will flop down with no trouble at all. If a little assistance and encouragement are given at this time, and if the words "down" or "lie down" are said over and over, the puppy will soon learn there is a connection between the command and the position in which he is lying.

First lesson in the Lie Down—Instructor pulls dog's legs forward

Second lesson—The hand pulls down on the leash

The hand signal must always be given even when the foot is used on the leash

Later he will drop whenever this signal is given

It is not so easy to train the adult dog to lie down. He will be inclined to struggle and to become panicky when he feels himself bound by the leash. Most animals do under these circumstances. Nevertheless, the grown dog can and should be taught to obey the command.

The dog is made to sit and face the trainer. If he is not too excitable and will permit himself to be handled, the trainer should pull the dog's front legs forward as he pushes down on the dog's back to force him to the ground. This is done once or twice so that the dog will know what is expected. When the command, "Lie down" is repeated quietly at the same time, the dog will associate the command with a prone position.

Success depends upon slowness of movement on the trainer's part and the giving of praise while the dog is being put down. No force, just gentle pressure until the dog settles to the ground. If the dog braces himself the owner, without giving in, should stop all action and wait for the dog to relax. I once out-waited a 160-pound Great Dane twenty minutes before he settled to a comfortable Down position. Some dogs fight violently on the Down exercise and become hysterical. Other dogs are just plain stubborn. Their attitude is one of "Make me if you can!" Both the stubborn dogs and those of an excitable nature, if handled quietly yet firmly, will give in without too much trouble if they receive the necessary praise.

To win out, the trainer should take his position close to and in front of the dog. The leash should be held in the left hand so that it just clears the ground. Before the trainer gives the command, the right foot should be placed over the leash in such a way that the leash can slide freely under the instep. The trainer's full weight is placed on the *right* foot. This will prevent him from being thrown over backward when the dog struggles and lifts his head. The command should be given in a low but firm tone of voice, and at the same time the leash should be pulled up slowly with *both* hands. This will lower the dog's head. He should be held in this position, even if he fights like a wildcat. Not that the trainer should choke the dog to death, but the leash is given just enough slack to permit the dog to breathe without giving in to him. When the dog stops struggling, the pressure on the collar should be eased and the trainer should push against the dog's shoulder or back to make him lower his entire body. When the dog finally goes down, the trainer should give the command, "Stay." But *the foot must not be taken off the leash*. It is kept there so that if the dog should leap up again, he can be pulled down quickly without loss of time or having him get out of control.

Whenever the dog is in a lying-down position the trainer should not be too enthusiastic in his praise. If he is, the dog will be tempted to

THE STUBBORN DOG

Step on leash

*Pull leash up
under arch of
foot*

*Push down on the dog's
back*

jump up in excitement. Instead, the trainer should merely stroke the dog gently or scratch his ear as a sign of approval.

When the foot is used for the downward pull on the leash, the dog can be made to obey faster and to perform more accurately for Obedience Trial competition. At the same time, the trainer will have complete control because the upright position in which he stands will not tempt the dog to creep forward. Even when the foot is used, the hand should still be raised in the down signal. The dog must clearly understand the signal so that he will later obey, even at a distance. The trainer should stand erect. The signal hand, in this case the right one, should be raised to the level of the right shoulder and held in that position until the dog obeys the command. The timing in this exercise is such that the voice and signal are given first and then are immediately followed by the correction with the foot on the leash.

Another way to make a dog lie down, providing the dog does not struggle too much, is to hold the leash short in both hands and to place the right foot on the leash close to the dog's collar. By stepping slowly downward and putting his full weight on the leash, the trainer will force the dog's head to be pulled to the ground. The dog should be held until the rest of his body drops down as well. Whatever method is used to get the dog down, the command and, later, the signal must be given so that the dog will learn to obey either.

The trainer should do a series of Downs and Sits, alternating one with the other; and he should see that the dog goes up and down in the same spot. In other words, he should imagine that the dog is sitting in the center of a small circle. If the dog doesn't lie down without moving outside the circle, he should be corrected.

One common mistake when teaching this exercise is permitting the dog to creep forward so that he is always groveling at the trainer's feet. Possibly the trainer was at fault during the early part of the dog's training by holding his hand so low that the signal was interpreted as a gesture to come rather than to down. This is why it is important for the trainer to hold whatever hand he uses to give the down signal at least on a level with the shoulder.

To cure a dog from creeping-in, the trainer should take his position as usual with the right hand raised above the shoulder. Just as the dog moves forward, he should drop his arm quickly and cuff the dog hard on the tip of the nose. (I do mean hard! Not a gentle love tap.) One good correction will get immediate results, but a dog will never stop moving forward if the owner makes no impression on the dog. After the hand raps the dog on the nose, it is held there for a second while the

ALL BREEDS ARE TAUGHT THE SAME WAY

The training class prepares for the Lie Down

The hand and foot are used together at first

command is repeated and until the dog lies down without creeping-in.

There are problems in all parts of the training, and the Down exercise is no exception. For instance, there is the dog that will roll over on his back. It does not help if the owner laughs at the dog's antics. The minute the dog starts to roll on his side the trainer should jerk him up quickly to a sitting position and then snap him down again. If he starts to roll over a second time, he should be jerked up and then down still again. This is repeated until the dog will no longer roll over on his back but will stay with all four legs underneath him.

There is the problem-dog that will growl and show his teeth or even lunge at the trainer and try to bite. For this type of dog the leash is held in both hands, and the right foot is placed over the leash where it just touches the ground. The leash is held in both hands, with eight or ten inches hanging free. The dog is told to lie down; and while the left hand takes up all slack in the leash to prevent the dog from leaping up at the trainer, the right hand serves as a barrier. If the dog growls or shows his teeth, or if he lunges forward, the end of the leash is brought down across his nose with a hard whack. The command is repeated in a tone of voice that implies that the dog had better obey if he knows what is good for him.

Another problem is the dog that will dart frantically off to either one side or the other instead of lying down quietly in front of the trainer. To correct this fault, the trainer should use his "signal" hand to block the dog and check him from moving forward in any direction. If the dog dashes to the right, the hand is dropped to the right with the palm toward the dog's muzzle ready to rap him on the nose. If he darts to the left, the same hand swings across to the left side, and the motion is like a backhand when playing tennis. The dog is then blocked in that position as well. It won't do any good just to hold the hand there unless the trainer will bounce the dog on the nose occasionally; the placing of the hand must have a significance.

An excellent rule for the trainer to keep in mind throughout the training, and especially when he is teaching the dog to lie down, is that whenever the dog ignores the trainer's signal or command and continues to move forward, the trainer in turn should move toward the dog and make his corrections more severe. When the opposite happens and the dog backs up from the trainer, the trainer should back away from the dog and ease up on his handling. The backing away is a sign the dog is afraid, and if he is pressed too far, he will be unhappy and become unsteady. For example, the dog that will obey the signal to lie down but will back up at the same time should be handled with little hand-motion.

The dog is

The trainer, instead of raising his hand high in the air, should hold it on a level with his waist and very slowly spread the fingers to give the signal. The dog is jittery and over anxious and he must be calmed down. Quiet handling is the best way to do it. Each and every dog will react differently, and the trainer must feel his way for that particular accord that will result in smooth-flowing teamwork.

When the dog lies down without assistance, the leash may be taken off. The dog is left in the sitting position and the trainer should face

d at a distance

him a few feet away. The dog is told to lie down. If he obeys, the trainer, by voice alone, should show his approval with a quiet, "Stay. Good boy!" or "Good girl!" After this the dog is made to sit and then is praised with enthusiasm. If the dog does not obey, the trainer should lean over and hold his hand just above the dog's head. When he gives the command he should cuff the dog lightly on the nose; but since the leash is not on to control the dog, the gesture should be done slowly or the dog may jump away. Sometimes it will help if the trainer will lift his right foot

147

slightly. Since this was the foot that was used to make the dog lie down in the first place, the motion will convey a meaning to the dog that he should not choose to ignore completely. Another method is for the leash to be left on and stretched full length on the ground. When the trainer tells the dog to lie down, the left foot pulls the leash taut while the right foot steps close to the dog's collar to jerk him down with a snap. In other words, the trainer should walk up the leash instead of having to pick the leash up in his hand to make the correction. If this fails to make the dog go down, the training should continue on leash and should be of a more severe nature.

The distances should gradually be increased until the dog will drop, either upon command or signal, when the trainer is at the far end of the training yard. Since the obedience rules for competition at dog shows require that a dog receive either the signal or the command, but not both, the dog should be trained in preparation for the trials. For instance, the trainer should first give the command only. If the dog is slow to obey, he should be corrected immediately with the leash. The trainer should then give the signal followed by the command, after which the leash is again used to make the correction if the dog doesn't respond at once.

A dog will not lie down when the leash has been taken off, nor will he drop at a distance, until he has learned to obey quickly when the leash is still on. *If the dog does not act immediately, the jerks on the collar have not been of a severe enough nature.*

The owner should train the dog to lie down at heel position, and not just when he is facing the trainer. This will be useful around the house as well as in Obedience Trials where the dog is left for the Down-stay exercise. The best way to teach this is to carry the leash short in the right hand and to use the left hand to push the dog down. The trainer should heel his dog for a short distance, and when he stops, he should command the dog to lie down. The left hand is placed on the leash close to the dog's neck to apply the pressure that will force the dog quickly to the Down position. At the same time, the right hand is raised to take up the slack so there will be room to snap the leash without hitting the ground with the left hand.

When this exercise is done without the leash, the dog will not confuse the signal to lie down with that of the stay if the wrist is bent and the fingers are held horizontal rather than vertical.

For practice, the dog should be made to lie down when he least expects the command, as when he is running about the house or is in the yard at play. He should be trained to lie down from the standing position as well as from the sitting one. The well trained dog will drop instantly wherever the command is given and whenever he sees the hand raised in the Down signal.

There are so many things that an owner will do incorrectly when he teaches his dog to lie down, I hardly know where to begin. Probably the most common mistake is that of giving up when the dog fights or yells with rage. The owner can't "take it." He would be more persistent if he would only realize that the moment he permits the dog to have his way, all is lost. Having succeeded the first time, the dog will try the same thing again.

On the other hand, many an owner makes the opposite mistake of holding the leash so tightly the dog cannot get his breath. Under these circumstances the dog will fight harder than ever. There is a difference between the dog that tugs and pulls at the leash because he is angry and the one that does the same because he is unable to get air. The trainer must recognize this point in order to know when it is necessary to ease up.

Then, too, the arm that is used to give the Down signal is very often held incorrectly. The trainer will hold it so close to the ground the dog will be tempted to come rather than to lie down. Many owners can't bring themselves to jerk the collars with sufficient force. As a result the response is slow. Nor will they cuff the little velvet noses to prevent the dogs from creeping forward. Owners will also inadvertently pull on the leash so the dog thinks he should get up. And trainers will say the dog's name, when special care should be taken not to use it when the dog is already in the lying-down position.

The Down and Stay

When a dog has learned Lie-down, it is not hard to train him to stay in the Down position if he already knows how to do the Sit-stay. When the trainer backs away slowly to the full length of the leash the first time, he must be ready to correct the dog at a moment's notice. The mistake that is made all too frequently is the slowness with which the trainer corrects the dog whenever he breaks from the Down position. The trainer should not take time to rearrange his leash and get his hands and feet placed just right before he makes his dog lie down again. The dog should be corrected quickly and with as little lapse of time as possible between the actual mistake and the correction he receives.

If the dog remains down, the trainer should walk back and forth in front of him and finally step back to heel position without circling. The

THE DOWN-STAY
(Note the dog's attention)

The instructor is prepared to make a correction

The dog is watched closely

All motions are slow

The dog is kept down after the instructor is back at heel position

Foot steps on leash

Off leash

dog is then told to stay, and the trainer leaves him a second time. If the dog is permitted to get up every time the trainer returns, he will get in the habit and may jump up too soon at an Obedience Trial, thereby losing points. Should the dog get up too soon, he should be quickly jerked down and told in a definite tone of voice to stay. The trainer, when he first circles around in back of the dog, may find it necessary to hold the dog by the muzzle so he can't get up or turn his body. After the trainer is back at heel position the dog must be kept down. If at any time the trainer thinks the dog is going to move, he may warn him with another command to "Stay." When the exercise is completed, the trainer gives the dog permission to move and makes a fuss over him.

From here on, the same procedure is followed that was used in the Sit-stay exercise: The leash is held in the hand but is kept slack; then it is placed on the ground but left fastened to the dog's collar. Finally, it is taken off completely. The dog is made to stay down while the trainer stands in back of him.

If at any time the dog gets up from this position before he is told, he is corrected in the usual way: The trainer takes the dog back, puts him down again with a sharp jerk on the collar, and demands in a severe tone of voice that he stay where he is. The distance is increased until the trainer can go out of sight for longer and longer periods of time.

The trainer should get in the habit of giving only one command for the Down-stay unless the dog actually breaks or the trainer thinks the dog is going to move, in which case the command is repeated with more force. A dog can be made steady on the Down position by the trainer tempting him to get up—and, thereby, inviting a correction. Clapping the hands, stamping the feet, whistling, and calling to other dogs are distracting. So is stepping over the dog's back while he is lying down, and tossing balls along the ground in front of the dog. The dog should be taught to resist the temptation to move under these circumstances.

The problems encountered in the Down-stay are handled about the same as those in the Sit-stay. Occasionally the dog will do only one of the exercises, but usually if he will hold the Sit-stay position he will hold the Down position. When he breaks on one of these exercises he will often break on the other. This means the trainer is probably at fault and has not been severe enough when making the corrections.

The long line is used for Sit-stay, Down-stay, Recall, and for run-away dogs

The obedience-trained dog will ignore other dogs

The Stand

One argument against Obedience Training is that a dog is made to sit every time he stops. Very often one hears the remark, "But I don't want my dog to sit. I want him to stand!" It is not difficult to keep a dog on all four feet. Early in his training the dog can learn to stand without becoming confused with sitting-at-heel, as required in Obedience Trials. The dog is trained to sit automatically when the trainer halts, but he should receive a signal or command to stand.

The trainer walks with the dog in the heeling position and with the leash held short in the right hand. When the trainer stops he commands the dog to, "Stand!" At the same time, the leash is tightened just enough to take up the slack. Care should be taken not to jerk on the leash because it will make the dog sit down. The left hand is dropped to the dog's side and touches him gently in front of his right back leg. If the trainer is quick enough, he can keep the dog standing and not have to lift him from the sitting position.

Very often on the Stand the dog will swing his tail end away from the trainer. In this case the left hand should reach over the dog's back and touch him in front of the left back leg. Until the dog knows what it is all about, the trainer may even have to place his hand underneath him two or three times and lift him to a standing position or to loop the end of the leash around the dog's body to keep him on all four feet.

Another way to teach a dog to stand is for the trainer to slip his left foot under the dog (heel or toe pointed up) just as the dog comes to a halt. When the dog starts to sit down, he will feel the trainer's foot there and will quickly come to a stand. This method is not used for an excitable dog because it will cause him to leap around in a frenzy. One might hold the dog by the muzzle and take a step forward every time he starts to sit. This will keep him in a standing position, and if the command is given at the same time he will soon learn what the word "Stand!" means.

A few dogs will respond by coming to a standing position when their backs are scratched. The trainer must find out what method pleases his particular dog and use that method. Nevertheless, he must remember to give the command at the same time so the dog will associate the word with the action.

The trainer should next stress the signal for the Stand-stay position. This is simply dropping the left hand down to the side, palm backward. It indicates that the trainer wants the dog to remain where he is. To reach this point of perfection, the trainer gradually works his left hand forward from the position in front of the dog's right back leg to, first,

154

THE STAND

Standing at heel
position. Note right
hand signal

Stand-stay on leash.
Note palm
toward dog's muzzle.

Stand-stay off leash

(King photos)

the side of the dog; then to the dog's shoulder; and later to just ahead of the dog's muzzle. If at any time after the dog has been told to Stand-stay he moves forward even a step or two, the habit should be broken immediately. The trainer should bounce the palm of his hand hard against the dog's nose and then hold it quietly about three inches in front of the dog while he repeats the command. If the dog moves forward again, the nose is banged harder than ever.

The trainer can simplify the training for the Stand if he will take an

The Stand-stay in an exhibition at Madison Square Garden given by the author during Westminster Kennel Club Dog Show

extra long step forward with the right foot when he gives the dog the signal. This will place him ahead of the dog when he stops, and the dog can see the signal more clearly.

Sometimes a dog may be slow to note the signal, or he may confuse it with a signal for some other exercise. In this case, the right hand can be used in either an upward or downward motion to cut across in front of the dog and to check his advance forward. The trainer should use the method that will get the quickest results.

After the dog has learned to remain on all fours and will obey either the command or the signal, the Standing-at-heel should be alternated with the Sitting-at-heel so the dog will clearly distinguish between the two positions.

The Stand-stay should be done while the trainer faces the dog at the full length of the leash. The dog must remain standing while the trainer circles around in back of him to heel position. This part will be easy because the dog already knows how to stay and is familiar with the command. The leash is taken off and the same procedure followed. The distance is gradually increased until the trainer can stand the length of the training yard without the dog breaking. And the dog should remain from three to five minutes.

A small dog will learn to stand more quickly if he is first posed on a table. The command, "Stand!" is said over and over while the dog is handled and made to remain in the standing position. Later, when the dog is placed on the ground, he will have some idea what it is all about; and even when the leash is looped under his stomach to keep him standing, he will not be afraid.

A dog with so bad a disposition that he will try to bite while he is being handled should be muzzled. Under no circumstances should he be permitted to get out of doing the exercise just because he doesn't like it. Even a grumpy dog must obey. The dog that snarls when he is touched underneath his stomach (and there are plenty that do), or the one that thinks he is a snapping turtle, can be kept under control if the leash is pulled forward and held tightly across the trainer's left knee, thereby preventing the dog from turning his head around far enough to grab the trainer's hand. This procedure is the same as that suggested for lifting a cross dog from the floor. It is not uncomfortable for the dog because the pressure from the collar comes on the back of the dog's neck; and yet the trainer will have complete control. A snappy dog should be handled firmly and with patience. The trainer, meanwhile, hopes the dog will soon get tired of his own cussedness.

The Stand for Examination

When a dog has learned how to stand and will remain standing for a period of time, the trainer should ask someone to handle the dog so that he will learn to accept examination. The importance of this training cannot be stressed too much. Altogether too many dogs object to being touched. The Stand for Examination has its practical uses as well. It will make the dog's trips to the veterinarian or to the beauty shops more pleasant. It will also make it easier for the family to handle the dog at all times.

The Stand for Examination is of value in the breed ring at dog shows

The purpose of the Stand for Examination is to reveal the dog's temperament. The dog should allow himself to be touched without showing resentment and moving away. In Obedience Trials, the Stand for Examination appears in two different places. The first is in the Novice Class. The dog is made to do the Stand-stay on leash while the owner faces him and the judge touches his head and back. In the Utility Class, the Stand for Examination is done in a group, and the length of time the dogs must remain standing is a minimum of three minutes. The owner who has successfully trained his dog to do the Stand, both on and off leash, should not have too much trouble in the Stand for Examination and the group examination; for these combine the Stand, the Stay, and the dog's permitting a person to handle him.

Unless actually vicious, almost every dog can be trained to take a certain amount of handling from someone other than his owner. The dog is first taught to do the Stand on command and to remain in the standing position. With the dog on leash and facing the trainer, the trainer next asks a number of different people to touch the dog while he is kept standing. At first, the examination should be casual, with the stranger just running his hand over the dog. Later, the examination should be more thorough, and the person testing the dog should touch the dog's hindquarters and tail; should open the dog's mouth to look at his teeth; and should pick up the dog's feet and examine the pads. Under no circumstances should the dog growl or move away. If he shows uncertainty, the trainer in a more severe tone of voice should command the dog to stay. If he sidles away, the trainer should put him back in place and, if necessary, hold him while the other person puts his hands on him. The trainer should bounce the palm of his hand off the dog's nose if he moves forward. If the dog growls when he is touched, he should be smacked hard by his owner and told in no uncertain terms to "Cut it out." Dogs with a questionable disposition should be muzzled until they get used to being touched and until the owners have a chance to see how their dogs will react toward a stranger.

With practice, the trainer should be able to leave the dog in the standing position and should be able to go the length of the training yard away. After that, it is only a matter of requiring the dog to remain longer and under more trying conditions.

The trainer should *always* return to heel position by circling the dog. Then he should stand quietly for a few moments before releasing the dog from the exercise and praising him. Special care should be taken to keep the hands motionless. If the trainer pulls up on the leash, the dog will be apt to sit down.

Even a shy dog can be trained over a period of time to the point where he will permit strangers to touch him. It is difficult because the shy dog's confidence must be won before much progress can be made. The shy dog is suspicious of everyone and he feels that if a person comes near he has an ulterior motive. Because of this attitude, it is better to have the strangers merely walk around the dog at first in a nonchalant manner and not try to put their hands on him. Later, they can brush lightly up against the dog "accidentally," while the trainer insists that the dog stay where he is and sees to it that he obeys. Gradually over a period of time, the owner, if he is firm enough, will get the dog to the point where he will permit a stranger to examine him—very gently at first, and later in a more natural way.

Owners whose dogs fail to do the Stand with any degree of accuracy are apt to be at fault in the following ways.

The trainer will be slow to give the command or the signal and the dog will be half sitting before he is told what to do. Whether the signal or the command is used, it must be given while the dog is still on all four feet and while the trainer is still moving forward.

159

The trainer who hesitates to bounce the palm of his hand against the dog's nose will have a dog that cheats on the Stand—that is, the dog will move up a step or so at a time until he finally closes the gap between the trainer and himself.

Another mistake the owner will frequently make is to pull on the leash. This results in the dog sitting rather than standing. While teaching the Stand exercise, *the leash must be kept slack.*

Failure to keep the dog standing in the first place has its disadvantage. It is always more difficult to lift the dog to the standing position than to keep him on his feet. When something is placed underneath the dog, he will very quickly learn to stand by himself. One of the best ways I found of making toy dogs remain on all four feet was the use of an "Oscar" I received a few years ago as an award. The trophy was in the shape of a dog whose ears were the most pointed I have ever seen. The whole statue was just the right size to slip under a toy dog when he stood on the table for grooming. With the statue in place, a dog would sit down only once.

Very often exhibitors in Obedience Trials have come to me with the problem that they cannot make their dogs stand when they move away from them. I suggest that the owner stand the dog so that he straddles a low bar or solid jump. With the owner at the full length of the leash, the dog may attempt to sit down, but he will correct himself when he feels something underneath him. With a little practice the dog will very quickly learn to stand even when the owner is at a distance.

The Drop on Recall

When a dog is said to do the Drop on Recall, it means that he lies down upon command as he is coming in to the trainer. A number of dogs have been saved through this act of obedience because the owner gave the command to drop when the dog started to dart across the street in the face of an oncoming automobile. Mastery of this exercise assures the complete control over a dog that is greatly to be desired and is not difficult to achieve.

The previous training, in which the dog was made to lie down on command and to drop in the distance, should be practiced from both a sitting and a standing position. The dog is now left in the Sit-stay or the Down-stay position, and the trainer faces him a short distance away, as for the straight Recall. After waiting a moment to see if the dog is going to break, the trainer gives the command to, "Come!" Before the

In the Drop on Recall the dog is commanded to lie down as he runs toward the instructor. Note hand signal. (King photo)

An excellent example of the Drop on Recall at Madison Square Garden before an estimated crowd of 15,000 people *Photo by Evelyn M. Shafer*

dog gathers too much speed he is given the command and the signal to, "Lie down!" If he goes down at once, the trainer should wait a moment, then call the dog again. The dog must complete the exercise by sitting in front of the trainer and then by going around to heel position upon command. It may be necessary to do this training on leash until the dog will obey the command more quickly. The dog is left in a sitting position at the full length of the leash, which the trainer holds in his left hand. The dog is called and the trainer runs backward while the dog follows on the run. While still moving and at the full length of the leash, the dog is given the command to lie down, at which time the trainer raises his right hand and cuffs the dog sharply on the nose. When the dog drops down he is told to stay, and the trainer steps back quietly to the full length of the leash, waits a moment, and repeats the exercise.

After the leash has been taken off and the dog is called and made to drop, the owner should occasionally return to the dog, pat him, and give him a word of praise for doing what the trainer asked. If the dog ignores the command and continues to come forward, the trainer should run toward the dog and cuff him on the nose. Before the dog is called the next time the leash should be wadded tightly in the hand that is used to give the signal; then if the dog doesn't drop when told, the leash is thrown on the ground just in front of him. Startling the dog this way will make him stop short, and then when the command and the signal are repeated he should go down immediately. The trainer must make it a point to check the dog at once by running toward him or by throwing something if the dog continues to come forward after he has been told to drop. If the training is done inside, a loud stamp on the floor is an excellent means of startling the dog.

On the other hand, there is the dog that will turn away or swerve sharply when he hears the command. In this case, the trainer should be gentle and give the dog more assurance.

Since the Drop on Recall will slow up a dog that is ordinarily fast moving, it is recommended that this training not be given too consistently until after a dog has won his C.D. title in Obedience Trials. The writer has found that if a dog is properly trained to drop in the distance, he will obey the command to drop on recall without slowing up appreciatively. Nevertheless, a word of warning: Do not make a practice of dropping the dog every time he is called, nor in the same place. The dog will then anticipate the order and automatically slow up at a certain point. The trainer should also practice giving just the signal to drop, then just the command. The dog must obey either one or the other but not both together.

Whether it is because a dog feels he is being punished when he is made to lie down on the Recall I do not know, but so often the dog will appear unhappy when he does this exercise. To keep his spirit gay, the trainer should reward the dog in some way when he drops on command so that the dog will know he is doing the correct thing. A piece of meat or some other favorite food may be tossed to the dog while he is in the Down position, or a quiet "Good boy" may be said. The dog should soon overcome any dislike of this particular part of the exercise if he anticipates the more pleasant reward he is to receive.

The Special or Review Exercise

The six basic steps of training make up the Special Exercise. It is really a review of all the work up to a certain point and includes the Heeling, the Come Fore, the Sit-stay, the Lie Down, the Come, and the Finish. If the owner is successful in getting his dog to do the commands that make up the special exercise he will, at least, have a well mannered and obedient dog.

With the dog walking at heel position, the trainer gives the command, "Come fore." When the dog is sitting in front, he is told to, "Stay." As the trainer moves back from the dog, he holds his right hand in front of the dog's muzzle and flips his fingers upward under the dog's chin as a signal to remain where he is. The leash is played out without jerking the dog forward. When the trainer gets to the full length of the leash, he commands the dog to, "Lie down," then, "Come" and, finally, "Heel." The commands and signals are used together at first, but after a fair amount of training the dog is made to obey the voice and later just the signals. When a dog is put through this routine exercise for ten or fifteen minutes a day, it is surprising how quickly he will learn the basic training; and the owner will be more than pleased with the results.

The leash should be kept on until the dog is letter perfect and until he receives almost no assistance from the trainer. The training may then be attempted without the leash. However, even the fully trained dog should be put through the Review Exercise every day with the leash on so that he can be corrected the first time he makes a mistake. The novice trainer, because of his enthusiasm, is always anxious to get his dog working without the leash, and, as a result, the dog will get away with murder. The experienced trainer is not ashamed to take advantage of the leash and will use it over a much longer period of time.

Heel

Come fore

Sit-stay

164

Lie down

Come

Heel

165

Heel Free

Even though the trained dog should be kept on leash at all times in congested areas, almost every dog owner harbors the fond dream of someday being able to trust his dog to walk close to his side when the leash is off—secure in the knowledge that the dog will be under complete control.

As soon as the dog will heel with the leash slack, will make all turns without corrections, and will sit without being told, the trainer should throw the leash across his right shoulder while the dog is put through the training routine. This way the dog is given more freedom. Up to this time the dog, having watched the trainer's hands, knew the leash was there ready to correct him if he did not do the right thing. If the dog now thinks he is no longer under control and tries to scamper off, a quick jerk on the leash will bring him back unexpectedly.

The leash should not be made too slack because this will give the dog too much leeway. There should be just enough sag to allow for a good correction and yet enough tightness to keep the dog under control. The left arm is held close to the body, with the elbow bent so that the hand is carried close to the leash where it crosses in front of the trainer's body. When a correction is made, it is done with the left hand, which snaps the leash in a short, hard jerk; but the leash is let go of immediately. When the trainer halts and the dog must sit, the left hand snaps the leash up but again lets go of it when the dog starts to sit down.

At this point, the trainer should realize the importance of being able to control his dog entirely by voice. With the leash off, the one way the trainer can make the dog obey is by using his voice. That is why the value of timing the command with the correction was stressed earlier. They never come together, but with a split second pause between each. In other words, the dog is given a command and a second later he receives the correction. This is immediately followed by the praise and patting. By the time the dog reaches the stage where he will work without the leash, this procedure should be so strongly impressed on his mind that he will obey the command whether the leash is on or not. The trainer will never succeed with proper free heeling until the dog has learned to perform faultlessly while the leash is still attached to his collar. The novice trainer should not be too impatient about hanging the leash back up on the wall.

If the training has proved satisfactory, there should be only a few corrections to make when the leash is taken off. If the dog lags, the

Heeling with the leash over the shoulder prepares the dog for—Free heeling

finger is hooked into the ring of the dog's collar and he is brought up close. If the dog darts ahead, the trainer should stand still and signal the dog back into place as he demands, "Heel!" in as firm a voice as he can muster. In fact, every time the dog steps out of line he should be brought back by using both the signal and the command. The dog must be taught that the minute he is given his freedom he cannot forget all his training. If he fails, the owner should put the dog back on the leash and, by keeping it slack, correct each mistake more severely. In other words, the leash should be used as little as possible, but when necessary it should be used in a definite manner that will get results.

There are always a number of training problems when a dog starts working without a leash. One of the most discouraging of all is the dog that lags behind. If the trainer jerks hard to make the dog come close, the dog will hang back more than ever. As suggested in the lesson on Heeling, the owner of such a dog would do well to keep a few morsels of food or dog candy in his pocket to tempt the dog to stay close, at the same time reassuring him with a quiet "Good boy." If the corrections

167

come from others rather than from the owner himself they will prove more effective. When the outside corrections are of the right nature, the dog will think that the safest person to be with is his owner or his trainer, and he will want to be as close to him as possible.

The dog that will wait for the leash to be taken off, then scamper to the far end of the field, should be given his freedom in gradual stages. A small thin clothesline tied to the dog's collar and permitted to drag along the ground may be helpful. The trainer should put him through the heeling exercise; but if at any time the dog attempts to dash away, the trainer can quickly call out, "Heel!" and, at the same time, step on the line to snap the dog backward. As the training progresses the line is shortened until only a small piece is left attached to the collar and, finally, it is taken off completely.

The dog that is slow to sit or that sits at an angle should be slapped down quickly with the left hand the moment the trainer halts. The voice no longer commands the dog to sit, but the hand immediately follows through with the action. When the dog refuses to lie down, the trainer will get obedience if, after he gives the command or the signal, he will lean over and cuff the dog sharply on the nose. If the dog won't obey the trainer when he is close by, it is hopeless to think that he will obey when the trainer is far away. So the dog should be kept on leash until he obeys instantly. Another suggestion is for the trainer to start to lift his right foot after he gives the command. The dog will remember that he was originally jerked down by this foot and should respond at once.

An owner will sometime give the signal to lie down and then, if the dog doesn't do it at once, will give up. When the hand is once raised, the owner should continue to hold it there until the dog obeys. The command can be repeated over and over again, but the hand should not be taken away except to cuff the dog on the tip of the nose when all else fails to make him lie down. This holds true whenever signals are used throughout the training. When the hand is once placed in any signal position, it should be held there until the owner gets obedience.

And now for the headache—the dog that won't come when he is called and knows that the trainer has no leash to persuade him from the error of his ways. I can only repeat what I have said a number of times before. All unpleasantness must come from the outside while the joyous things must come as much as possible from the trainer. The dog should want to come of his own accord and not obey because he is afraid.

There are a number of things that can be tried to make the dog hurry when he is called, but the trainer will have to decide between those that will bring the best results and those that may lead to disaster. At various times I have used throwing chains, pellets shot from an air-rifle, or an object that would make a noise. In fact, anything that will cause a dog to hurry to his owner for protection will get the desired results. Care must be taken not to frighten the dog to extremes by using these methods, or he may become unsteady throughout. There is no definite rule to follow when training a dog to work off leash, for the trainer must invent new ways to deal with every situation. The idea is to get results without a serious or unfavorable reaction from the dog. If the dog will do better heeling when the trainer's left hand is carried behind his back (many dogs will), it should by all means be kept there. If the dog prefers the speed of an express train to that of a local, there is nothing wrong in that. The one obligation that every owner has to his dog, though, is to keep him happy and to work in a gay and cheerful way. The dog's every mood is registered in the way he carries his tail (if he has a tail). It is the "stop" and "go" sign to be closely observed by the trainer and is his signal either to proceed with caution or to go full steam ahead. The trainer will do well to heed this warning!

Part 3: ADVANCED OBEDIENCE TRAINING

C.D.X. (COMPANION DOG EXCELLENT)

Retrieving is the basis of all advanced training and the most difficult to teach. All dogs at some time or other carry objects about in their mouths and retrieve them when they are thrown in play; but in Advanced Obedience Training the dog is taught to do this on command from the trainer.

There are two kinds of retrieving. The first is when the dog retrieves of his own accord without having been actually trained. The other is when the dog is given systematic instruction to obey a given command. Personally, I like to combine the two. When the puppy is small, he is encouraged to retrieve in play; then, as he gets older, he is gradually transferred to the more serious work. I believe this will result in a happier response from the dog. Chasing a ball or a stick can be fun for every puppy, and when it is time to settle down to Obedience Training, the dumbbell can be substituted for the toys. Even in play, the retrieved objects must always be brought back to the trainer. The owner should insist on this, as it will pave the way for more accurate training later on. The dog who takes the attitude, "Catch me if you can!" is cute but not conducive to the getting of high scores in Obedience Trials.

At no time should the dog be permitted to play with his dumbbell or work-articles as he would with a toy. Such things should be kept entirely for training purposes and the dog given a tennis ball or a hard rubber bone for entertainment.

171

A dog is taught to hold a rolled magazine. (Note how the foot steps on the leash)

A dog is taught to hold a dumbbell

Holding the Dumbbell
(or Rolled Magazine or Newspaper)

The first lesson in retrieving is to teach the dog to hold an object in his mouth. With the dog on leash, sitting and partly facing the trainer, the leash is laid on the ground but stretched tight as the trainer steps on it with the right foot. This will leave both hands free to work with the dumbbell. The left hand is placed over the dog's muzzle and pressure is brought on each side of the jaw with the thumb and middle finger to make the dog open his mouth. The dog is commanded to, "Take it!" and the dumbbell or rolled magazine is slipped in quickly.

The trainer should pull the dog's lips back so he will not bite them. While the dog's head is held up with the left hand, the right hand should press the jaws together on the object so the dog cannot spit it out. The trainer should stroke the dog's head gently and repeat over and over, "Take it. Take it. That's it. Good boy. Take it!"

After a moment or two, the trainer commands, "Out!" and the dumbbell is removed quietly and the dog praised and patted.

The exercise is repeated but not for too long a time. Otherwise, the dog will get bored and learn to dislike the dumbbell.

If the dog doesn't let go of the dumbbell when he is commanded, "Out!" the trainer should never fight the dog by pulling against him. The dog's jaws should be pried apart as the dumbbell is gently removed and the dog told, "Out!" in a more demanding tone of voice. If the dog still doesn't let go and retains his bulldog grip, the end of the dumbbell should be held firmly in one hand while the free hand cuffs the dog hard on the side of his nose. The dog is again told, "Out!" Still another way is to blow lightly into the dog's nostrils. The owner should never pull the object from the dog's mouth but should force the dog to let go by himself.

A dog will sometimes put up a terrific fight when made to hold the dumbbell. Some will back away and try to claw it out while others will scream with rage. If the owner has the patience to quietly hold out until the dog gives up struggling, he will win a major battle.

When the trainer stands on the leash with his right foot, the dog cannot back away no matter how hard he tries. The trainer should automatically take this position every time he teaches a dog to hold something so that he will be prepared, no matter what happens, to keep the dog under control.

If the dog makes a half-hearted attempt to push the dumbbell out with his front feet, the trainer should press the dog's jaws together onto

174

No—Phooey! (The dog is corrected for dropping the dumbbell)

the dumbbell and hold them firmly with one hand. The other hand gives a sharp jerk on the leash every time the dog starts to lift his feet. This will throw the dog off balance. He is sharply commanded to, "Stop that!"

The type of dog that rears up on his back legs and fights like a maniac is handled quietly but very firmly. The left hand is hooked underneath the collar and takes a tight hold on the flap of loose skin under the dog's throat. Whenever the dog rears up or struggles to get away, the trainer should lift the dog's front feet completely off the floor and sharply demand that the dog behave. When the dog stops struggling he is lowered to the ground. The right hand in the meantime is cupped over the top of the muzzle and presses hard against the lower jaw to prevent the dog from dropping the dumbbell. The object is to keep the dumbbell in the dog's mouth in spite of everything. When the dog ceases to struggle, he is made to sit down quietly while the dumbbell is taken away and he is praised and patted. The dog will soon learn that he is not harmed in any way when he is made to hold something, and he should then accept it willingly. If the dog is very stubborn and spits out whatever the trainer

175

offers, he should be cuffed hard on the tip of his nose and told, "No! Phooey!" in a very displeased tone of voice.

When the dog allows the dumbbell to hang on his teeth without gripping it, the trainer should tap the ends to make it wobble. The dog's natural reaction should be to tighten his grip. If instead he permits it to fall out, the trainer should place it in his mouth again and cuff him harder than ever when he drops it a second time.

The dog should hold the dumbbell while the trainer steps back from the dog and while he circles completely around him—in other words, while the dog does the Sit-stay exercise. The dog must never drop the dumbbell of his own accord but must always wait until the trainer takes it away from him.

Take It

The command, "Take it!" means for the dog to take something in his mouth. In the previous lesson he learned to do this when the trainer placed the article there; but the dog must next learn to reach for the article himself.

With practice the dog may open his mouth of his own accord to take whatever the trainer offers; but the chances are he won't, so the dog must be given the usual training. The collar is swung around on the dog's neck so that the leash is on top. It is then pulled forward until it rests just behind his ears. It is held taut in this position with the left hand. The dog is made to sit as close to the left side as possible, so that he is supported against the left leg and cannot turn away. The trainer gives the command, "Take it!" and then starts tightening the collar gradually until the dog opens his mouth and gasps for air. The dumbbell is slipped in quickly and held there while the pressure on the collar is released immediately. The dog is told, "That's it. Good boy. Take it." Whenever the dog rears up on his back legs and tries to claw the dumbbell away with his front paws, the trainer should quickly jerk the dog off to the side to throw him off balance. When the dog is again sitting in the proper position, the training continues.

If the dog clamps his teeth together in defiance, the trainer should pry the dog's jaws apart by inserting either the middle or the ring finger of the right hand just in back of the dog's eyeteeth. Meanwhile, the left hand pulls steadily upward on the leash. When the dog opens his jaws, the dumbbell is eased in gently. Under no circumstances should the trainer push the dumbbell against the teeth to force the dog to open his mouth. This exercise is repeated until the dog will open his mouth

176

"TAKE IT"

e chain collar is
lled tight as the com-
mand is given

by himself when told to "Take it." If he responds immediately, no pressure is applied to the collar, but whenever he hesitates, the collar is tightened a little harder than the previous time.

Next, the collar is jerked with a snap. The trainer should hold the dumbbell close to the dog's mouth and give the command, "Take it!" Immediately afterward the collar is jerked hard and held tight momentarily. When the dog opens his mouth, the dumbbell is eased in gently. The pressure is then released and the dog praised and patted. If the dog will make no attempt to open his mouth when he hears the command, *the jerks on the collar must be more severe.* Each successive snap must be harder than the preceding one if the owner is to get the results he is looking for. Until the dog will respond instantly to the trainer's command, "Take it!" while he is sitting at heel position, and until he will reach for the dumbbell by himself, he will never learn to retrieve properly on command. This is especially true with a dog that is not interested in playing and is stubborn about learning to retrieve.

The training for the command, "Take it!" should be so intense that if the owner should, for instance, point to a chair and say, "Take it!" the dog would at least make an attempt to take hold of the chair, even if he does look disgusted and thinks the owner needs to have his head examined.

Carrying the Dumbbell and Other Articles

When the dog will take the dumbbell willingly by himself and will hold it without dropping it, he is taught to carry. With the dog sitting and facing the trainer, the leash is shortened in the left hand. At the same time the dog's head is supported from underneath. The right hand is placed on top of the dog's skull and the head is dipped quickly toward the ground to get the dog to stand on all four feet. Still holding the dog's head, the trainer walks slowly backward and repeats. "Come! Come! Come!" At intervals, the trainer halts and the dog is made to sit with the dumbbell still in his mouth. When the dog gets the idea of holding the dumbbell while he is walking, the trainer should gradually release his hold until the dog will carry the dumbbell without having his head supported. The command is, "Take it—carry!" The leash is kept slack and the trainer is generous with his praise as the dog walks at heel position. When the dog drops the dumbbell, the leash is jerked sharply and the trainer, in a very displeased tone of voice, says, "No—phooey!" "Phooey" is a good word to use when correcting a dog, for it has a very displeasing and relatively unique tone. The dog can learn to associ-

arrying while heeling on leash   **Carrying while free heeling**

ate the word "Phooey" with everything he does wrong if the trainer will take the time to train him in this manner.

If the dog persists in dropping the dumbbell, even after a lot of training, the correction is a harder cuff on the nose. Each slap should become more severe than the preceding one, until the dog would rather keep the dumbbell in his mouth than to be punished for dropping it.

The dog should carry the dumbbell while he walks along at heel position, and he should continue to hold it when he sits either at the side of his trainer or in front of him. Later, the dog should hold the dumbbell in the Sit-stay position, after which the trainer should call the dog from across the training yard. The dumbbell must not be dropped or spit out, but must be held and the dog made to sit in front of the trainer to wait to have it taken from him.

Since carrying and retrieving is one of the most difficult exercises, the trainer should not hold the dog to a strict obedience routine during this part of the teaching. In other words, the dumbbell work should be stressed even if some other part of the dog's training must be temporarily sacrificed. When the dog is holding the dumbbell, the trainer should play

179

with him and pat him and make him think he is doing something wonderful by keeping the dumbbell in his mouth. When the dog is given a great deal of praise and made a fuss over, he will not think too badly of this chore and will take pride in his accomplishment.

To train the dog so he will know that the command, "Take it" means to take whatever is given to him, the trainer should use an assortment of articles while training the dog to carry and not just the dumbbell. Otherwise, the dog will learn to dislike the dumbbell and will refuse to take it willingly when asked later to retrieve.

It is best to start with an old glove or something the dog has a particular liking for. Articles of different material should also be used, such as those made of wood, leather, and last but not least, metal and glass. When a dog is forced to carry an assortment of objects he will not associate any one thing with the unpleasant part of his training. At the same time, it will help to prepare the dog for the more advanced work of Seeking a Lost Article, Scent Discrimination, and Tracking. The trainer should use the words "Take it" whenever he gives anything to the dog, even things he likes. This is so the dog will have a happy association with the command and not feel that it means doing something disagreeable.

With practice, the dog should heel and sit, should stay on command, and should come when called—all with the various objects in his mouth. When he holds them, he should be given credit for doing so; but when he drops them, he should be reprimanded sharply.

The dog must be prevented from mouthing his dumbbell or any other article he may be carrying. When the dog chews on whatever he is holding, he should be given a sharp rap on the nose and told to, "Stop it!" If he continues, he should be rapped again, harder than ever. Persistent mouthers can be cured by training them with a dumbbell or a tightly rolled burlap bag that has sharp nails projecting throughout to teach the dog to hold the object lightly and not to clamp down too hard with his teeth.

When the household pet knows how to take an article on command and how to carry he can be made very useful. I have used such a dog to run errands, to carry messages, and to act as delivery boy.

An excellent demonstration of how well a dog will respond to a command, if the training has been thorough, was given recently in Rockefeller Plaza during National Dog Week. Without rehearsal, the Standard Poodle Ch. Carillon Jester, U.D.T., Int. C.D., was handed a leash on the other end of which was a Toy Poodle, Casey. Jester was told to "take it" to the opposite end of the plaza. Casey had other ideas and proceeded to brace all four feet. I am still wondering what Casey's posterior felt like after being dragged from Forty-ninth to Fiftieth Street!

In this same exhibition, numerous signs from four to eight feet long were carried by the different dogs. There is no limit to what can be done in the entertainment field when the basic lessons have been well established.

Taking the Dumbbell and Other Articles from the Ground

Until now the dog has been taught how to take, hold, and carry the dumbbell as well as other articles, but he must next be trained to pick them up from the ground and to retrieve them when thrown. If the trainer will keep in mind that the Retrieve is the continuation of "Take it," he should get excellent results. Unfortunately, an owner will sometimes think the dog should pick things off the ground after one or two lessons. Some dogs will, but the majority require anywhere from one to two months' training before they can be relied upon to obey under all conditions. So much depends upon the ability of the owner as well as upon the type of dog he is training that no time limit can be set for teaching a dog this work. In the training classes which I conducted in New York City from 1944 to 1960, perhaps half of the owners succeeded in getting their dogs to retrieve during the nine-week period of the Advanced Course. Others find it necessary to repeat the Advanced Course a second and even a third time before they receive their diploma.

If a dog will open his mouth by himself when he hears the command, "Take it," a major step in retrieving has been learned. Next, with the dog sitting at heel position, the leash is held short in the left hand. The dumbbell is held about four inches from the dog's nose and he is given the command, "Take it." If the dog fails to reach for it, the leash is jerked hard in the direction of the dumbbell. Sometimes it is better to have the leash come over the top of the dog's head and between his ears to bring pressure on his throat when the leash is pulled tight. Other dogs will respond just as well when the leash is held at the side and is pulled forward with a snap. The main thing is that the dog must open his mouth the moment the command is given. If he does not, the leash must be snapped harder. *No dog will pick up the dumbbell from the ground on command until he first "picks" the dumbbell out of the air*—that is, until he reaches forward by himself to take the dumbbell.

The trainer should next walk with the dog at heel position and with the leash carried short in the left hand. *While walking*, he holds the dumbbell close to the ground just ahead of the dog so he will have to stretch

PICKING DUMBBELL FROM GROUND

A jerk toward the dumbbell is given

The dumbbell is held lower

Finally it is placed on the ground

out his neck to pick it out of the trainer's hand. If the dog shows no interest, the leash is jerked with a snap every few steps until the dog will open his mouth. The trainer, *while still moving*, should reach down and take the dumbbell from the dog with the command, "Out!"

For practice, the dog is made to face the trainer in a Sit-stay position. The trainer should walk backward and tell the dog to come and, *while walking*, hold the dumbbell in front of the dog close to the ground until he takes it. Every time the dog reaches for the dumbbell the trainer should let go of it, but he should be in no hurry to take his hand away. The hand is kept there momentarily to give the dog the feeling of having picked the dumbbell out of the trainer's hand.

As time passes—and it will pass—the trainer next circles slowly to the right as he drags one end of the dumbbell along the ground ahead of the dog. When the dog reaches for the dumbbell, the trainer should again let go of it. In the meantime, both the trainer and the dog should still be moving forward. When a dog is learning to retrieve, he seems to do better work when he is kept in motion than when permitted to stop all activity for any length of time.

This preliminary training will get the dog into the habit of taking the dumbbell every time he hears the command and, all of a sudden, one day he will surprise both himself and his owner by picking it up off the ground where it was dropped "accidentally." Another major battle in retrieving will then have been won!

When the dog is extremely stubborn about reaching to pick up the dumbbell, a series of snaps on the leash will sometimes work where just one will fail. With the dumbbell dragged along the ground ahead of the dog, the leash is given a number of short jerks, each one harder than the last, while the trainer commands, "Take it. Take it. Take it!" Point to the dumbbell until the dog picks it up.

If a dog shows the least inclination to play, the trainer at this point would do well to take advantage of it. The dog should be kept on leash but given plenty of freedom. He can be teased into having a game with the dumbbell in which the owner makes believe he is going to throw it but doesn't. Or, the dumbbell can be hidden behind the trainer's back or scuffed back and forth between the dog's front paws. The objective is to get the dog interested enough to make a grab for the dumbbell. When he does, the trainer should let the dog have it immediately but at the same time use the command, "Take it. Good boy" so the dog will associate the command with the action.

At times the trainer may have to assist by actually slipping the dumbbell into the dog's mouth, and the dog should be given as much praise as though he had made all the effort. If the trainer feels he is making no progress, he should start over from the beginning and review the first lessons of the Advanced Training.

When the trainer has the dog taking the dumbbell from the ground on command, he should get him interested in running after it. While teaching the dumbbell work, the trainer should not insist upon perfect obedience, such as the dog sitting before he retrieves or going to heel position after he picks up the dumbbell. The important thing is to get the dog to do it by himself, and to do it happily. The steadying down will come later.

About this time the trainer may become discouraged with his efforts because he has learned a great deal more than the dog. The basic lessons have not been difficult because the exercises have been simple, and the dog did not object to doing them. His attitude may well have been one of, "Oh well, if you want me to sit here and stay, I will. It doesn't make much difference to me one way or the other." But when the more difficult work begins and the dog is forced to do something he does not like nor want to do, he may take on a new attitude. An owner cannot be considered a successful trainer unless he is able to make a dog obey even though "the poor little dear doesn't like it." It is surprising how many owners will take this attitude toward their dogs, and expect to get results.

In the exercise where the dog is taught to hold and carry the dumbbell, the dog at first will express displeasure at holding something that he considers distasteful. It is up to the trainer to see that when the dumbbell is put into the dog's mouth it stays there, even if it has to be held. The dog will learn that it isn't so bad; and I have yet to see one dog that sooner or later has not learned to love his dumbbell and take great pride in carrying it about and showing off with it.

The following pages will cover such exercises as Retrieving, Jumping, Seeking a Lost Article, Scent Discrimination, Speaking on Command, Directional Jumping, and Tracking. All of this work is difficult, and the owner will have to be firm if he wishes to complete the training. If he becomes discouraged and takes a defeatist attitude of "I can't do it" after one or two attempts, he will get no place. One can do it if one has the patience and the perseverance. Granted, it is more difficult to train a dog for Obedience Trial competition than it is for hunting and field work where the dog's natural instincts are employed. Even though certain instinctive qualities are made use of, Obedience Training for the most part is foreign to the way a dog would normally behave. But if he learns his ABC's before the more advanced work is approached, the training will be simplified.

184

When an owner has once given a command, the dog should be made to mind even if it means forcing him against his will. If the trainer will only hold out until the dog gives in, every time the exercise is repeated it will become that much easier. The trainer who feels sorry for the dog that is made to do something he does not want to do is no longer master —the dog is.

About now, the trainer will have to watch that he himself does not become bored with everyday training. It is exciting to make headway in the simple exercises, such as the Sit, the Down, and the Stand; but when the trainer cannot make the dog learn the more difficult exercises, he is certain to become discouraged and will want to give up. This, of course, is always fatal. The trainer should also take stock of things in general, both from his own as well as the dog's point of view. It is so easy for the trainer, without realizing it, to confuse his dog to the point where he will be affected permanently. This was brought home to me years ago when I was learning to train dogs for attack work.

I had been handling a particular dog over a period of weeks—teaching him to protect me and to guard my personal property. One day, one of the other trainers who had been doing the "teasing" (which consisted of aggravating the dog to the point where he would attack) wanted to demonstrate some particular part of the training. He said he would handle the dog and asked me to do the teasing and to be the victim. What the trainer failed to do was to have me go away and reappear in other clothes and with my face covered so the dog would not recognize me. I was new at the work and did not realize the importance of such small details.

The trainer gave the dog the command to advance. It is hard to describe the utter confusion that appeared in the dog's eyes. For weeks he had been taught to guard and protect me, and now, for no apparent reason, he was told to attack. The dog refused in a most definite manner.

For the trainers the lesson ended right there, but the dog was not so quick to forget. The following day when this same trainer tried to turn the dog out for exercise, the dog would not permit him near the place where he was kenneled and growled and tried to bite at him through the wire mesh. Finally, I had to be called to take charge of the dog. It was a long time before the dog fully trusted that particular trainer again. This is to show that when things do not progress as they should, the trainer may easily be at fault.

"Sit-stay"

"Take it"

"Come"

"Sit"

"Out"

"Heel"

Retrieving

When a dog is made to retrieve, he must go out by himself to pick up an article and return with it to his owner. With the dog on leash, the trainer starts by throwing the dumbbell out six or eight feet in front of the dog and telling him to, "Take it!" The trainer should keep the leash slack and then start toward the dumbbell with the dog. When the dumbbell is picked up, the trainer should run backward and make the dog bring it to him, then sit in front while the dumbbell is taken away. After this the dog goes to heel position.

The dumbbell should be thrown at a number of different angles until the dog will retrieve whenever he hears the command. Although the trainer will want to make the dog steady so he will not anticipate the Retrieve by darting out the moment the dumbbell is thrown, it is better to have the dog overly keen at first than to discourage his enthusiasm. A dog that will retrieve in a happy spirit is a joyous sight to behold, and he can be calmed down later by being made to wait longer.

When the leash is off, the dog should be controlled almost entirely by voice commands. This will come naturally if the trainer used the voice for all parts of the exercises while the dog was learning. For instance, the first command is, "Stay!" and the dumbbell is thrown. Then, "Take it!" after which the dog goes for the dumbbell. Just as the dog picks it up, the trainer quickly demands, "Come," then, "Sit!" to make the dog sit in front, then "Out!" and finally, "Heel!" The trainer should get into the habit of using these commands because they can always be dropped when the dog is so good he no longer needs them. In the meantime the dog is kept under control.

The dog that is slow to start after the dumbbell may be tempted to move faster by having a game. The trainer throws the dumbbell, then runs after it himself. He picks it up and throws it again. The dog may soon realize he must start after it at once if he is to get there ahead of the trainer. If the dog has been retrieving satisfactorily and then all of a sudden gets stubborn about picking things up, the leash should be kept on. If the dog goes out for the dumbbell and just stands there, or if he starts to return without it, a second command of, "Take it!" is repeated and the leash is given a hard jerk. This will act to remind the dog of the first lesson in which he was taught to, "Take it" on command. If the dog will do a perfect retrieve when the leash is on, he will be more dependable when the leash has been taken off.

Occasionally in my training classes there have been dogs that would retrieve nicely without the leash and then balk completely when the

188

A dog should retrieve quickly and gaily

leash was put on. The owners would invariably try to sneak the leash off without my noticing so that the dogs would make a good showing in class, but they were fooling no one but themselves. Such dogs had not been trained to retrieve. They did it only because they wanted to and not because they had been commanded. Until a dog has learned to retrieve on leash, he will never be dependable.

There are many problems on the Retrieve that will also apply when the retrieving is done over a hurdle. There is the dog that starts for the dumbbell too soon, and there is the dog that won't start at all. There is the one that goes through the act of retrieving, but in slow motion. And there is always the dog that throws the dumbbell at the trainer's feet as though to say, "You pick it up!"

The dog that anticipates and starts before he is told must be put on leash and made to sit at the trainer's side while the dumbbell is thrown not once, but several times without the dog being permitted to go after it. If he attempts to do so, the leash should be jerked so hard it will throw him back on his haunches. If the trainer wishes, he may slap the dog's nose with his left hand to make him draw back.

The dog that won't go after the dumbbell when he hears the command should be jerked in the opposite direction with enough force to put him on his feet at once. At the same time, the trainer can swing back with his right foot to boot the dog in the rear end to urge him forward. The main thing is to give the command first and then the correction.

The owner of the dog that moves at a snail's pace has my sympathy. There is little he can do except to use all the devices that have been suggested thus far to speed a dog to act more quickly. Very likely the most effective way of getting a fast return is, when the dog starts back with the dumbbell, to have a second person throw a chain or make a loud noise. If it is on the going out that the dog is slow, the persuasive methods must come from behind the trainer.

The dog that tosses the dumbbell at the trainer's feet as much as to say, "Throw it again!" can be prevented from spitting it out by the use of voice commands. Just before he reaches the trainer, he should be given the command to, "Sit," followed by a quick command, "Stay!" The word "Stay" should cause the dog to stop whatever he is doing so that the dumbbell will be kept in his mouth. By repeating this over and over and letting the dog get a little closer to the trainer each time, the dog can be prevented from dropping the dumbbell and will deliver it in the proper way.

This training applies when the dog drops an article even though he is already sitting in front of the trainer. It will not be necessary to give

190

the command to sit, but the command to stay will help to make the dog keep a firm hold on whatever he has.

It is recommended that the trainer keep the dog on leash and do a series of "Comes" while the dog holds the dumbbell and is made to sit in front of the trainer. If at any time the dog drops it, the trainer should not hesitate to cuff him sharply on the nose, making each correction more severe than the last.

Finally, there is the dog that does not wait for the command to go to heel position but jumps around the moment the trainer takes the dumbbell away. To get the dog over this habit, the trainer should quietly give the command, "Stay!" as he takes the dumbbell out of the dog's mouth. The dog should be made to wait an extra long time before he is allowed to finish the exercise.

Jumping

A dog should be taught to jump early in his training. The fact that most dogs enjoy it can be used to advantage to keep up their interest in the work. Knowing how to jump has its practical uses as well, such as when a dog is taken for a ride and must jump in and out of a car, or when he is put on the table for grooming, or taken to the veterinarian for treatment. Some people object and say that when a dog is taught to jump, he can no longer be confined. This may be justified to a certain extent, but jumping as it is taught here is not the scaling of a high barrier but the clearing of a low hurdle. Only occasionally have I found that it interfered with keeping a dog in an enclosed area.

The trainer can start by using a jumping stick. The stick is carried in the right hand and the leash held short in the left. The leash should be wadded up so it will not dangle in the dog's face or drag on the ground in front of him. The trainer should walk with the dog at heel position, then quietly place the stick low (a foot or so from the ground) and squarely across the front of both himself and the dog. At first, the end of the stick is placed against some permanent object, such as a post or the side of a building. This will steady it and prevent it from moving if the dog knocks against it. The trainer should step over the stick with his *left* foot, at the same time pulling the dog over with the left hand. The command is, "Jester, hup!" The leash should be slack when the dog lands and the trainer should immediately turn and start walking in the opposite direction. This will make the dog check himself after he jumps, and he will learn to come back to heel position by himself.

There are few dogs that will not balk the first time they see a jumping

The trainer steps over with the left foot

The dog jumps with less assistance

Carrying dumbbell and off leash

*The same method is followed
as in the stick jumping*

stick; but if the trainer will slowly drag the dog over once or twice, he will soon understand that he will not be harmed in any way and will quickly learn to clear it properly.

The dog is next made to jump without the trainer stepping over the stick with him. The stick is held level and the trainer throws his left shoulder forward, at the same time giving the leash a sharp tug. The dog is commanded to "Hup!" Again the trainer turns and walks in the opposite direction to check the dog from going ahead. It is surprising the number of owners who expect their dogs to jump over a stick while at the same time they will hold the dogs back with the leash. Every time a dog is made to jump, the trainer should pause for a moment and look at the position of his left arm. If it is held in back of his body it is wrong. It should be ahead of the body and pointing in the direction the dog is to go.

As the dog gets accustomed to jumping, the stick should be raised higher and be approached with a fair amount of speed. The stick should also be held motionless while the dog is jumping. I have watched owner after owner command a dog to jump and at the same time keep moving the stick ahead of the dog so that it was impossible for him to catch up in order to obey the command.

The dog should be trained to jump in either direction—in other words, over the stick and back again without the trainer turning his body. If after the dog goes over the stick he does not jump back but sneaks around in back of the trainer, the trainer should swing the stick around to the left side and into the dog's face. He will think better of making the same mistake twice. The dog should also be taught to carry his dumbbell over the jumping stick. At the first attempt he will probably drop it, but when it is replaced in his mouth and the leash kept slack, he should do this exercise without any trouble.

By now the dog may be enjoying his jumping and start to get out of control. In this case he must be steadied down, both before and after the jump. The dog is made to sit and told to stay. The trainer takes one or two steps ahead of the dog and holds the stick in position. He gives the command to jump. The minute the dog lands on the other side, the trainer tells him to sit or lie down. If the dog doesn't obey, the leash is there to make the correction.

When the dog will immediately jump over the stick upon command, and will return to heel position on a slack leash, the exercise can be tried without the leash. The dog, when he knows he is free, may jump as ordered but keep right on going. If the trainer will use his voice to control the dog and command him to either sit, to lie down, or to come, the basic training should have such a strong hold the dog will obey instantly. But if he doesn't, back on the leash he goes to be given more practice.

When working with a lazy dog, the trainer should tap the front legs with the jumping stick to make him pick his feet up more quickly. Then, by lifting the stick, the trainer can force the dog to raise his back feet higher in order to clear the stick completely. This should always be done on leash at first, otherwise the dog will try to duck away.

I have noticed in the classes that Boxers, for instance, are always amused with the jumping stick and think it is something to take in their

Most dogs enjoy jumping, and it's good exercise

mouths in play. There are other breeds that feel the same way. The trainer should never rush this type of dog. In fact, he should do the opposite. Every movement is slower than usual and when the stick is put in place it is done in a quiet manner. When the dog attempts to grab it with his mouth, the trainer should never jerk the stick away. He should hold it perfectly still and *demand* that the dog behave. *Without* changing the position of the stick, the trainer should hold the leash taut until the dog obeys the command to, "Hup!"

After the dog has mastered the jumping stick, he is next made to jump over a slow solid jump. This exercise is done on leash so that the trainer can correct all mistakes. The trainer steps over with the dog a few times,

195

just as he did with the stick. If the dog refuses to jump, the trainer again holds the leash tight and steadily pulls, pulls, pulls the dog over until he finally makes it. The dog later jumps over and back while the trainer remains on the same side. The trainer should always approach the hurdle with the leash held the proper way. For everything except the jumping stick, the leash is held in the *right* hand, just as when the dog is taught to heel. It is then grasped with the left hand a short distance above the dog's collar. When the trainer walks toward the hurdle, the left hand takes up all slack and "lifts" the dog up and over the jump. Should the dog refuse to go over, or should he attempt to go around to the side, the leash is held taut and the dog is dragged over the top instead. When he lands on the opposite side, the left arm should drop quickly toward the ground so the dog will be given plenty of leash while landing and not be jerked too severely.

In practice, the dog is made to jump over the hurdle and back and to sit in front of the trainer. Should the dog hesitate to jump on the return, a jerk on the leash will usually start him over. The trainer commands, "Jester, hup! Come on. That's it. Good boy!" The trainer pats the top board of the hurdle to encourage the dog to jump, but moves backward quickly to give the dog plenty of room in which to land.

The jumping exercise is continued, but now a bar hurdle is used instead of a solid one. When a dog has been properly trained to jump over a stick, he seldom will refuse the bar; but if he does not know stick jumping, nine times out of ten the dog will try and duck underneath.

When he does this, the trainer should hold the bar firmly in place, either with his hand or his foot, and pull the leash tight as he did when he practiced the Figure Eight around a post. When the dog corrects himself, the trainer should coax him to jump by patting the top of the bar and using a coaxing tone of voice. It is surprising how much the tone of voice will influence a dog in his work.

If in spite of everything the dog still refuses to jump, the hurdles should be lowered until he gains confidence. Then they should be gradually raised. All hurdles should measure from one and one-half to two times the height of the dog at the shoulder. If a dog is trained to jump higher than required in Obedience Trials, the chances are there will not be so many failures at dog shows.

From now on the trainer combines the Carry with the Jump. The dog is encouraged to carry his dumbbell over the hurdles to give him a preview of the more advanced work that is to follow. This preliminary training will make the other lessons easier.

Almost every mistake that is made in the first jumping lessons can be

196

FIRST LESSON IN JUMPING
THE SOLID HURDLE

At first the leash is always used to control the dog

Note slack leash

"Come—Good boy"

traced to the owner's holding the leash the wrong way. This applies to the jumping stick, the solid hurdle, the bar hurdle, and even the broad jump that has not yet been discussed. The trainer often acts as though his left arm were in a cast. He immobilizes it to such an extent that it is of no help in guiding the dog; and yet the left arm is the one thing the dog will watch more closely than anything else. He depends on it for all his signals. Whether the leash is on or off, the trainer should be very careful about the way he uses the left arm when the dog is learning his jumping lessons.

Retrieving over Hurdles

Only when a dog will retrieve perfectly on the flat will he retrieve over an obstacle on command. That is not to say a dog won't retrieve over the jump in play; but he won't do it to the point where he will be dependable under all conditions.

For the first lesson, a low solid jump should be used. The dog should be kept on leash while the trainer tosses the dumbbell on the ground two or three times in an ordinary retrieve to get the dog interested in picking it up. When he is interested, the trainer should approach the hurdle and throw the dumbbell over the jump just ahead of the dog. The dog is commanded, "Hup!" and the trainer passes to the side of the jump while the dog goes over it. The trainer then commands the dog to, "Take it. Carry!" When the dog picks it up, both the trainer and the dog should keep on walking. Then they do an about-turn and repeat the exercise by approaching the hurdle from the opposite direction.

When the dog will leap over the obstacle and pick up the dumbbell by himself, he next must return over the obstacle as well. He must be trained to wait for all commands in order to steady him down so he will not anticipate the exercise. For instance, the dog must sit at heel position while the trainer stands about four or five feet in front of the hurdle. The dog is given the command, "Stay" while the trainer throws the dumbbell. He is then told to, "Jester, hup. Take it (or Carry)!" The trainer moves with the dog toward the hurdle but remains on the same side while the dog goes over alone. The leash is held in both hands but is kept slack so as not to interfere with the jumping. When the dog lands on the other side, the trainer should point to the dumbbell and give the leash a sharp snap as he repeats the command, "Take it!" When the dog picks it up, the trainer should give the command, "Come" and step back from the hurdle to give the dog room in which to land. The dog is then told to "Sit!" in front; then commanded "Out!" to make him let go of the dumbbell; and, finally, "Heel" to make him finish the exercise.

During all this time the leash, though slack, is there ready for a correction. When it is necessary to use the leash, it must be jerked as though by accident. The dog must not blame the trainer for the correction. When the dog becomes dependable the exercise can be tried without the leash. The trainer should stand close to the jump so the dog will not be tempted to run around the end. All motions and commands should be given in the usual way, and the trainer should control the dog as much as possible by using his voice for the different parts of the exercise. The extra commands can be dropped as soon as the dog will perform reasonably well.

If the dog returns around the jump instead of over the top, the trainer should wad the leash up in his hand and throw it on the ground just in front of the dog as he comes around the end. This should be done with a great deal of force and the dog commanded, "No. Phooey!" He is taken back and made to come over properly by a jerk on the collar or by patting the top of the hurdle.

The height of the jump is gradually increased until it is equal to twice the height of the dog at the shoulder. The trainer should remember the suggestions that were given when teaching a dog to jump—namely, that when the dog balks, the obstacle should be lowered until he clears the hurdle with ease, then gradually built up again. The trainer should stand close to the jump to discourage the dog from running around the end. If on the return trip the dog is tempted to go around, the trainer should be ready to throw the leash in front of him. And last but not least, if the dog goes haywire, he should be put back on the leash for more thorough training.

The dog should clear all jumps and not scale them or balance on top. To break the habit of touching the top board, several sharp branches may be tied or nailed along its edge, or a cloth can be stretched across so that there will be no permanent footing to support the dog. The hurdle can be constructed in such a way that the top board will spin around when the dog steps on it. In fact, anything that will give with the dog's weight should help to overcome the habit of balancing on top of or climbing over the hurdle.

With practice, the trainer should be able to make fewer commands and motions, until the dog will obey instantly either the signal to retrieve or the command, "Take it!" The trainer will do well to practice throwing the dumbbell off to the side so the dog will have to make an effort to go out of his way to return over the hurdle. If he gets in the

199

RETRIEVE OVER THE HURDLE

"Stay"

"Hup"

"Take it"

"Come"

"Sit"

"Heel—Good boy"

habit of jumping only when the dumbbell falls in a direct line, there will come a time when the unavoidable happens at a dog show and he will not have been trained to take care of the situation.

The dog that overshoots his mark on the return and goes past the trainer, instead of sitting directly in front, can be controlled if the trainer will call out the word, "Sit!" while the dog is still in mid-air and just before he lands. This basic command should remind the dog of his earlier lessons and he will eventually learn to correct himself.

If the dog should start to retrieve before he is commanded, the trainer should use the leash to correct him in a very definite manner. If the leash is off, he should hook the index finger through the ring in the collar and jerk the dog off balance when he starts before he should. Another way is for the trainer to hold his left hand around in front of his body. The dog is watched closely when the dumbbell is thrown, and if he starts before he is told, the left hand is swung around and the dog is slapped hard on the muzzle. At the same time, the trainer should repeat the command, "Stay!"

One of the most aggravating things that a dog will do at a show is to go over the hurdle and pick up the dumbbell and then just stand and wait for the trainer to call him back. At such a time, nothing can be done except to say a little prayer; but during the practice sessions the trainer can do plenty. We come back to the box or rolled magazine. The object is tossed in back of the dog by an assistant who stands on the opposite side of the jump from the trainer. The object is not thrown until after the dog has picked up the dumbbell and after he has turned away from the assistant. No extra commands are given, only the correction. When the dog jumps back, which he should do immediately, he is given a word of praise.

Broad Jump

The purpose of the Broad Jump is to teach a dog to clear a wide area such as a ditch or a small body of water. The jump consists of four separate hurdles which, when set in place, will give an over-all length up to six feet. The four hurdles are built so they will fit one within the other for convenient handling. When teaching the Broad Jump, the trainer should keep in mind that while the High Jump requires a thrust upward, the Broad Jump requires a thrust forward. Thus a longer take-off is necessary to give the dog the momentum to carry him forward over the longer distance. A dog can stand close to the High Jump and still clear it

Use two hurdles at first and step over with the dog

The trainer steps to the side as the dog jumps

with ease, since he springs upward, but he will need a good running start to do the Broad Jump properly.

The over-all length of the Broad Jump varies with the different breeds. In Obedience Trials the dog is required to do a length that is equal to twice the height of the High Jump for that particular dog. If the dog is trained to jump farther than necessary, the Broad Jump at dog shows will be easier to manage.

The trainer should at the start use two of the four hurdles. With the dog on leash and walking at heel position, the trainer and the dog jump over together. The leash is held in the right hand, but the left hand, at the same time, holds the leash out from the body to keep the dog under control. The command is the same as for all jumping—namely, "Jester, hup!" When the trainer and the dog land on the opposite side, they continue to move forward with more heeling, do an about-turn, and repeat the jump going in the opposite direction. When the dog is jumping freely, the trainer side-steps the jump while the dog goes over alone. But the trainer immediately snaps out the command, "Heel!" when the dog lands on the other side. The purpose of this is to teach the dog to jump in a straight line and not to cut the corners.

If the dog *walks* on the hurdles they should be tilted on their sides. With nothing to step on, he will be more inclined to leap over and clear them properly.

Extra hurdles are added until the distance measures the required over-all length. The dog is still kept on leash. Before he jumps, the dog is always given the command to "Hup," after which the leash is snapped hard. When he lands on the opposite side, the trainer should command, "Come!" and snap the leash a second time. Both the trainer and the dog then circle around, and the dog is made to go over the hurdle again. This is done over and over without stopping. The success of the exercise will depend upon the timing of the voice with the action.

When the dog will take the hurdle without assistance and return to the trainer when he hears the command, "Come!" he should then be made to wait between the different parts of the exercise; this will make him steady.

The dog is taken to a position from six to eight feet in front of the jump and told, "Stay!" The trainer walks to the right side of the hurdle and stands in the area between the first and the last hurdle and about two feet to the side. The trainer should wait to see if the dog is going to break and then command, "Jester, hup!" When the dog lands on the other side, he is told, "Come!", is made to sit in front of the trainer, and later finishes the exercise by going to heel position.

Both hands are used on the leash. The right hand holds the loop, while the left arm is stretched out as far as the trainer can reach to support the weight of the leash. When the dog is commanded to jump, the right hand pulls the leash through the palm of the left hand to take up all the slack. The left hand controls the direction in which the dog jumps and helps to lift the dog up and over. The left hand is also used to snap the leash, both at the beginning and at the completion of the jump. *The leash must be entirely slack when the dog lands on the opposite side.* Otherwise, the dog will be thrown off his feet and will think ill of doing the Broad Jump again.

The exercise is next tried without the leash. The trainer should stand with his back three-quarters toward the dog and he should give the signal with his *left* hand. If the dog's performance was perfect when the leash was on, it should be nearly perfect when it is taken off. Conversely, all mistakes that are made while the leash is fastened to the dog's collar will be repeated when the leash is taken off. So the trainer will do well to strive for perfection during the training period.

The problems that come up when one is teaching a dog to do the Broad Jump are such things as not waiting for the command, refusing to jump, running around instead of jumping over, walking on top, making a wide return, et cetera. The owner who will systematically train his dog from the very beginning to do all jumps as perfectly as possible will run into less trouble than the owner who gambles on his dog's performance—even though all preceding tries were unsuccessful.

The dog that won't wait for the command to take the Broad Jump should be left in the sitting position in front of the hurdle while the trainer takes his place at the side. Instead of letting the dog jump, the trainer should return to him. This is done several times and, since the dog will not know when to expect the command, he will no longer anticipate.

The dog that refuses to jump or goes around instead of over will have to be jerked more severely. The one that circles wide on the return should be given the command, "Come!" just as he lands, and then the leash should be snapped hard but given slack immediately. If the dog does not sit close in front of the trainer, he should not be jerked in but coaxed—just as when he was trained to do the Recall.

A way to correct the dog that has been in the habit of cutting corners is for the trainer to stand ahead of the jump with his back to the dog. The dog is given the command to jump and when he lands on the opposite side, close to the trainer, the trainer lifts his left knee quickly and knocks the dog hard to the left. The trainer then works his way gradually back to the side of the jump, but he should always be

205

"Stay"
(Waiting for
command)

"Hup"
(Note how dog is
pulled forward)

Note slack leash
on landing

OUR HURDLES

"Come"
"Sit"

"Heel"

The broad jump off leash (Note left hand signal)

ready to step toward the jump to make a correction if the dog gets careless.

The lazy jumper should be trained to leap higher in the air by either one of two methods. An assistant stands in back of the trainer and holds a long bar across the width of the jump just above the first hurdle. If this doesn't teach the dog to lift himself over, the trainer may build a special bar attachment that will cause the first hurdle to tip on its side when the dog knocks against it. The resulting discomfort should teach the dog to clear it as he should.

To achieve perfection in Jumping, the trainer should set up all three hurdles in a row. The solid, the bar, and the broad jump are placed ten to twelve feet apart. With the dog on leash, he is made to take all three jumps, one after another, but must heel both before and after jumping each hurdle. The dog is not rushed over the hurdles but is made to jump them quietly and to return to heel position immediately after each jump. Later, the trainer may halt halfway between the hurdles and make the dog sit at heel. This practice will teach him to jump in a straight line. It will also steady the dog down in his performance. The dog should be made to carry his dumbbell as well as other articles over the three hurdles, and should be made to perform either with the leash on or off. When the dog is working without the leash, the trainer should give the signal with the left arm and control the dog by voice commands to prevent too many mistakes in the beginning.

The trainer should not make a practice of using just one set of hurdles for jumping and retrieving but should practice with jumps of all shapes, sizes, and colors. And the dog should be made to jump and retrieve in a number of places and under all conditions. This will avoid the disappointment that comes when a dog fails to work in an Obedience Trial because the conditions were not quite the same as those under which he was trained. Just as the command, "Take it!" means for the dog to take something in his mouth, the command, "Hup!" or "Over!" should mean for the dog to get all four feet off the ground and into the air at once.

A few years ago during an exhibition at Rockefeller Plaza in celebration of Be-Kind-to-Animals Week, I was directing a group of children in Obedience Training. The youngsters, in some cases, were handling trained dogs that were owned by other people. During the exercise in which the dogs were required to take the three hurdles, a lad of thirteen started toward the first hurdle with his dog. Just about that time the dog caught sight of his owner at the side of the Plaza and, therefore, was not paying attention to the boy at his side. The boy gave the command "Hup!" but he had misjudged the timing and the command was given far too early. In the meantime the dog, whose attention was not on his work, heard the command "Hup!" and must have thought to himself, "Here, what am I doing? I should be jumping!" With that he took off without looking and came down squarely on top of the bar.

This little story proves two things. First, it is important that the trainer time the command with the action. When the owner is at fault, the dog cannot be blamed for the mistake. Second, if a dog is properly trained, he will obey regardless of circumstances. He will not need to be excused because conditions are different and he can usually be depended upon to obey at all times.

Part 4: MORE ADVANCED TRAINING

U.D. (UTILITY DOG)

The more advanced training which will be outlined in this chapter is really that training necessary to compete in the Utility Classes at dog shows. Even though the owner has no desire to enter his dog in Obedience Trials, he can have a glorious time teaching his dog to do the Utility exercises. Seeking a Lost Article, Scent Discrimination, and Tracking are more exciting than all the other training put together; and when a dog already knows how to retrieve, these exercises are not as difficult to teach as one would think. They offer the opportunity to amuse one's friends of an evening, and they make the dog useful in many ways around the home.

The trainer should remember that the More Advanced Training is only a continuation of the Novice and Advanced work. He should bear in mind that all training is progressive, and that once the basic lessons are instilled into a dog's mind, each new exercise will smooth the way for the ones to follow. When a dog is weak in his Utility work, it usually means that he is weak in the Novice and Open class work as well. The trainer should not attempt to teach a dog to seek a lost article or to do scent discrimination, for instance, if the dog is not good at picking up articles on command and does not know how to retrieve. Otherwise the trainer will be forced to make corrections for something entirely apart from what he is trying to teach the dog. Such corrections will cause more harm than good.

Before attempting the advanced lessons, the trainer should make certain his dog has had the high-school education necessary to enroll in what is equal to the college or university course—in other words, the Ph.D. of dogdom.

211

Speaking on Command

What is the advantage of having a dog speak on command? There are several. One is security. The mere barking of a dog is often sufficient reason to cause an intruder to turn away. If an owner is able to make his dog speak when he lifts a finger to give the signal, it is reassuring to say the least. There have been cases in which an injured person has been able to get help by drawing attention to himself through the barking of his dog. Many times it has been easy to locate a lost dog or one that has been accidentally locked up some place because the dog responded to the owner's command to speak, even at a distance. There is the advantage of having a dog ask to go outdoors or to come into the house, instead of just standing by the door and waiting for attention that the owner is sometimes slow to give.

Although Speaking on Command is no longer required in Obedience Trials, it still has many practical uses and it may be something an owner would like his dog to do. Whether a dog becomes a nuisance once he is taught to speak is debatable. By right, the dog that is trained to speak on command should be quieter than the one that has not been trained. In the process of learning when to speak, the dog also learns when not to speak. On the other hand, the dog that is made to speak in fun, or for every reward he receives, is more apt to "talk back" to his owner when he wants something, for he has found out that by asking he will get it.

The owners of Sporting dogs complain that if a dog is taught to speak it will make him give voice in the field. This was undoubtedly the reason why the exercise was dropped from Obedience Trials. The Trials are intended for *all* breeds of dogs, so an exercise that is harmful to any one breed should be excluded.

Ordinarily, a noisy dog will be noisy whether he has been told to voice his opinions or not. If a dog is naturally quiet, the command or the signal to speak will hardly cause him to bark unnecessarily at other times.

Some dogs will bark at the slightest provocation. Others will be slow to become aroused. The yappy dog will naturally learn to speak more quickly than the one that is quiet. To train the dog to speak on command, the trainer should take advantage of any noise the dog will make with his voice. The command or the signal to speak should be given at the same time so the dog will associate the two. The occasion might be barking at strangers, asking for food, yapping at play, or gurgling in jealousy. It may be when the dog anticipates something pleasant. The trainer will have to determine, in each case, the way to get results. If

212

SPEAKING ON COMMAND
*(All to be done later
at a distance)*

Stand position

Sit position

Down position

the owner has two dogs, for instance, he can tie the one he wishes to make speak at one end of the room and let the other dog run around. By playing with the free one and getting him excited so he will bark, the other one may bark as well. If he does, the trainer should praise him with, "Attaboy. Speak!" At the same time, the speaking signal should be given. This is the right index finger moved up and down in short snappy motions. The owner can also take one dog out for exercise and leave the other behind. The latter will think he has been forgotten and may remind the trainer that he wants to go as well, at which time the owner again takes advantage of the noise the dog makes to give the command and the signal to speak. If the owner has only one dog, some other method must be used. He may be successful using the dog's training equipment as bait. When a dog has passed the preliminary training he will usually look forward to his obedience lessons. The rattle of the chain collar will, therefore, excite the dog. If he speaks through anticipation when the trainer asks him if he wants to go—fine! That is just what is wanted.

A city dog can be taught to speak by using a routine habit such as going for a walk. If it has been customary for the dog to have an eleven o'clock airing, and then, all of a sudden, the trainer starts to go without the dog, the dog may bark to say it is time for his walk as well. If the dog is keen about food, the trainer can use the dog's dinner or a tidbit to bribe him into speaking. Another way is for the owner to blow gently in the dog's face and make him sneeze. Later, the sneeze may turn into a real bark when the dog gets sassy and answers the owner back.

One dog was taught to speak through his enthusiasm in trying to catch a cat. The dog was kept on leash and the cat was allowed to roam freely around the place. At first the dog squealed when he saw the cat, but, with a little encouragement from the owner, the noise soon changed into a real bark. This method may also work if the dog's one desire in life is to chase squirrels or pigeons. It does not make any difference what method is used as long as the trainer succeeds in getting his dog keyed up to such a point he will make some sound or other.

After the trainer has taught the dog the meaning of the word "speak" by any of the above methods, the next thing is to teach the dog Speaking on Command. To do this, the dog is kept on leash and made to sit and face the trainer. The leash is held short in the left hand and waist high. The right hand is used to give the signal, and the up-and-down motion is made with the index finger. The trainer should be warned at this point not to confuse the dog by making the speak signal too much like the signal for Lie Down. Whereas in the latter the hand is held

214

so that the dog can see the entire palm of the hand, in the signal for the speak the hand is kept close to the body and only the index finger is extended. Also, the hand moves out from the body instead of down toward the ground.

The trainer should look the dog straight in the eye as he gives the command, "S-s-speak!" The trainer's approach should be a creeping-in motion to "press" the speak out of the dog. When the trainer gets results, he should move back and drop the index finger quickly. The routine is then repeated. If the dog is disinterested and just looks the other way, the trainer should start to jerk the leash with the left hand so the movement will arouse the dog's attention. If the dog jumps around excitedly, the chances are he wants to please the owner but he doesn't know what to do. The leash is then jerked hard enough to make the dog give a little cry or a whine—after which he is praised more than ever so he will understand he is not being punished but is doing exactly what the trainer wants him to do. During the next few attempts, the dog should be given a chance to speak without being jerked. If after several tries he still refuses, the leash is again snapped quickly to make the dog squeal.

Occasionally a dog will not cry out no matter how hard the leash is pulled. I remember one dog that could not be induced to make a sound, either from joy or from pain. He wasn't the "crying" kind. Jerking on the collar had no effect. I only went through, daily, the motions of giving the signal to speak and the make-believe jerk on the collar. I repeated the word, "Speak!" over and over. Each time I said the word, my right index finger came close to the dog's nose, and occasionally I flicked the tip of the dog's nose with my finger. This would make the dog sneeze, for which he was praised. For two days during the training period we went through this routine in an attempt to "press" the speak out of the dog. The first indication of ultimate success came on the third day when, in the excitement, the dog backed up a little, then started to get up, sat down, then got up again. At this point, all training was discontinued until the next morning when, at the very first command to, "Speak!" the dog burst forth in an enthusiastic bark. To this day, no matter where the dog is, the owner can get the dog to speak immediately by merely lifting a finger.

When a dog will speak on command from a sitting position, the trainer should make him speak from a lying down position and from a standing one. He should try it from a short distance, then from a greater one. The dog should be made to speak when he is running around in play and when he least expects it, to speak for his dinner, and when he is taken for a walk. If the trainer will take advantage of all these opportunities to make his dog give voice on command, the dog will soon learn he must obey at any time and under all conditions.

Stop Speaking

A dog that is trained to speak on command must also be trained to stop speaking when he is told. This is not so much stopping the uncontrolled barking, which was covered in an earlier chapter, but is the signal that is used to make the dog stop barking at the time he is taught to use his voice.

There is no question that when a dog is trained to stop speaking on command, either in his early training or during the routine Obedience Training, he will be more responsive in every way.

In this particular exercise, the left hand is used to give the signal. The hand is held waist high. When the trainer wants the dog to stop barking, the hand is opened up palm down, with fingers spread. It is moved from the wrist in a short, horizontal, side-to-side motion. This is done with a threatening gesture, while at the same time the trainer commands, "Quiet!" "Stop," or "No!" The dog is kept on leash so he cannot back away from the trainer. The trainer should first give the signal with the right hand for the dog to speak, then the signal with the left one to stop speaking. The dog should obey both. When the dog is slow to stop barking, the left hand in a sideward motion should whang sharply across the dog's nose. The trainer should alternate the signal to speak with the command to speak, and the signal to stop speaking with the command to stop. A well trained dog will obey either one.

The Signal Exercise

In the Signal Exercise, a dog is required to do the basic-obedience exercise entirely by signal, with no verbal commands. If the trainer has taken care throughout the dog's training to alternate the signal with the command on such things as Sitting, Standing, Lying Down, Coming When Called, and Going to Heel position, he will probably have only a few minor corrections to make in order to have the dog perform the Signal Exercise creditably well.

At the start the leash should be kept on while the dog is made to review all the work required in this particular exercise. When the trainer starts walking, he should step forward on the *left* foot. No verbal command is given but the left hand motions forward along the ground to give the dog the signal to start. If he doesn't start immediately, the right hand, which is holding the leash, should jerk the dog forward with a snap. The trainer should halt and the dog be made to sit. The exercise is then repeated. Only if the dog starts to move when the signal is given should the trainer refrain from jerking the leash. Otherwise the leash is jerked right after the signal is made with the left hand. All the heeling routine should be reviewed and the corrections should be made without once speaking to the dog. The trainer should then signal the dog to stand at heel position. Either the left or the right hand may be used to give the signal, but neither one should come in contact with the dog except for the purpose of making a correction.

If the dog creeps forward on the Stand, the trainer should bounce the palm of his hand off the dog's nose as hard as he finds it necessary to make the dog stay in one place. Another way is to let the leash pass between the dog's front legs and drag along the ground. When the trainer signals the dog to stand, a second person should step on the leash or snap it back quickly to check the dog from moving forward. Some trainers tie the leash to the dog's front feet and when it is snapped back by a second person, it makes the dog trip head first. He soon pays more attention to the trainer's signal to stand and to stay.

From a position facing the dog, the trainer next signals the dog to lie down. If the response is not as quick as it should be, the trainer should not hesitate to step on the leash and snap the dog to the Down position quickly. The hand is kept raised until the dog lies down. No command is given—only the correction which follows the signal. The dog is then signaled to sit. This is one of the first lessons in which the dog is taught to sit from a down position. The signal is the right hand drawn backward then forward with the palm toward the dog. After the first signal, if the dog doesn't obey, the signal is repeated in the form of a correction. The same hand jerks up on the leash, and the foot is used to tap the dog's paw hard enough to make him jump up immediately.

To get the dog to sit when the trainer is at a distance, a second person should stand near the dog and hold the leash. If when the trainer gives the signal the dog does not obey, the assistant should snap up on the leash. The trainer should keep his hand low so the dog can clearly see the palm.

When signaling a dog to come, the trainer must be careful not to confuse the signal to come with the signal to lie down. All the dog can see is a motion with the hand, and from where he is it is hard for the dog to judge the direction the hand takes unless the signal is distinct. Probably the least confusing signal to use for the "Come" is an exaggerated motion made with the right hand moving across the body from the right hip to the left shoulder. The position the hand takes in this motion is similar to that which was used when the dog was taught to come in the first place. It is also a signal that will not confuse the dog as it is in no way similar to any other.

If the owner is having trouble making his dog come on signal, the leash should be held in the left hand, chest high and away from the body. The right hand signals across the body under the left arm and lands with a snap on the leash. Once the initial jerk is made, the voice is used to praise the dog and to coax him to come closer. When the dog gets used to seeing the signal, and is not so uncertain about coming-in, the trainer should refrain from jerking the leash. Instead, he should use his voice to let the dog know he has done the correct thing by starting forward when the motion was made with the hand. The dog is praised when he sits in front of the trainer and again when the entire exercise has been completed.

The signal for teaching a dog to go to heel position was covered in an earlier chapter. If the jerk on the leash is severe enough, the dog will obey at once when the hand drops to the owner's left side.

While teaching the Signal Exercise, the owner must keep in mind the following: Only one signal should be given; then, if the dog does not obey, it is immediately followed by the correction. The hand is not moved from any signal position even though it may be necessary to give several voice commands to get the dog to obey. All signals must be clear and distinct and must not be so similar that the dog will become confused. The trainer should take care to make as little excess motion with his body as possible. The dog, as he waits for the signal, will misinterpret the trainer's slightest movement as an excuse to act.

Everyone who witnessed the twenty-four dogs at the obedience exhibition held at Madison Square Garden during the Westminster Dog Show a few years back, remembers the Standard Poodle that pulled a "Wrong-Way Corrigan" when he did the three hurdles in reverse. The dog started before he was called. Then, realizing his error after he took the first two, he turned around and went in the opposite direction to wait to be called again. The dog didn't make a mistake. The handler, when she moved forward to get into position to call the dog, moved her body in such a way that the dog interpreted the gesture as the signal to come.

Scent Discrimination

The unknowing person, when he witnesses an exhibition of Scent Discrimination for the first time, will often think it is a trick and that, in some way, the dog was given a cue to pick out the right article. Here's one remark heard at Madison Square Garden after a demonstration of nose work: "There must have been some liverwurst on it!"

When a dog is trained to use his nose, he learns to distinguish one scent from another and to recognize corresponding scents. The object that is picked out by the dog will have the same smell as that which was given to him at the start.

One way to give a little preliminary training on this exercise is for the dog to retrieve his dumbbell from among one or two dumbbells that belong to other people. A dog will recognize his own belongings, so, although he may be curious about the strange dumbbells, he should retrieve his own without hesitation—that is, if the dog knows how to retrieve. When a dog selects one special dumbbell from among several, he is using his nose to recognize a particular scent.

Before the trainer gets too involved in the training for Scent Discrimination, he should gather together an assortment of articles made of wood, leather, and metal. These may include gloves, wallets, clothespins, blocks of wood, spoons, or bottles. There should be five or six of each kind of article used.

The trainer should then take one of each article and should keep them apart from the others, as they will be used as the trainer's scent articles. The others may be put together in a basket or container and must be handled only with a pair of tongs so the trainer will not leave his scent on more than one. If a second person helps with the exercise, the tongs are not necessary.

The dog is kept on leash so the trainer will have control over him and so there will be no need to yell or speak too harshly to the dog. The tongs are used to place one unscented article on the ground. Let us assume it to be a glove. The trainer then takes the similar glove from his own basket and, to leave his scent, holds it in his hand for a few moments. The dog should watch while the trainer tosses the scented glove next to the unscented one. The dog is told to, "Take it. Look for it!" The leash is held just slack enough so it will not interfere with the dog when he moves forward to obey the command. If the dog has been properly trained to retrieve, he should immediately go to the gloves and pick up the one he saw the trainer throw. Out of curiosity he may sniff at the other, but he should bring back the one which the trainer touched. The dog is praised with, "That's it. Good boy!"

If the dog starts to pick up the unscented glove, the leash is not jerked nor does the trainer scare the dog by yelling at him. He quietly says, "No-o-oo!" in a low voice that will make the dog realize he has made a

219

"Stay" (A scented glove is dropped next to an unscented one)

The dog is given the scent by placing the hand over nose

"Look for it" "Take it"

"Come"

"Sit"

"Heel—Good boy"

The articles should be similar and should include metal

mistake, and, at the same time, the trainer pulls the dog gently away from the wrong glove.

If the trainer does not act fast enough and the dog succeeds in getting the wrong glove in his mouth, the trainer should press the dog's jaws apart until the article falls out. Then he should point to the proper glove and encourage the dog to pick it up. When the glove is finally retrieved, the exercise is completed in the usual way.

After the dog gets accustomed to seeing two gloves that look alike and will bring back the one the trainer threw, the next thing is to cover the dog's eyes so he cannot see the glove being thrown. Under these conditions the dog will have to use his nose if he is to find the correct one. Before the dog is given the command to find the article, the trainer must give the dog the scent so he will know what to look for. The trainer must be extremely careful not to frighten the dog by yelling at him if he goes near the wrong article. Even though he will be tempted to call, "No!" and to jerk the dog away, he should, instead, ease him back by a

The dog picks his article from among many

gentle tug of the leash. When the dog approaches the correct one, he should be encouraged and at just the right moment.

More unscented gloves are added as the dog becomes proficient in selecting the scented one. Eventually, all five gloves are placed on the ground and the dog must bring back the scented one every time. The position of the scented glove should be changed occasionally so it will not always be found in the same spot; and the articles should be placed further away until the dog will go out to the full length of the leash by himself. Still using the glove as the scented article, the trainer next uses in turn wallets, blocks of wood, or metal spoons for the unscented articles. Finally he uses an even wider assortment.

The entire procedure is repeated—but a wallet or a block of wood replaces the scented glove. The dog must retrieve each newly scented article from a number of unscented similar ones and later from an assortment of articles. The exercise may then be tried without the leash. As in all parts of the training, when the leash has been taken off, the trainer will have to control his dog by voice. But the commands must not be given too severely or the dog will become depressed and he will make no attempt to find the right article. If the dog is yelled at, he will be so afraid of what will happen if he picks up the wrong article that he won't pick up any.

One way to train the dog that has a difficult time doing scent work is to use several clothespins—the snap variety—and to fasten those that are unscented to a line stretched along the ground. The scented clothespin is laid down without fastening so that when the dog attempts to pick out the scented article the only one that can be lifted from the ground will be the correct one. For which he receives generous praise.

By using articles that are similar, the dog will very soon learn to recognize the right one by scent alone. The trainer must never fail to place his hand over the dog's nose and to give the dog time to get the scent.

A lad of nine years, after watching a test of Scent Discrimination, turned to his mother and in a loud voice for everyone to hear remarked, "Golly, ma, that lady sure must stink." For this particular exercise, the more "stink" there is, the better. The dog must know what he is to look for.

The scented articles should be partially hidden at times and should be placed at some distance from the unscented ones. This is to train the dog not to become discouraged if he does not find the scented article immediately but to continue hunting over a larger area until he locates it. Many dogs will fail in Obedience Trials because the owner has made the work too easy during the practice sessions. Instead of finding out how well a dog will work under difficult conditions, they make it as easy for the dog as they can. As a result, the dog will either fail in a trial or he will just skim through.

When a dog has been trained in Scent Discrimination, he should be tested on his ability to perform by having all the articles mixed together. The trainer should select one article at random and hold it for a few seconds before placing it with the other articles. If the dog is successful in this test, he can then be tested on a stranger's scent, whose hand is placed over the dog's nose just as the trainer's was; but, in this case, the dog should pick out the article which was placed there by the stranger. In other words, the dog should learn that the object he is to retrieve must correspond to whatever scent was given at the start.

When Scent Discrimination is properly done, the dog should smell the various objects and when he comes to the one with the corresponding scent he should hesitate, go on and sniff the others, return to the scented one and pick it up. By right, a dog will retrieve the most recently touched article even though two articles have the trainer's scent. On the other hand, it cannot be said that the dog is wrong if he retrieves the first scented article he finds without checking the remaining ones—that is, if he has been taught only to get something with the trainer's scent and not the most recent thing the trainer touched.

If at any time during the teaching of Scent Discrimination the dog reaches the point where he is making no progress, the trainer should go back to the beginning and start over again. The entire routine should be reviewed until the dog gains more confidence and knows what he is doing.

Even in this work a dog will be lazy and take the shortest and easiest way out. In 1937, when Mrs. Whitehouse Walker and I took our now famous 10,000-mile trailer trip throughout the Southwest, we had a Poodle, Carillon Epreuve, U.D.T., give exhibitions of Obedience Training wherever our caravan stopped. By the time we reached Dallas, Texas, the exhibitions were an old story to "Glee," and when it came time for the scent work, she was pretty well fed up with the whole idea.

To make it more amusing to the public, golf balls were used for the scent work because they were identical in appearance and the spectators could tell there was nothing deceiving about them. Glee sniffed the first ball she came to, which was the scented one, and immediately picked it up. To make certain that she had the correct one before she brought the golf ball back, she went on down the line and smelled all the others, still holding the first ball in her mouth. Perhaps she wasn't lazy after all, but was using her head as well as her nose.

Just where the idea originated that it is necessary to boil all the scent articles after they have been used in a trial, I wouldn't know. I, for one, strongly object to a brew of wood, metal, and leather and see no reason for having one. A good airing of the articles after each test, or wiping them off with a damp cloth, is sufficient precaution for the owner to take. By experiment, it has been proved that a dog will pick out the most recently touched article, even though only a few hours have lapsed since the others were also handled.

If a dog runs to the articles and pounces upon the first one he sees, it is certain the dog has not received systematic training in Scent Discrimination. This kind of dog should be classed with those that retrieve the dumbbell because they think it is fun. Such a dog should be put back on leash and started from the beginning. Until he learns to recognize or to distinguish one scent from another, he will never be serious about his work.

The dog that goes to the articles and then just stands (the most mad-

Placing a scented golf ball among five unscented ones

dening thing in the world) may do it for one of two reasons. The dog is either poor at retrieving, or the training for the scent work was too severe and he is afraid he will pick up the wrong article. The correction for our apparently disinterested friend should be the same as on the Retrieve. With the leash on, the dog is sent for the article, and if he waits even a moment before he goes to work, the leash should be snapped hard in the same motion as that of cracking a whip. No second command is given. Just the correction. The frightened dog should be handled in just the opposite way. The leash is left on and used gently to avoid a mistake. No harsh words are spoken—only encouragement and praise when he does right and a quiet "No-o-oo!" when he does wrong. The work should be reviewed from the beginning and the dog's confidence gradually restored.

The dog that works in a sulky or bored manner should have the scent work take on the aspects of a game. The one that drops his articles undoubtedly dropped his dumbbell as well and should be given the same corrections. Other mistakes made throughout the exercise will be the

A real test in scent discrimination

same as those made in the Novice and Open class work. The best thing to do is to put such a dog back into kindergarden for a little while.

Seeking a Lost Article

When a dog knows how to retrieve and can recognize corresponding scents, he is next taught to look for a lost article. This exercise is known as the Seek Back and combines the Retrieve with the Scent Discrimination.

As stated previously, if the trainer will teach his dog to retrieve a number of different articles as well as the dumbbell, the ground work for the Seek Back, the Scent Discrimination and the Tracking will have been laid. Each of these exercises is a retrieve of one form or another. It will be to the owner's advantage if he will start the dog with the idea that the Seek Back is a game. If he will permit the dog to retrieve a special glove or change purse in play, and will later hide the article so the dog must use his nose to find it, it will give the dog some idea of

227

what it is all about. At this point, the owner should change his command from, "Take it" to "Take it! Look for it!" The last expression means that the dog must hunt around for an article that is not in plain sight. When the dog is finally trained, the first part of the command, which is "Take it," can be replaced with the word "Go" to lead up to the Directed Jumping and to encourage the dog to leave his trainer on command.

The first serious attempt to teach the Seek Back should be done with something the dog likes and with the article left in a place where it will not be difficult to see. It might even be a good idea to let the dog see it thrown the first few times and to treat the Seek Back more as a retrieve.

Later the training should be done where the grass is long and where the article will be harder to find. Again, the trainer should continue to make a game of this exercise and should permit the dog to see the article thrown in the tall grass, after which the dog is given the command, "Go! Look for it!" The dog will know the article is there as he saw it being thrown, but he will have to use his nose to find it. The Seek Back may be done by either sight or scent; but since the dog's keenest sense is that of smell, he will soon rely more upon his nose than his eyes. By training a dog to use his nose to find a lost article the trainer is preparing him at the same time for the Tracking which is even more difficult.

With the dog at heel position but not necessarily on leash, the trainer should walk in a straight line and carry the article in his right hand. When the dog is not looking, the trainer should drop the article and continue walking fifteen or twenty paces, then make an about-turn and halt. If the leash is on, it should be taken off. The trainer should hold the dog quiet by hooking a finger of his left hand through the ring of the collar, and then placing his right hand over the dog's nose to give him the scent. This last is very important if one is to teach the dog to seek back for articles that belong to a number of people. The dog will otherwise bound off by himself with the idea he is to find just any article that is hidden or one that belongs only to his trainer. If all the previous training has been successful, the dog should start at once when he receives the command, "Go! Look for it!" When he has found the article, even though it was in plain sight, he should be praised with, "That's it. Good boy!" He is then made to come and sit in front while the trainer takes the article away, just as he did on the Retrieve. Finally, the dog is made to go to heel position.

If the dog makes no attempt to go after the article, or if he starts in the wrong direction, the trainer should review the lessons on retrieving on the flat. He should walk with the dog toward the article, point to it,

228

and demand, "Take it! Look for it!" He should then move back to his original position and make the dog bring it to him.

After several lessons where the Seek Back is done in a straight line, the trainer should make a single right-hand turn, or a single left-hand turn, and later a number of turns. The article should be dropped in different places and each time farther away. The dog is not required to follow where the trainer walked as he is entirely on his own and is permitted to cast around in all directions as long as he finds the "lost" article.

The Seek Back problems are not too serious. The conditions under which the Seek Back is held at dog shows make this exercise an easy one. If the article is dropped in the open the dog can see it immediately and will run and retrieve it. Some judges will attempt to make the exercise more difficult by having the owner drop the article behind some obstacle. The chances are that the dog will go directly there if he was trained at home for just such an occasion. The greatest annoyance is when the dog returns without the article. Because a second command means a heavy penalty, the owner usually just stands and glares at the dog while the dog glares back at the owner. If the dog has been receiving a second command at home during the practice sessions, he will wait for it during a trial. To train the dog not to wait, the trainer should hold the rolled-up leash or some other object in his hand, and, when the dog returns to the trainer without the article, the object should be thrown hard at the dog's feet or the trainer should start walking toward the dog. If the dog starts back to look for the article, he should be encouraged with, "Good boy"; but if he returns without it he should have something thrown at him again. When the dog finally locates the article, a lot of encouragement should be given and the dog praised and fussed over to make up for the corrections.

The average owner ordinarily leans too much toward keeping the dog in close while he is working. It should be a question of how great a distance the dog will travel to do the Seek Back. He should be trained to cover a wide area and to keep looking until he finds the article he is seeking.

Undoubtedly many an owner has had the painful experience of having a judge mark his dog zero because the dog passed underneath the rope and went outside the obedience ring while looking for the article. A dog that has his nose to the ground and is working every minute of the time is not a failure, even though he technically leaves the ring. The dog has no way of gauging the specified area when a mere piece of rope is stretched above his head.

A dog should never be marked down when he goes to the trouble of jumping the hurdle on his way back with the article if the hurdle is in a direct line with the trainer. The dog is showing sense by jumping over instead of going out of his way to avoid taking it. Even if it is not in a direct line, the dog still cannot be blamed for occasionally jumping it because in the retrieve over the hurdle the dog received punishment if he *didn't* circle back to return over the hurdle. After all, the trainer must be sensible about such things and not expect the dog to be a mind reader.

The owner who trains his dog to seek lost articles around the house should use the name of the article the dog is seeking. Dogs can very easily learn to distinguish articles by their names; so the words "leash," "ball," "slipper," et cetera, will have a definite meaning, and the dog will seek the corresponding article.

Group Examination

The Group Examination is little more than the Stand-stay done off leash combined with the Stand for Examination as covered in an earlier chapter. The minimum length of time the dog must remain standing is three minutes and the test is made with a number of other dogs. Again, I repeat. If the individual parts of this exercise have been carefully taught, the owner will have little difficulty training his dog to do the Group Examination.

The problems that come up include such things as the dog creeping forward a step or so at a time or the dog that will sit either before or after he has been examined. For the latter, the owner should make the training more strict during practice so the Group Examination at a dog show will be simple in comparison. During training, the person who is giving the examination can help if he will tell the dog to stay as he approaches him and will help to make the correction by forcing the dog to stand up again if he sits down.

The dog that is naturally reserved toward strangers will be more inclined to move or shift his position when he is approached. Under these circumstances, the owner should call out the command "Stay!" from the distance and he should use a very demanding tone of voice. If the dog creeps forward or shies from the person examining him, a second person holds the handle of a leash looped around the dog's hindquarters. If the dog moves, the owner sternly commands "STAY!", after which the second person pulls the dog back into position.

Directed Jumping

The only part of the Directed Jumping exercise that is actually new in the dog's training is the Go, by which, for the first time, the dog is trained to leave the owner on command. Almost every dog can be taught to stay and to come when called with little or no trouble; but to train him to leave his master and go off by himself, for no apparent reason, is another story. Unless the training is done with care, the dog's reaction may be similar to that of the dog who has been punished or told to "Go home," "Get out of here," or "Scat."

When the dog left the owner on all other occasions there was a reason for going. This was in the form of a reward, such as when finding the dumbbell on the Retrieve or locating the "lost" article on the Seek Back. In the Directed Jumping there is no imminent reward. The dog is sent out for something that is not there. He is then recalled to the owner by a circuitous route whereas before he had always been taught to come in straight. The dog is also made to go out of his way to jump over a hurdle—a black mark against him if he does it on any other exercise.

There is a definite value in teaching a dog to Go on command. The obedience-trained dog should obey an order to leave his owner as well as to come to him. The training is similar to that received by the messenger-dogs in times of war. For the home pet, the value lies in being able to send a dog back when he follows someone or chases after a car. Because the immediate reward is lacking in the Directed Jumping, care should be taken that the dog does not feel he is being reprimanded when made to leave the trainer.

Directed Jumping should be taught as systematically as any other obedience exercise. By this I mean that the dog should be confined by a rope or a line so that all mistakes can be corrected immediately and he will not get into the habit of doing it the wrong way. No dog should be started in the Directed Jumping unless he has been well trained and the owner is able to control the dog entirely by voice. I have watched owners waste time by attempting to teach this exercise to dogs that were not steady even in the Open class work.

The Directed Jumping should be taught without hurdles at first. The trainer should work on the Go exclusively until the dog understands what the word means and will obey. There will be some trainers who will say the hurdles should be used because they furnish an incentive for the dog to Go—he enjoys jumping and will anticipate this as a reward. The dog should obey whether he is permitted to take the hurdles

1. When teaching the Go on line,
   the pulley is placed higher
   than the dog's head

2. The trainer supports the weight of
   the line and slowly walks
   with the dog

3. After obeying the command "Sit!"
   the dog receives his reward

4. The trainer walks with the dog
   as he is being pulled out by the
   line, giving constant praise

232

5. *The trainer begins to drop back*

6. *The dog is commanded to sit*

7. *The trainer walks to the dog to reward him*

8. *The dog is made to "Go" from a sitting position with his back to the pulley*

(King photos)

or not, and he should respect the command or the signal regardless of where he is and under what circumstances he must work. After the dog has learned how to do the Go, the hurdles may be used to speed the dog up in performance and to keep him in a happy frame of mind.

The trainer will find an automatic fishing reel and line useful when teaching this exercise or a plastic or nylon line and pulley. Of the hundreds of dogs that I have taught Directed Jumping, I had only one that did not take kindly to the line. My own U.D. Poodles have all been trained on the line. After two weeks of training they entered the obedience ring and gained their U.D. degree. The line is successful but it must be used properly and with care.

When using a reel the trainer should select a large tree or a fence behind which the assistant can stand so he will not be too conspicuous. When using the pulley, the pulley should be fastened to a stationary object three to four feet above the dog's head. The 100-foot line is run through the pulley, then fastened to the dog's collar and held in the trainer's left hand. After the trainer tells the dog "Jester, go!" he walks with the dog, giving continuous praise, while the assistant takes up the slack in the line by walking away from the pulley. When the pulley is reached, the trainer takes a step backward, calls out "Jester, sit!" After praising the dog he leads the dog back to the original position.

Several such trips will get the dog accustomed to the line and the pulley. The next step is for the trainer to walk with his dog without holding the line. The assistant gently pulls the dog forward. Both the trainer and the assistant give continuous praise. The trainer next starts with his dog when he gives the command, then he slowly drops back and lets the assistant take the dog out by himself. If the dog balks to any great extent, the trainer runs forward and goes with the dog. If the dog will let himself be pulled out, when he reaches the pulley he is told "Jester, sit!"

At this point the trainer should walk to the dog where he is still sitting and reward him with a special tidbit, a pat, and a word of praise. The dog is then taken by the collar and walked to the full length of the line and the whole thing is repeated. This is done day after day until the dog will go out immediately on one command and will keep on going until told to sit. The trainer should give the one command at the start and a second or third command only when the dog stops moving, at which point the assistant gives another tug on the line.

The training will be more successful if the dog is walked to the pulley the first few times, rather than to run him out. The dog will speed up

234

The dog obeys the command "go" by passing between the hurdles

Calling his name turns the dog and he is commanded "Sit!"

The trainer handles the line by walking backward after telling the dog "Go!"

(King photos)

after he knows the exercise. The training will also be more successful if the trainer is generous with his praise while the dog is being taken out by the pulley.

The next step is to leave the dog sitting in the center of the training area while the trainer faces the dog, quite some distance away. He tells the dog "Go!", this time without using his name, after which the assistant gives one tug on the line to turn the dog and make him start toward the pulley. It takes only three or four such corrections to make a dog realize that "Go!" means the opposite of "Come!"

The exercise is next tried without the line. Very often the trainer will expect the dog to go the full distance and to perform perfectly the first time he is ordered out. By right, the dog should be sent only a few feet and then halted unexpectedly. After this he is given liberal praise for his actions. A short Go well done is preferable to a mediocre longer one.

The distance can be gradually increased, and, if the trainer will not always send the dog to the same spot, the dog will not anticipate the command to sit. If the dog moves out only a little ways and then waits for another command, or if he just stands and looks back at his trainer, a second command should be given in a more demanding tone. If the dog still doesn't go, he should be put on a strong line and jerked hard by the assistant. If the corrections are severe enough, the dog should learn not to stop before he receives the command from the trainer. Success has been achieved by sending the dog for his dumbbell or for a toy at the other end of the yard, then stopping him before he reaches it. Personally, I think this is a dirty trick and is apt to interfere with the regular retrieving exercises. On the other hand, the trainer should try the various methods and use whichever one he finds will get the best results. Systematic training on the line will make the dog more reliable in the long run, but the other tricks of the trade may pick a dog up just when he needs picking up most.

If the trainer finds difficulty making the dog go in a straight line, he should choose a long, narrow passageway in which to train the dog. This may be done between two fence lines, between two walls, or in the middle of the roadway. After the dog gets into the habit of going straight, the test should be done in the open field and he should be sent in a number of different directions.

The owner who has no one to assist him when he is teaching this exercise can train the dog by himself if he will use a line and a pulley, but it is more difficult. The pulley is fastened to a tree or a post, and the line is carried back to the trainer who stands with the dog at heel position.

The dog waits for the directed signal

The dog is directed to the right

"Hup" the dog is directed to the left

"Come" "Sit"

(King photos)

After the dog is given the command to Go, the trainer slowly walks backward, giving continuous praise as he pulls the dog forward on line. If the dog is slow to start he gives the line a single tug, then slowly moves backward to take up the slack. If the dog draws back he uses a steady pull with lots of praise. The rest of the training procedure remains the same.

For the second part of the Directed Jumping, the hurdles are moved in and set close together. The dog is made to do the Go between the two hurdles and to sit at the other end of the training yard. The trainer then walks to the dog and rewards him. The dog is then sent in the opposite direction. This is done several times without permitting the dog to jump over the hurdles at all. The dog must learn to do the Go by always passing between the hurdles. If he is permitted to jump them, even on the way back, he may be tempted to jump when going in the wrong direction. With the same thought in mind, the dog must never be permitted to return to the trainer by passing between the hurdles. Otherwise, he may do the same thing in an Obedience Trial, which, of course, he should never do. That is why the trainer, unless the dog is doing the complete exercise, should walk to the dog after each Go before sending him in the opposite direction. When the dog is ready to take the hurdle on the way back, the trainer should signal the right hurdle with the right hand and the left hurdle with the left hand. The arm is extended at right angles to the body, palm toward the dog, and is held outstretched until the dog starts toward the hurdle. The command to "Hup" is given an instant after the signal so the dog will know which hurdle he is to take before he hears the voice. In other words the trainer should point first, then give the command.

In this exercise it is important that the trainer avoid using the dog's name. Almost every trained dog will come when he hears his name called, and this may be the means of starting him on a straight Recall rather than on the Directed Jumping.

If the dog has been trained to respond immediately to the command "Hup" and recognizes it as the jumping command, he should very quickly associate the hurdle he is to go over with whatever arm is used to give the signal. When the dog is first made to jump either hurdle, the trainer should start him close to the one he is to use. The dog should continue to work close until he will obey the first command to jump. When he does and while he is in mid-air, the trainer should snap out the command "Come"—so that when the dog lands he will already know he must come directly to his trainer. Instead of doing the complete exercise, the trainer should work on the individual parts of the Directed Jumping until the dog is perfect. This means he should do a series of right-handed jumps, then a series of left-handed ones. He should then alternate one with the other and finally combine the jumping with the "Go" for a complete performance.

When the dog has been signaled to take either hurdle, he must never be permitted to return without jumping. The trainer should block the dog by immediately moving in the direction of the hurdle and insisting that the dog go over.

The hurdles can be spaced wider apart as the dog becomes more proficient. With practice, the dog should be able to go in an almost forty-five-degree angle in order to jump each hurdle in turn. If he doesn't— back to the beginning and start over again. The trainer should avoid a set routine for the Directed Jumping, and the hurdles should not always be placed in the same way lest the dog's work become automatic.

Trailing and Tracking

When one looks up the definition of Trailing and Tracking, one finds that, basically, they mean the same thing. If an attempt is made to train a dog to do these exercises we think of one as being distinct from the other.

When a dog trails, he follows the scent left by a body as it passes through undisturbed air. The air-borne scent, as it settles to the ground, falls on the grass, on the leaves, and on the surrounding area. Thus a dog may trail a scent, even though the object that left the scent did not actually come in contact with the ground or the material things over which it passed.

When a dog tracks, he follows the broken path that is the result of the laying of the track. A dragged object or a person's footsteps disturb the ground. The crushed grass, the broken twigs, and the pebbles and stones that have been shifted about give off a scent of their own that combines with the body-scent of the track-layer. This simplifies the dog's task because, even though in reality he is following the scent left by the track-layer, at the same time he is following an assortment of scents.

When a dog performs in a Tracking Test under the present rules and regulations of the American Kennel Club, he may work by trailing, by tracking, or he may combine the two. In other words, given a dirt track or one on short grass, and with little or no wind, a dog will work with his nose close to the ground and will scent the footsteps where they disturbed the surface of the ground. Under these conditions, a dog will stay close on the track and will follow almost exactly where the person walked.

In a strong wind, the track-layer's scent will descend from his body and may be blown quite some distance from the actual path of travel. A dog will work with his nose high, in this case, as he trails the air-borne scent rather than the ground scent. The dog will cast about more than usual, and his direction of travel will not always be direct. There have been instances, in a high cross-wind, when a dog has worked 75 to 150 feet off the actual course, and yet was trailing the scent.

Tracking comes easily to the long-nosed breeds of the Working, the Hound, and the Non-Sporting groups. Probably most sporting dogs can be trained to follow a person's scent, providing they are not tempted by a stray bird or two. Terriers have good noses but they must be taught to concentrate. To the breeds with the short, pushed in faces—such as the Bulldog, the Boston Terrier, and the Pekinese—tracking is difficult. But, regardless of the breed of dog one is training, there are certain existing conditions that affect every dog's ability to track.

A strong odor, such as that of tar or gasoline, will overpower a scent. Also, when the track is laid over a moving object, the dog's work will not be so accurate. Running water and leaves that are blown about will cause the trailing-scent to shift and to be broken.

The time of day has an influence, too. Late afternoons or early evenings, when the air is heavy and the dew begins to fall, are ideal. This atmospheric condition will hold the scent close to the ground and make it more potent. Early morning before sunrise is also a good time. After the sun comes out and the moisture evaporates, scenting becomes more difficult. The hot dry part of the day is the hardest of all.

Will a heavy rainfall destroy scent? One would ordinarily think that it would be washed away immediately. Instead, although the scent is temporarily lessened while it is raining, when the rain stops the scent will still be prescent.

When a dog tracks, he is controlled by means of a harness and a light line thirty to sixty feet long. If a harness is not available, the regular training collar can be used, but the line should be fastened to the ring so it will not tighten the collar and choke the dog while he is working.

When laying the track, the track-layer, according to the American Kennel Club rules, must not wear shoes soled with rubber or rubber composition. I have not found this precaution to be necessary because the dog follows a person's scent as it falls from the body, and not just from the soles of the feet. Then, too, the ground over which the person walks will become disturbed whether the shoes have rubber or leather soles. If it were true that a dog is unable to follow a person who has worn rubbers, it is doubtful if so many criminals and lost children would be found. The strong odor of rubber may make it more difficult for a dog to track under such conditions, but it is not impossible.

There are one or two different ways to start training a dog to track, the one chosen depending upon the circumstances. If the trainer has an assistant, the ideal way is for the dog to see the person he is most fond of, then walk off into the distance and out of sight. This should be done at first in a straight line. The one holding the dog immediately gives the command, "Go look for him" and permits the dog to hunt for the track-layer. The handler follows at the full length of the leash, restraining the dog gently so he will not break into a run. When the dog locates the person he is hunting (which will be easy under these conditions), he should have a fuss made over him and be given something as a reward. A few simple tracks done this way will teach a dog to use his nose and at the same time make him realize the fun there is in this game of playing hide-and-seek. The trainer and his assistant then change places so the dog will get into the habit of looking not just for one particular person but for many.

It is rather unfortunate that the rules for Tracking Tests are not based on the same principle as those used by the police when tracking down lost persons or criminals. Their procedure is just the reverse of the Obedience Trials. The dog is given an article belonging to the "lost" person, or at least one that was handled by him, and then, with no assistance, must pick up the trail and follow it to the end, where he finds not a dropped article but an individual. In Obedience Trials, the dog is given a scuffed up section of the ground where the person walked, and he then must complete the track by finding a "lost" article. Frankly speaking, this test is more like a glorified Seek Back and lacks the practical value tracking should have. It is hoped the time will come when the dog is at least given an article at the start of the trail, even if he must still find another lost article where the trail ends.

A demonstration of real nose work was given several years ago during a tracking contest in which five of the six dogs entered failed to complete the track. Articles that belonged to five different track-layers were left

TRACKING

Shoes must not have rubber soles

The direction of the wind is checked

The dirt is well scuffed up at the start

A stake is placed as marker, and the trail is laid against the wind

The article is dropped

The return is made over the same trail

*The scent is given
to the dog*

*The command
"Look for it"
is given*

*Encouragement
is important*

The article
is found

"Come"

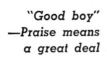

"Good boy"
—Praise means
a great deal

in the field. They were articles of value and each had a personal sentiment attached to it. One dog, in this case a Standard Poodle, was taken to the spot where the first track began. The track-layer held her hand over the dog's nose for a moment and then the dog was turned loose. As the gallery watched, the dog did a perfect track and found the article at the end. The dog was then taken to the second track, and the person who laid the second track gave his scent to the dog. By repeating this on all trails, the dog successfully retrieved all five articles.

The point of this story is to show that a dog, if he is properly trained in Scent Discrimination, Seek Back, and Tracking, will follow or pick out the scent that corresponds with the scent given at the start. Before a dog will do this he must *know* what he is looking for.

It is interesting to note that in Germany, where training has been carried on longer than any place else, the dog is given an article to scent and must find the individual, who mixes with a crowd of people. When the dog locates the person whose scent he is following, he holds him by barking. No harness or line is used.

The next step in Tracking is for the person who lays the track to carry along a number of articles that may be dropped at intervals along the way. After the articles are dropped, the track-layer circles around and returns near the starting point. The track is still laid in a straight line, with no turns. The dog is told to, "Go find it" or "Go look for it," and when he comes to the first article, he should be encouraged to pick it up and return with it to the person who is handling. The dog is given a second command and is sent on for the second article. This is repeated until all articles are found, one after the other. There should be an understanding between the trainer and his assistant as to how many articles there are in the field. Then the dog will not be forced to look for something that isn't there.

If the trainer has no one to assist him while training, he can start the dog off on his own scent. Before he does, he should have a number of articles and one or two pointed stakes that can be pushed into the ground with ease. The stakes may be from three to five feet long and tied at the end with a white cloth so they can be seen at a distance.

The trainer should choose a day with little wind and should pick an open field where the grass is fairly long and the ground slightly damp. The dog may be allowed to see the first track laid. The owner should scuff up the dirt at the start and drive in the starting stake. Since the first track will be laid in a straight line, the other stakes will not be needed until later. If no stakes are available, the trainer can use a tree or a post as a marker. The trainer should walk *against* the wind for fifty to seventy-

246

five yards and then drop the articles he is carrying at eight- or ten-feet intervals. When the last article has been dropped, he returns over the track to the starting stake. The alternative is for the trainer to make a wide circle and return to his dog in a roundabout way. But since the dog will look upon the first few tracks as an extended Seek Back, he will not be confused to any extent by having the trainer reverse the direction in which he walks. Moreover, this procedure saves a great deal of time and will use up less ground, since no two parts of a trail must ever cross.

It is a recognized fact among those who work with dogs that a dog will never back track. There is no explanation for this, except that possibly the dog is seeking the strongest part of the scent, which at all times lies ahead. When a person retraces his footsteps over a certain pathway, one would expect the dog to become confused. Possibly under perplexing tracking conditions this would be so, but many dogs that have been trained have successfully passed their Tracking Test using the method by which the track-layer walked back over the original track. Carillon Epreuve, U.D.T., the first dog to receive all obedience titles, was one example. Perhaps the fact that she located a "lost" article at the end of the track made the test take on the appearance of an extra long Seek Back.

At the start of Tracking, the dog is brought up to the starting stake while heeling on the trainer's left side. The line is coiled up and carried in the left hand. The dog is made to lie down so that his nose is just over the scuffed up earth. The coiled line is thrown backward, but the single line is still held in the hand.

The trainer pushes the dog's head gently to the ground and *holds* it for several seconds to give the dog plenty of time to fill his nostrils full of scent. After all, he must know what he is to look for. I have seen a number of dogs fail their Tracking Test just because the owner failed to give the dog the proper length of time at the start of the track, and, consequently, the dog was urged to look for something that he didn't know was there.

The trainer should motion forward along the ground and give the command, "Go look for it!" or, "Go find!" If the dog makes no attempt to follow the track, the trainer should walk along with him and coax him step by step. The dog is encouraged with, "That's it. Good boy. Look for it!" When he reaches the first article, even though the trainer did most of the work, the dog should feel that finding it was a great accomplishment. He is then sent on for the next one, and the procedure is repeated until all the articles have been picked up.

Two or three short trails are enough for one lesson. Tracking is hard work, and the dog has to concentrate a great deal. The trainer should be satisfied with a limited number of tracks well done.

When the dog becomes familiar with tracking in a straight line, the track-layer, after walking 75 to 100 paces, should make a right- or a left-hand turn, drive in the extra stake he is carrying, then proceed another 100 or so paces and drop whatever article he has. The track layer then makes another sharp turn and circles back near the starting point. Both stakes are left in the ground at first.

If the trainer does not lay the track, he should watch the track being laid so he will know where it goes; or he should have some one he can rely upon watch the dog while he is working to see that neither he nor the dog gets into a complete dilemma. Personally, I prefer the latter because, when the handler knows where the track is, he interferes too much and throws the dog off the scent. The handler must also learn to judge for himself whether his dog is actually working or just fooling around. The best way for the amateur to learn this, and thereby to gain confidence in himself, is for him not to know or at least think he knows more than the dog. By prearranged signals it is possible for the assistant to prevent a complete fiasco, and, at the same time, the dog's handler will not be tempted to guide the dog in any way.

The American Kennel Club rules governing Tracking Tests state that an extra stake should be placed in the ground thirty yards from the start, thereby letting the handler know the dog is traveling in the right direction. This, of course, is a point in the handler's favor.

Although a second stake is not necessary, the practice conditions should be nearly identical to that of a trial. The second stake should be used so that the dog will not be surprised when he sees it. Although he may attempt to retrieve it once or twice (for which the dog cannot be blamed), he will soon learn to pick up the scent again at the second stake. In practice, when the dog is put on a track that has a sharp turn the trainer should check him slightly as he comes near the stake that marks the turn. Otherwise the dog may overshoot. If he does, the trainer should stand still and cast him around in a circle until he picks up the scent again, going in the same direction. This time, the dog will probably slow up of his own accord and make the turn without a fault.

Let me repeat the warning that, although a dog will stay almost directly on the track when he is working, either with the wind or against it, the same dog may be a dozen feet to the side when he is working in a cross wind.

The trail is next laid with a number of turns but with a stake placed to mark each turn. This will help to keep an accurate check on the dog's progress, and if he fails repeatedly to track correctly, the distances must be shortened and all turns eliminated until the dog understands more clearly.

Very soon, the only stakes that will be used are the one where the dirt is scuffed up at the beginning and the second stake thirty yards farther on. When the trainer lays the track himself, the stakes may be left in to mark the pattern of the trail and then picked up on the way back if the trainer returns over the same trail.

No part of a trail must cross over another part of the same trail. It isn't that the dog will not be able to follow. He will because he would naturally pick the more recent of the two tracks; but in a tracking test, the dog must follow the general pattern of the track or he will be marked a failure. Neither should two tracks, by the same person, be laid so close together that the scent from one will be blown to the other.

If two different people lay tracks, it will not interfere if they cross one another. Neither will it interrupt when a stray dog, or some other animal, chooses a path that is directly across that of the track-layer's. But when a dog is first learning, the trainer should try to avoid the unexpected and make the work as simple as possible.

My advice to those persons who plan to enter a tracking test is to practice, and then to do still more practice. Tracks should be laid in the early morning, in the late afternoon, and after dark. They should be laid during the hottest part of the day, and the dog should track in a wind of almost hurricane force, as well as on the calmest of days. Open fields with long grass, a plowed up section of ground, mowed lawns, woods, and even cement surfaces will also give the dog experiences which will prove beneficial.

The dog should be made to track every type of person. The degree of scent that is given off by an individual will vary, and it may be the owner's misfortune to have a track laid by someone whose scent will be hard to follow.

I have seen dogs fail their Tracking Test because the owner was careless at the start. When a dog is taken to the starting stake, the owner should observe the wind direction *beforehand*. If the wind is blowing crossways, the trainer should approach the stake from the *opposite* side. If the track is laid directly into the wind, the approach is made from behind the stake. But when the track is laid *with* the wind, the trainer must go beyond the stake before he lowers the dog's head to the ground.

If at any time the owner thinks the dog has lost the scent, he should not urge the dog to keep on but should *go back* to the last place where the dog was tracking enthusiastically. Many dogs have failed a Tracking Test because the owner urged the dog forward when the scent was not there to be picked up.

The speed with which a dog tracks is not important. Very often a fast-working dog is a handicap because he is more inclined to overshoot the turns. Were the dog not confined on leash this would not matter so much because the dog would swing around by himself and pick up the scent a second time. Being unrestrained, he covers a great deal more ground as he casts about looking for the trail. When the dog is kept on a line his actions are checked, and unless the scent is within a given area, he will not be able to reach out far enough to find the track in order to carry on.

A dog has been marked "failed" in a test because he worked on the wrong side of the track in a cross wind. Such tracking conditions will actually exist if the track was laid in a cove or in a field pocketed between a solid wall of ground or of woods. The wind when it hits the embankment may rebound and go in the opposite direction. The same holds true when a dog walks over a knoll or goes up a hill. The descending scent does not settle on just one side of the knoll but may settle on any part of the ground at the base of the hill. Thus the scent may completely encircle a small mound. When a track crosses a moving stream of water, the scent ends at the edge of the stream. The water carries away any scent that is present. The dog, when following such a track, will emerge on the opposite bank and will cast both upstream and downstream until he locates the scent he was following on the opposite side. If he is confined on leash, he may not be given the necessary freedom to travel far enough to find the place where the track left the water. That is why the tracking line, although essential, is at times a drawback to the dog's ability to do good nose work.

The Show Ring

The *Regulations and Standards for Obedience Trials*, published by the American Kennel Club and reprinted as an Appendix of this book, are final when it comes to the dog competing in Obedience Trials at dog shows. To keep abreast of the times the standards and regulations are changed once in a while. The exhibitor, as well as the judge, should make it his business to familiarize himself with the rules and to know that he has the most recently revised set. In one instance, a judge scored an entire class on the basis of rules that had been out-dated the previous year.

The American Kennel Club booklet gives a complete description of each exercise and outlines the show-ring procedure. It explains just what can and what cannot be done. Obedience people should study these rules so that they will know what to expect when they enter their first Obedience Trial, either as an exhibitor or as a judge.

If the owner is new in the dog game, there will be a number of things he will have to have explained that the veteran exhibitor takes for granted. For instance, how to get information about the different trials and how to make an entry for a particular show. There are superintendents who run dog shows to comply with the rules of the American Kennel Club. By writing to the superintendents that manage the shows in a particular part of the country, a person's name may be put on the mailing

A collie retrieves over the hurdle at a recent dog show where he is competing for his C.D.X.

list to receive the premium folders for the different dog shows. The owner will then know what trials are coming up and he will have ample time to enter his dog. All entries must be in about ten days before the show. Local inquiries and dog publications will furnish the names of the superintendents. The premium folder will give instructions on how to fill out the entry forms. If a show is what they call a "benched show," it means that the exhibitor must have his dog in the stall that has been assigned to him by a certain time in the morning and that he must leave the dog there until the closing hour of the show. If the show is "unbenched" the dog may be kept in the car, in a crate, or tied under a tree.

*The author timing dogs on the long down
at an obedience trial*

In either show, the dog is given a number which, together with the dog's name, is published in the catalog. The obedience entries always appear at the back unless it is a specialty show and they have a catalog of their own.

Although the ruling is not compulsory, the exhibitors are usually taken in the order in which they are listed in the catalog. Frequently the dogs will not have arrived or else the owner is exhibiting in the breed ring, in which case the next dog in line will be called. Upon arrival at the show, the exhibitor should immediately look to see how many entries there are in his classes and where his name appears. If it is among the first, the owner should get ready to be called at the scheduled time. If there are a number of names listed ahead of his the chances are there will be no immediate rush.

Here I would like to mention the courtesy due every judge by the exhibitor whose name is listed first in the catalog. Such a person should be ready and willing to enter the ring on time. All too often, the owner of the first dog is not to be found until a number of other dogs have been in the ring. The exhibitor is only fooling himself by hiding in back of the benches or sneaking under the ropes. The judge, as well as the other exhibitors, know the owner is present and that the dog is in his stall. By refusing to go into the ring first, the exhibitor shows very poor sportsmanship.

The exhibitor should take care to exercise and water his dog prior to going into the ring. This is especially true of dogs that have been left on the bench for a long period of time. If the dog has had no chance to relieve himself, it is only natural for him to think the obedience ring is an exercise yard.

By experience the owner will learn to what extent his dog must be left alone before he competes. A dog may do his best work when he hasn't seen his owner in a long time. The dog will be so joyous when he is taken off the bench that he will show his enthusiasm in the way he performs. Another dog will work himself into a frenzy when he is left by himself for even a few moments. Such a dog will be on the verge of a nervous collapse and when required to do the obedience routine will be completely out of control. By watching the dog's behavior at one or two shows the owner can judge what precautions he must take.

The exhibitor (providing, of course, he is not the first) should stand at the ringside and observe the other exhibitors. A lot can be learned just from watching. There is a certain etiquette maintained in every obedience ring and the exhibitor should be aware of it and follow it to the best of his ability. Every judge has his own judging procedure and it will be to the exhibitor's advantage to know what the requirements may be that day.

The moment the exhibitor and his dog enter the obedience ring they become the center of attention and the subject of conversation. There are eccentrics who wait for just such an opportunity to display themselves blatantly, but the obedience ring is not the place to do it. The owner, even though his knees are knocking together like two piston rods and his heart sounds like a Model-T Ford, should act as natural as he can under the circumstances. Almost every judge remembers the first time he walked into the obedience ring and he will be sympathetic in spite of the scowl he is wearing. Although it is not advisable to talk to the judge prior to working in the ring, the owner should not hesitate to ask a question if something is not clear and if it has a bearing on the trial that day. Usually the judge will give the exhibitor all special instructions so that a great deal of talking with the judge will not be necessary. A pleasant "Good morning" or "How do you do" is always welcome and it will give no cause for complaint.

Each exercise, in turn, will come naturally if the owner trained his dog correctly from the start. The Heeling calls for walking in a brisk manner. The turns should be sharp and done with the correct footwork as described earlier in the section on Heeling. When the judge asks for a Fast the owner should do a fast forward run, not a fast up and down in the same spot. A Slow means a normally slow pace that will not immobilize the dog to the extent that he will start to sit down every few inches because he thinks the trainer has already stopped moving. When doing an about-turn, although the trainer was told to step back with one foot while he was training the dog, this extra motion should now be avoided and the trainer should execute the turn in a smooth fashion and in such a way that he will not walk away from his dog. The same is true when doing the Figure Eight. When the dog is on the inside of the circle the trainer should take long strides. When the dog is on the outside, the trainer should slow up a little and take shorter steps in order to stay with the dog.

All commands should be spoken clearly and distinctly and the dog should not be screamed at under any circumstances. A display of affection by giving the dog a pat or a kind word is a natural reaction and should be evident even in the obedience ring. The owner should not be ashamed to let the ringside know he approves of the way his dog has behaved. One thing that is on the black list, though, is correcting a dog severely or exhibiting uncontrolled temper. I agree that when a dog gets away with making a mistake it is to the disadvantage of both the owner and the dog because the same mistake will be repeated at some future show. But most persons are not careful in the way they correct a dog, and, very often, the spectators will not understand why a correction was made in a certain way. If the obedience ring were permitted to be used as a training yard, obedience, on the whole, would eventually suffer.

The owner should guard against talking unnecessarily to the dog while he is in the ring. He should not attempt to inform the judge of what dog he has in the ring that day nor of the dog's previous high scores. Calling the dog by name is allowed but it shouldn't be overdone.

Before he is entered in an Obedience Trial, the dog should be trained to the point where the owner will have confidence in him. A well trained dog will make the owner feel more secure. There is a tendency among the novices to work in close and this results in the dog making a poor showing. When the judge asks to have the dumbbell thrown, the exhibitor should heave it out a reasonable distance—not four and one-half feet ahead of the dog. Contrary to this is the exhibitor who just doesn't use his head. He will throw the dumbbell so far it goes out of the ring completely or he will throw it in the most difficult of places. I have watched an exhibitor deliberately throw the dumbbell so that it landed underneath the four hurdles that make up the Broad Jump. Such action is not good handling.

Since all the competing dogs in a class take the Sit and the Down

Twenty-four dogs, representing nineteen different breeds, take part in an obedience exhibition during the *Westminster Kennel Club Dog Show*

A few of the owners and their dogs that under the direction of the author gave obedience exhibitions at *Yankee Stadium* for three consecutive years before crowds of 70,000 people

exercises together, the exhibitor who is considerate of the judge and of the other exhibitors will stay close to the ring or will report in ever so often. Nothing is more annoying to a judge and his ring-stewards than to try to locate a number of dogs whose owners have vanished into thin air.

There are exhibitors who like to impress the judge with their knowledge, and those who are sticklers when it comes to the rules. If the hurdle is as much as a quarter of an inch off, one hears, "I shall report it!" An exhibitor is entitled to fair play but he should not be ridiculous. In a class by themselves are the owners and the trainers who think they are getting away with something by using body motions to signal their dogs. The judge is not being fooled. He recognizes every one of them.

The obedience dog is, or at least should be, scored on his willingness to obey and his enjoyment of his work. The owner should make an effort to have his dog exhibit such an attitude throughout the whole performance. If for any reason the dog should stop working and stand idle, the owner would do well to give the second command and take a penalty. If he doesn't, it may be necessary for the judge to mark the dog "failed" and he will receive a zero for the exercise. I might add that it gets a little boring when a dog is permitted to stand idle. Usually it ends with the judge glaring at the exhibitor, the exhibitor glaring at the dog, and the dog continuing to just stand. There is no ringside appeal under these circumstances.

Good sportsmanship and good fellowship on the part of the exhibitor are qualities upon which no value can be placed. The exhibitor who has the reputation of always complaining and making excuses is his own worst enemy. So what? It is just another dog show. If the owner doesn't make the passing grade that day there will be other shows coming up and —he still has his trained dog.

The owner who is lucky enough to come away with the blue ribbon must expect to make a few enemies. The winner is all too frequently maligned. When he hears it said that the reason for winning was because he had lunch with the judge a couple of years before, the best thing he can do is to toss such a remark off with a smile.

Very often I am asked how one secures a license to judge Obedience Trials. An individual who wishes to "stick his neck out" and become an obedience judge should apply to the American Kennel Club for permission. The Kennel Club will send the necessary papers for the applicant to fill out in which he must answer all kinds of questions pertaining to his experience in obedience. If the information meets with the approval of the Kennel Club, the applicant's name is published in their official publication, *The American Kennel Gazette*, for comment, favorable or otherwise. If there is nothing to the person's discredit, the applicant is approved by the Board of Directors as an apprentice judge. Such a person is permitted to sit in the obedience ring but in no way interfere with the running of the trial. The apprentice judge makes a report on how the different dogs worked, how he scored them and why. This report is forwarded to the American Kennel Club. If the account of the show is satisfactory and meets with their approval, it becomes official and the applicant's name is placed on the American Kennel Club's list of approved judges.

Conclusion

The real purpose in training a dog is to make him a better pet and companion. My chief reason in writing this book has been to simplify the training. If one has followed the outlined instructions carefully, his dog by now should show a definite improvement; but if the owner is having trouble accomplishing what he set out to do, he should stop for a moment and analyze himself as a trainer. It is sad, but probably true, that in nine cases out of ten it has not been the dog's fault. How about patience? It takes more of it than one realizes to train a dog. Training is not the result of a miracle but of good hard work over a long period of time. Has the owner made it clear what he wanted the dog to do? Since the dog cannot speak for himself the trainer must do the thinking for both. The trainer should reconsider the dog's temperament. Perhaps he has not been firm enough, or on the other hand maybe he has been too hard and, through nagging, has made the dog resentful. Above all, has the owner kept in mind just how a dog learns to be obedient? The dog must associate his acts with pleasing or displeasing results. The owner should think back for a moment and decide whether the results really have been pleasing or displeasing.

The owner should study and restudy the twenty-one Do's and Don't's on page 91. There is a wealth of information to be had from these few pages. One should ask: Have I used the correct tone of voice? Have I confused the dog by giving the wrong signals? Have I timed my corrections properly? Perhaps the dog was permitted to get bored. Or maybe he was punished without knowing the reason why. When the dog fell down on a particular exercise did the owner review all the work leading up to that exercise? And, above all, who took the blame for the corrections? Is the dog holding a grudge? In other words, if the owner has not been successful in training his dog, he should try to find out why he has failed and how he can improve his technique. If, in training his dog to

The author gives a training class exhibition at Rockefeller Plaza during 1944 National Dog Week

Carillon Jason, owned by John Livermore, makes his radio debut with his trainer, Miss Saunders, during "Be Kind to Animals Week"

Photo by Warren McSpa

be a better pet and companion, the owner has been given the incentive to help the dog gain his titles in obedience, he should naturally strive for a lot more finish in all the work. The rules and regulations for Obedience Trials, as approved by the American Kennel Club, are published in the Appendix. These rules should be read and studied carefully. *Training You to Train Your Dog* outlines the procedure the owner should follow to train his dog for Obedience Trials, but the rules and regulations as drawn up by the American Kennel Club are final.

If the owner feels his dog is ready to compete with other dogs, and if he, himself, is familiar with the obedience routine, he would do well to attend one or two dog shows and watch the Obedience Classes from the sidelines. This will give the owner some idea of what goes on at a trial and will make him more familiar with the actual procedure. Then the dog should be entered in a show for experience. This is for the sake of the owner as well as for the dog. The owner will have the opportunity to see how his dog behaves when in the presence of other dogs, and he will be able to compare his own handling with that of the other exhibitors. If the dog has been trained indoors the first attempt should be at an indoor trial. Otherwise, the grass and outdoor smells will be a temptation to the dog and he will not do his usual good work.

The owner should not feel discouraged when his dog fails, for even the best of workers will play the clown. Since no corrections are allowed at a dog show, when the dog gets away with making a mistake he is apt to repeat the same error at the very next dog show he attends. To overcome this, the owner should attempt to create a dog-show atmosphere wherever the training is done; then if the dog makes the same mistake again, he can be corrected immediately.

I would like to repeat that the owner who wants to keep his dog for protection or for attack work should send the dog to some well known professional trainer who is familiar with this type of training and can give the dog the required specialized schooling. A little knowledge is dangerous under the best of conditions, and it is doubly so when the objective is to teach a dog to guard property and to attack on command. The average owner lacks this knowledge and it is, therefore, far better to rely upon someone with experience.

This book on training has been written for the millions of people who appreciate the dog and value his love and friendship. It has also been written for those who have yet to learn what a dog's love and friendship can mean. I hope the suggestions that have been given here may bring about a better understanding of, and will make more friends for, the greatest of all animals—the dog!

Voice Commands Used in Obedience Training

"COME"   Command used to make the dog run to the handler.

"COME FORE"   Command used to bring the dog from the side of the handler to a position where he sits and faces him.

"DOWN"   Command used to make the dog drop to the ground in a prone position.

"GO"   Command used to send the dog away from the handler.

"GOOD DOG"   An expression of approval when the dog does the right thing.

"HEEL"   (a) Command used to make the dog walk at the handler's side. (b) Command used to make the dog go to heel position from the come-fore position.

"HUP" or "UP"   Command used for jumping.

"LOOK-FOR-IT"   Command used to make a dog seek an object that he will recognize only by smell, such as when seeking a lost article, doing scent discrimination or tracking.

"NO"   A word used to caution the dog or to let him know he has done wrong.

"OUT"   Command used to make the dog release his hold on whatever object he has in his mouth.

"PHOOEY"   An expression used to correct a dog when he has made a mistake.

"SIT"   Command used to make the dog sit down.

"STAND"   Command used to keep the dog on all four feet.

"STAY"   Command used to make the dog remain by himself in either the sitting, the lying down, or the standing position.

"TAKE IT"   Command used to make the dog take an object either from the handler's hand or off the ground.

Hand Signals Used in Obedience Training

COME   A motion across the body from the side toward the opposite shoulder.

COME FORE   A motion from the side to in front of the handler to make the dog come around and sit in front.

260

DIRECTED JUMPING   Arm extended full length to the side and parallel to the ground. Right arm indicates right hurdle. Left arm indicates left hurdle.

DOWN   (a) Arm raised above shoulder in a striking motion if handler is facing the dog. (b) Arm hanging straight down with wrists bent and fingers parallel to the floor if the dog is at heel position.

GO   Arm extended full length in front of the handler.

HEEL   (a) A forward motion along the floor to make the dog start walking at heel. (b) A swinging motion from in front of the handler to his side to make the dog go to heel.

JUMPING (Broad Jump)   The arm nearest the dog moved with a quick motion parallel to the hurdle.

SIT   When facing the dog, hand extended palm upward. Fingers flip up with a quick wrist motion. (No signal is used to make the dog sit at the handler's side.)

STAND-STAY   Same as signal to Stay.

STAY   Arm extended downward, palm back, and held momentarily in front of the dog's muzzle.

Commands of Instructor or Judge to Handler

"ABOUT TURN"   Handler makes a counter turn to the right to go in the opposite direction.

"ARE YOU READY?"   The question asked the handler before starting each exercise.

"BACK TO YOUR DOG"   Handler to return to his dog that has been left by himself.

"DOWN YOUR DOGS"   Handlers to prepare for the Long Down.

"DROP IT"   Command used for handler to drop his article in the Seek Back.

"EXERCISE FINISHED"   An expression indicating the dog is no longer being judged in that particular exercise.

"FAST"   Handler executes a running pace.

"FINISH"   Handler to complete the exercise by making the dog go to heel position from the come-fore position.

"FORWARD"   Handler to walk briskly with the dog at heel.

"HALT"   Handler to stop walking and dog to sit at heel.

"LEAVE YOUR DOG"   Handler to leave the dog by himself.

"LEFT TURN"   Handler to make a 45-degree-angle turn to the left.

"NORMAL"   Handler resumes a natural brisk walking pace.

"RIGHT TURN"   Handler to make a 45-degree-angle turn to the right.

"SEND YOUR DOG"   Handler orders the dog to obey a command or signal.

"SIT YOUR DOG"   (a) Handler prepares for the Long Sit. (b) Handler sits the dog from the down position at a distance in the signal exercise.

"SLOW"   Handler executes a slow walk.

"STAND YOUR DOG"   (a) Handler poses or stands his dog for the Group Examination. (b) Handler signals the dog to stand at heel in the signal exercise.

"STAND FOR EXAMINATION"   Handler to pose or stand his dog, then faces him at the end of a loose leash.

"TAKE IT"   Handler takes whatever object the dog is holding.

"THROW IT"   Handler throws the dumbbell.

APPENDIX

SUGGESTIONS FOR THE FORMATION
OF A DOG OBEDIENCE TRAINING CLASS

(Approved by the American Kennel Club, the American Humane Association, and the A.S.P.C.A.)

How Many Can Participate?

A Training Class may be formed with any size group, children or adults.

When?

Classes may be held outdoors in the spring, summer, and fall; in a gymnasium or drill hall in winter or when weather is bad.

Your Dog's Age Limit

An 8-month-old puppy to an 8-year-old dog may be safely and successfully trained in Obedience.

YOUR NEEDS

What You Will Need

(1.) The book *Training You To Train Your Dog* by Blanche Saunders, published by Doubleday & Co., Inc., in a new and revised edition. This will be used by each member as the instruction manual for both class and every-day homework. Pages 75–171, Novice or Basic Obedience.

(2.) Films and television lessons are available (in color or black and white) for use with training classes, the showing of which has been found helpful before and during the course.

By viewing repeatedly the correct and incorrect way of handling, owners grasp more quickly the technique of training.

(3.) Equipment: Training collar (plain, chain choke collar, 6-ft. leash, and a jumping stick). These items are all obtainable at local pet shops or department stores.

(4.) If possible, engage a competent instructor to conduct class sessions, and to assist with the major Do's and Don'ts in both the films and the book. Such services should be available at a nominal fee or as a courtesy.

Local kennel clubs can aid in securing a list of competent instructors. An ex-K9 serviceman may be located and the idea presented to him. If no in-structor is available, appoint a responsible member of your group to give commands and outline instruction.

Next, choose someone who will act as business manager. He should collect dues, set schedules, inform members of all activities, and keep records of attendance.

It is advisable that the training course consist of a definite number of lessons. Groups should meet for 2-hour periods once or twice a week for 8 to 10 weeks. The class should be divided into halves, to provide rest periods for the dogs and also to permit the handlers to observe others in their work.

Fighters should be barred from the class unless properly muzzled.

Run Films

Before the course begins, run the films in order that owners may study correct procedure.

LESSON: ONE

Course Outline

Always check to see that collars are on correctly and leashes held properly.

(A) "Heeling" and "Sitting" (heeling to include Right turns, Left turns, and Right-about turns) if there is room. At each halt, the dog sits at Heel position.

(B) "Sit-stay" on leash. The instructor's commands are: "Forward" . . . "Halt" . . . "Right-turn" . . . "Left-turn" . . . "Right-about turn" . . . and after the Sit-stay, "Handlers back to Heel position." (Handlers always return to Heel position by circling the dogs to the right.)

LESSON: TWO

Review:

(A) "Heeling" and "Sitting."
(B) "Sit-stay" with leash on ground, foot on leash.

New Exercises:

(C) "Come-fore" and "Going-to-heel" positions. Instructor's commands: "Come-fore" . . . "Dogs to heel position."
(D) Recall on leash. This is done from the "Sit-stay" position. Instructor's command, "Call your dog."

LESSON: THREE

Review:

(A) "Heeling" and "Sitting" (Right turns, Left turns, Left-about turns, Right-about turns, Left-U-turns, Fast, and Slow.)
(B). "Sit-stay," with leash on ground, handlers short distance from dogs.
(C) "Come-fore" and "Go-to-heel" positions.
(D) "Recall" on leash.

New Exercises:

(E) "Lie-down" (using foot on leash). Instructor commands: "Drop your dogs."

LESSON: FOUR

Review:

(A) "Heeling" and "Sitting"—leash thrown over shoulder.
(B) "Sit-stay"—handlers distance from dog increased.
(C) "Come-fore" and "Going-to-heel" positions.
(D) "Recall" on leash.
(E) "Lie-down" (foot on leash, hand raised in down signal).
(F) "Down-stay" (with handlers away from dogs).
(At this point a "Special Exercise" is practiced which is a review of all work, namely: "Heeling," "Come-fore," "Sit-stay," "Lie-down," "Come," "Sit," and finally "Heel.")

New Exercises:

(G) "Stand-at-heel" and "Stand-stay."
(H) "Stick-jumping." Although jumping is advanced work, Stick-jumping keeps up interest, gives a dog exercise, and is practical training for the novice. The first jumping is done with stick placed against some object for support, such as the wall, a chair, a bench, or a post.

LESSON: FIVE

Repeat the Films

At this halfway mark run films to refresh memory.

Review:

(A) "Heeling" and "Sitting"—leash over shoulder.
(A-B-C-D-E-F) *Special Exercise.*
(B) "Sit-stay" (handlers across room).
(F) "Down-stay"—same as "Sit-stay."
(G) "Stand-at-heel" and "Stand-stay."
(H) "Stick-jumping" (done in the open).

LESSONS: SIX TO EIGHT
or SIX TO TEN

A review of all preceding work with each exercise made more difficult, and all work done OFF leash, if the dog's work warrants it. (If the dogs fail, back on leash for next few lessons.) The "Sit-stay" and "Down-stay" are done with handlers gradually going out of sight for longer and longer periods of time. Dogs should be made steady through whistling, loud clapping and stamping. The "Lie-down" is done with handlers at a distance from their dogs and the dogs made to obey through alternating the command to drop with the signal to drop. On the "Recall," dogs are called and occasionally commanded to lie down halfway in.

During the "Stand-stay" the instructor should examine each dog. The "Stick-jumping" calls for a series of jumps the length of the room with the dog heeling between each jump.

Final Film Review

At the final lesson, depending upon the length of the course, run the films again so the owners may compare their handling with that of Miss Saunders.

After classes have been formed and started, Miss Blanche Saunders, if her schedule permits, will be glad to attend one of the sessions to help with any urgent problems.

FOUR IMPORTANT REASONS WHY YOUR DOG
SHOULD BE TRAINED

What this Obedience Training Will Do for You

1. For your own pleasure, comfort, and satisfaction.
2. For your dogs happiness, well-being, and safety.

3. To avoid annoyance to your friends and neighbors.
4. For the good of your community.
The above suggestions developed by Blanche Saunders cover Basic Obedience Instruction, Practical Home Value, and will qualify you and your dog to enter the Novice Obedience Trials at Dog Shows held under the Rules of the American Kennel Club, where your dog may earn his Obedience title —C.D. (Companion Dog).

GRADUATION EXERCISES

Graduation

This can be made an important event with coverage by the local press. Local civic and church officials are always glad to attend and lend their support to such a constructive cause. Well-known Obedience judges can be counted upon to co-operate, acting as judges without fees. Consult local Kennel Clubs for names of judges in your immediate vicinity.

DIPLOMAS AND PRIZES

Diplomas—Prizes

Diplomas, signed by the instructor and director, may be awarded to the members of the class who successfully complete the course. Local merchants and pet shops are generally pleased to contribute graduation ribbons and prizes when credit for these is given in the program. Prizes are awarded for:

Best Performance 1st, 2nd, 3rd
Best Handling 1st, 2nd, 3rd
Greatest Improvement 1st, 2nd, 3rd

IF YOUR DOG COULD TALK, HE WOULD SAY,
"THANK YOU FOR TRAINING ME."

OBEDIENCE TRIALS

SPECIAL REGULATIONS AND AWARDS APPLYING TO DOGS COMPETING IN OBEDIENCE TRIALS

Copyright 1952, 1963, 1964 The American Kennel Club

Chapter 1   Obedience Trial Regulations

SECTION 1. OBEDIENCE CLUBS. An obedience club that meets all the requirements of The American Kennel Club and wishes to hold an Obedience Trial at which qualifying scores toward an obedience title may be awarded, must make application to The American Kennel Club on the form provided for permission to hold such trial. Such a trial, if approved, may be held either in connection with a dog show or as a separate event. If the club is not a member of The American Kennel Club it shall pay a license fee for the privilege of holding such trial, the amount of which shall be determined by the Board of Directors of The American Kennel Club. If the club fails to hold its trial at the time and place which have been approved, the amount of the license fee paid will be returned.

SECTION 2. DOG SHOW CLUBS. A dog show club may be granted permission to hold an obedience trial at its dog show, and a specialty club may also be granted permission to hold an obedience trial if, in the opinion of the Board of Directors of The American Kennel Club, such clubs are qualified to do so.

SECTION 3. OBEDIENCE CLASSES. An obedience trial need not include all of the regular obedience classes defined in this chapter, but a club will be approved to hold an Open class only if it also holds Novice classes, and a club will be approved to hold a Utility class only if it also holds Novice and Open classes. A specialty club which has been approved to hold an obedience trial, if qualified in the opinion of the Board of Directors of The American Kennel Club, or an obedience club which has been approved to hold an obedience trial may, subject to the approval of The American Kennel Club, offer additional non-regular classes, provided a clear and complete description of the eligibility requirements and performance requirements for each such class appears in the premium list.

SECTION 4. TRACKING TESTS. A club that has been approved to hold obedience trials and that meets the requirements of The American Kennel Club, may also make application to hold a Tracking Test. A club may not hold

268

a tracking test on the same day as its show or obedience trial, but the tracking test may be announced in the premium list for the show or trial, and the tracking test entries may be included in the show or obedience trial catalog.

SECTION 5. OBEDIENCE TRIAL COMMITTEE. If an obedience trial is held by an obedience club, an Obedience Trial Committee must be appointed by the club, and this committee shall exercise all the authority vested in a dog show's Bench Show Committee. If an obedience club holds its obedience trial in conjunction with a dog show, then the Obedience Trial Committee shall have sole jurisdiction only over those dogs entered in the obedience trial and their handlers and owners; provided, however, that if any dog is entered in both obedience and breed classes, then the Obedience Trial Committee shall have jurisdiction over such dog, its owner, and its handler, only in matters pertaining to the Regulations and Standards for Obedience Trials, and the Bench Show Committee shall have jurisdiction over such dog, its owner and handler, in all other matters.

When an obedience trial is to be held in connection with a dog show by the club which has been granted permission to hold the show, the club's Bench Show Committee shall include one person designated as "Obedience Chairman." At such event the Bench Show Committee of the show-giving club shall have sole jurisdiction over all matters which may properly come before it, regardless of whether the matter has to do with the dog show or with the obedience trial.

SECTION 6. SANCTIONED MATCHES. A club may hold an Obedience Match by obtaining the sanction of The American Kennel Club. Sanctioned Obedience Matches shall be governed by such regulations as may be adopted from time to time by the Board of Directors of The American Kennel Club. Scores awarded at such matches will not be entered in the records of The American Kennel Club nor count towards an obedience title. American Kennel Club sanction must be obtained by any club that holds American Kennel Club obedience trials, for any type of match for which it solicits or accepts entries from non-members.

SECTION 7. DOG SHOW RULES. All of the dog show rules, where applicable, shall govern the conducting of obedience trials, and shall apply to all persons and dogs participating in them except as these Regulations and Standards for Obedience Trials may provide otherwise.

SECTION 8. TRAINER. As used in these regulations, the word "trainer" means any person who trains dogs other than those belonging to himself and his immediate family or who instructs obedience classes, whether or not he accepts any remuneration for his services. It includes assistant or stand-by trainers or instructors and any person who may reasonably be considered to be a trainer or instructor by obedience people familiar with his activity as a trainer.

SECTION 9. IMMEDIATE FAMILY. As used in this chapter, "immediate family" means husband, wife, father, mother, son, daughter, brother, or sister.

SECTION 10. PURE-BRED DOGS ONLY. As used in these regulations the word "dog" refers to either sex but only to dogs that are pure-bred of a breed eligible for registration in The American Kennel Club stud book or for entry in the Miscellaneous Class at American Kennel Club dog shows, as only such dogs may compete in obedience trials.

SECTION 11. LISTING. No dog that is ineligible for registration with The American Kennel Club may be entered in an Obedience Trial unless, following application, the owner has received American Kennel Club approval of an indefinite listing privilege.

SECTION 12. DOGS THAT MAY NOT COMPETE. No dog belonging wholly or in part to a judge or to any member of his immediate family or household, shall be entered or shown in any dog show, obedience trial or tracking test at which he is judging. This applies to both obedience and dog show judges when an obedience trial is held in conjunction with a dog show. However, a tracking test shall be considered a separate event for the purpose of this section.

No entry shall be made at an obedience trial or tracking test under a judge of any dog which the judge or any member of his immediate family or household has owned, sold, held under lease, handled in the ring, boarded, or has regularly trained or instructed, within one year prior to the date of the obedience trial or tracking test, and no such dog shall be eligible to compete. "Trained or instructed" applies equally to judges who train professionally or as amateurs, and to judges who train individual dogs or who train or instruct dogs in classes with or through their handlers. However, the above limitations as to trainers and instructors do not apply at sanctioned matches.

SECTION 13. WHEN TITLES ARE WON. Where any of the following sections of the regulations excludes from a particular obedience class dogs that have won a particular obedience title, eligibility to enter that class shall be determined as follows: a dog may continue to be shown in such a class after its handler has been notified by three different judges that it has received three qualifying scores for such title, but may not be entered or shown in such a class in any obedience trial of which the closing date for entries occurs after the owner has received official notification from The American Kennel Club that the dog has won the particular obedience title.

Where any of the following sections of the regulations requires that a dog shall have won a particular obedience title before being entered in a particular obedience class, a dog may not be entered or shown in such class at any obedience trial before the owner has received official notification from The American Kennel Club that the dog has won the required title.

SECTION 14. DISQUALIFICATION. A dog that is blind or deaf or that has been changed in appearance by artificial means (except for such changes as are customarily approved for its breed) may not compete in any obedience trial or tracking test and will be disqualified. Blind means having useful vision in neither eye. Deaf means without useful hearing.

270

A dog that is lame may not compete at any obedience trial and will be disqualified unless an official veterinarian, after examining the dog at the judge's request, certifies that the lameness is due to a temporary condition and that competition will not be injurious to the dog. Lameness means any derangement of the function of locomotion.

If a judge has evidence of any of these conditions in any dog he is judging at an obedience trial he must, before proceeding with the judging, notify the Superintendent or Show or Trial Secretary and must call an official veterinarian to examine the dog in the ring and to give the judge an advisory opinion in writing on the condition of the dog. Only after he has seen the opinion of the veterinarian in writing shall the judge render his own decision and record it in the judge's book, marking the dog disqualified and stating the reason if he determines that disqualification is required under this section. The judge's decision is final and need not necessarily agree with the veterinarian's opinion except in the case of lameness to the extent specified above. The written opinion of the veterinarian shall in all cases be forwarded to The American Kennel Club by the Superintendent or Show or Trial Secretary.

When a dog has been disqualified under this section as being blind or deaf or lame or as having been changed in appearance by artificial means, all awards made to the dog at the trial shall be cancelled by The American Kennel Club and the dog may not again compete unless and until, following application by the owner to The American Kennel Club, the owner has received official notification from The American Kennel Club that the dog's eligibility has been reinstated.

Spayed bitches, castrated dogs, monorchid or cryptorchid males, and dogs that have faults which would disqualify them under the standards for their breeds, may compete in obedience trials if otherwise eligible under these regulations.

No dog shall be eligible to compete if it appears to have been dyed or colored in any way or if the coat shows evidence of chalk or powder, or if the dog has anything attached to it whether for medical or corrective purposes, for protection, for adornment or for any other reason, except for certain breeds to the extent only that they are normally shown in the breed ring with the hair over the eyes tied back. The judge, at his sole discretion, may agree to judge such a dog at a later time if the offending condition has been corrected.

An obedience judge is not required to be familiar with the breed standards nor to scrutinize each dog as in dog show judging, but shall be alert for conditions which may require disqualification or exclusion under this section.

SECTION 15. DISTURBANCES. Bitches in season are not permitted to compete. The judge of an obedience trial or tracking test must remove from competition any bitch in season, any dog which its handler cannot control, any handler who interferes willfully with another competitor or his dog, and any handler who abuses his dog in the ring, and may expel from competition any dog which he considers unfit to compete, or any bitch which appears so attractive to males as to be a disturbing element. In case of doubt an official veterinarian shall be called to give his opinion. If a dog or handler is expelled by a judge, the reason shall be stated in the judge's book or in a separate report.

SECTION 16. NOVICE A CLASS. The Novice A class shall be for dogs that have not won the title C.D. Only one dog that is owned or co-owned by any particular individual may be entered in this class. Each dog in the class must have a separate handler who must be its owner or a member of his immediate family. No licensed handler, no trainer, no kennel employee, nor any person who has been approved to judge licensed obedience trials, may enter or handle a dog in this class.

SECTION 17. NOVICE B CLASS. The Novice B class shall be for dogs that have not won the title C.D. Dogs in this class may be handled by the owner or any other person. Owners may enter more than one dog in this class, but each dog must have a separate handler for the Long Sit and Long Down exercises when judged in the same group. No dog may be entered in both Novice A and Novice B classes at any one trial.

SECTION 18. NOVICE EXERCISES AND SCORES. The exercises and maximum scores in the Novice classes are:

1. Heel on Leash ....35 points
2. Stand for Examination ....30 points
3. Heel Free ....45 points
4. Recall ....30 points
5. Long Sit ....30 points
6. Long Down ....30 points

    Maximum Total Score ....200 points

SECTION 19. C. D. TITLE. The American Kennel Club will issue a Companion Dog certificate for each registered dog, and will permit the use of the letters "C.D." after the name of each dog that has been certified by three different judges to have received scores of more than 50% of the available points in each of the six exercises and total scores of 170 or more points in Novice classes at three obedience trials, provided a total of at least six dogs actually competed in the Novice Classes at each trial.

SECTION 20. OPEN A CLASS. The Open A class shall be for dogs that have won the title C.D. but have not won the title C.D.X. Only one dog that is owned or co-owned by any particular individual may be entered in this class. Each dog in the class must have a separate handler who must be its owner or a member of his immediate family. The same person must handle each dog in all exercises including the Long Sit and Long Down. No licensed handler, no trainer, no kennel employee, nor any person who has been approved to judge licensed obedience trials, may enter or handle a dog in this class.

SECTION 21. OPEN B CLASS. The Open B class shall be for dogs that have won the title C.D. and dogs may continue to compete in this class after having won the titles C.D.X. and U.D. Dogs in this class may be handled by the owner or any other person. Owners may enter more than one dog in this class but the same person who handled each dog in the first five exercises must handle each dog in the Long Sit and Long Down exercises, except that if a person has handled more than one dog in the first five exercises he must have an additional handler for each additional dog when judged in the same group. No dog may be entered in both Open A and Open B classes at any one trial.

SECTION 22. OPEN EXERCISES AND SCORES. The exercises and maximum scores in the Open classes are:

1. Heel Free	40 points
2. Drop on Recall	30 points
3. Retrieve on Flat	25 points
4. Retrieve over High Jump	35 points
5. Broad Jump	20 points
6. Long Sit	25 points
7. Long Down	25 points
Maximum Total Score	200 points

SECTION 23. C.D.X. TITLE. The American Kennel Club will issue a Companion Dog Excellent certificate for each registered dog, and will permit the use of the letters "C.D.X." after the name of each dog that has been certified by three different judges of obedience trials to have received scores of more than 50% of the available points in each of the seven exercises and total scores of 170 or more points in Open Classes at three obedience trials, provided a total of at least six dogs actually competed in the Open Classes at each trial.

SECTION 24. UTILITY CLASS. The Utility class shall be for dogs that have won the title C.D.X. Dogs that have won the title U.D. may continue to compete in this class. Dogs in this class may be handled by the owner or any other person. Owners may enter more than one dog in this class, but each dog must have a separate handler for the Group Examination when judged in the same group.

SECTION 25. DIVISION OF UTILITY CLASS. A club may choose to divide the Utility class into Utility A and Utility B classes, provided such division is approved by The American Kennel Club and is announced in the premium list. When this is done the Utility A class shall be for dogs which have won the title C.D.X. and have not won the title U.D. Only one dog that is owned or co-owned by any particular individual may be entered in the Utility A class. Each dog in the class must have a separate handler who must be its owner or a member of his immediate family. No licensed handler, no trainer, no kennel employee, nor any person who has been approved to judge licensed obedience trials, may enter or handle a dog in the Utility A class. All other dogs that are eligible for the Utility class but not eligible for the Utility A class may be entered only in the Utility B class to which the conditions listed in Section 24 shall apply.

SECTION 26. UTILITY EXERCISES AND SCORES. The exercises and maximum scores in the Utility Classes are:

1. Scent Discrimination—Article No. 1 ....20 points
2. Scent Discrimination—Article No. 2 ....20 points
3. Scent Discrimination—Article No. 3 ....20 points
4. Seek Back ....30 points
5. Signal Exercise ....35 points
6. Directed Jumping ....40 points
7. Group Examination ....35 points

    Maximum Total Score ....200 points

SECTION 27. U.D. TITLE. The American Kennel Club will issue a Utility Dog certificate for each registered dog, and will permit the use of the letters "U.D." after the name of each dog that has been certified by three different judges of obedience trials to have received scores of more than 50% of the available points in each of the seven exercises and total scores of 170 or more points in Utility classes at three obedience trials in each of which three or more dogs actually competed in the Utility class or classes.

SECTION 28. TRACKING TEST. This test must be judged by two judges. With each entry form of a dog which has not passed a tracking test there must be filed a written statement, dated within six months of the date of the entry, from a person who has been approved by The American Kennel Club to judge tracking tests, certifying that the dog is considered by him to be ready for such a test. These original statements cannot be used again and must be submitted to The American Kennel Club with the entry forms. Written permission to waive or modify this requirement may be granted by The American Kennel Club in unusual circumstances. Tracking tests are open to all dogs otherwise eligible under these regulations.

This test cannot be given at a dog show or obedience trial. The duration of this test may be one day or more within a 15 day period after the original date in the event of an unusually large entry or other unforeseen emergency, provided that the change of date is satisfactory to the exhibitors affected.

SECTION 29. T.D. TITLE. The American Kennel Club will issue a Tracking Dog certificate to a registered dog, and will permit the use of the letters "T.D." after the name of each dog which has been certified by the two judges to have passed a tracking test at which at least three dogs actually competed.

The owner of a dog holding both the U.D. and T.D. titles may use the letters "U.D.T." after the name of the dog, signifying "Utility Dog Tracker."

SECTION 30. OBEDIENCE RIBBONS. The following colors shall be used for prize ribbons in all classes except at sanctioned obedience matches:

    First Prize...Blue
    Second Prize...Red
    Third Prize..Yellow
    Fourth Prize..White

      All prize ribbons shall have the words "Obedience Trial" printed on them.

SECTION 31. MATCH RIBBONS. If ribbons are given at sanctioned obedience matches, they shall be of the following colors:

First Prize..Rose
Second Prize..Brown
Third Prize..Light Green
Fourth Prize..Gray

All prize ribbons shall have the words "Obedience Match" printed on them.

SECTION 32. PRIZES. Prizes and trophies at an obedience trial must be offered to be won outright and to be awarded automatically on the basis of scores attained by dogs competing at the trial with the exception that a trophy or prize which requires three wins by the same owner, not necessarily with the same dog, for permanent possession, may be offered for the highest scoring dog in the regular classes, for the highest scoring dog in one of the regular classes, or for the highest combined score in the Open B and Utility classes.

Class prize ribbons and trophies offered for the four official placings in a class shall be awarded on the basis of total final scores without regard to more than 50% of the points required for a qualifying score in each exercise.

Such other trophies and prizes as are offered for outright and automatic award at the trial may stipulate a condition that the score or scores be "qualifying."

Prizes may be offered for the highest scoring dog of a group as defined in Chapter 2 of the Registration and Dog Show Rules, or of a breed, but not of a breed variety. Prizes offered only to members of certain clubs or organizations will not be approved for publication in premium lists.

SECTION 33. RISK. The owner or agent entering a dog in an obedience trial does so at his own risk and agrees to abide by the rules of The American Kennel Club, and the Regulations and Standards for Obedience Trials.

SECTION 34. DECISIONS. At the trial the decisions of the judge shall be final in all matters affecting the scoring and the working of the dogs and their handlers. The Obedience Trial Committee, or the Bench Show Committee if the trial is held by a show-giving club, shall decide all other matters arising at the trial, including protests against dogs made under Chapter 20 of the Dog Show Rules, subject, however, to the rules and regulations of The American Kennel Club.

SECTION 35. DOGS MUST COMPETE. Any dog entered and received at an obedience trial must compete in all exercises of all classes in which it is entered unless disqualified or expelled by the judge or by the Bench Show or Obedience Trial Committee, or unless excused by the official veterinarian to protect the health of the dog or of other dogs at the trial. The excuse of the official veterinarian must be in writing and must be approved by the Superintendent or Show or Trial Secretary, and must be submitted to The American Kennel Club with the report of the trial. The judge must report to The American Kennel Club any dog that is not brought back for the Group Exercises.

SECTION 36. JUDGING PROGRAM. Any club holding an obedience trial must prepare, after the entries have closed, a program showing the time scheduled for the judging of each of the classes, and this program shall be printed in the catalog. This program shall be based on the judging of no more than 8 Novice entries, 7 Open entries, and 5 Utility entries, per hour during the time the show or trial will be open as published in the premium list, taking into consideration the starting hour for judging if published in the premium list, and the availability of rings. No judge shall be scheduled to exceed this rate of judging after allowance of at least one hour for rest or meals following five hours of judging as computed under this formula.

SECTION 37. LIMITATION OF ENTRIES. If a club anticipates an entry in excess of the club's facilities, it may limit entries in any or all classes by prominent announcement on the title or cover page of its premium list, or immediately under the obedience heading in the premium list for a dog show, stating that entries in one or more specified classes or in the obedience trial will automatically close when a certain limit or limits have been reached, even though the official closing date for entries has not arrived. If entries are limited non-regular classes will not be approved.

SECTION 38. ADDITIONAL JUDGES, REASSIGNMENT, SPLIT CLASSES. If when the entries have closed, it is found that the entry under one or more judges exceeds the limit established in Section 36, the club shall immediately secure the approval of The American Kennel Club for the appointment of one or more additional judges, or for reassignment of its advertised judges, so that no judge will be required to exceed the limit.

If a judge with an excessive entry was advertised to judge more than one class, one or more of his classes shall be assigned to another judge, and the class or classes selected for reassignment shall be those with the minimum number of entries which will bring the advertised judge's schedule within the maximum limit. If a judge with an excessive entry was advertised to judge only one class, the Superintendent, Show Secretary, or Obedience Trial Secretary, shall divide the entry evenly between the advertised judge and the other judge by drawing lots.

Immediately after the drawing the club shall mail to the owner of each entry affected, a notification of the change of judge. The owner shall be permitted to withdraw such entry at any time prior to the day of the show, and the entry fee shall then be refunded. If the entry in any one class is split in this manner, the club in such notice to owners, shall also announce the judge for the run-off of any tie scores that may develop between the two groups of dogs, after each judge has first run-off any ties resulting from his own judging.

SECTION 39. SPLIT CLASSES IN PREMIUM LIST. A club may choose to announce two or more judges for any class in its premium list. In such case the entries shall be divided by lots as provided above, but no announcement of the drawing need be made to the owners in advance of the trial, and no owner shall be entitled to a refund of entry fee. In such case the premium list shall also specify the judge for the run-off of any tie scores which may develop between the dogs in the different groups, after each judge has first run-off any ties resulting from his own judging.

SECTION 40. SPLIT CLASSES, OFFICIAL RIBBONS. A club which gives a split class, whether the split is announced in the premium list or made after entries have closed, shall not award American Kennel Club official ribbons in either section, but may offer prizes and trophies on the basis of scores made within each section if the split class is announced in the premium list. The four dogs with the highest scores in the class regardless of the section in which they were made, shall be called back into the ring and awarded the four American Kennel Club official ribbons by at least one of the judges of the class who shall be responsible for recording the entry numbers of the four placed dogs in one of the judges' books.

SECTION 41. ABUSE OF DOGS. The Bench Show or Obedience Trial Committee shall not permit severe training, correcting, or disciplining of dogs, or any use of spiked or other special training collars, on the show or trial grounds or premises. The Committee shall investigate any reports of such conduct. Any person who conducts himself in a manner prejudicial to the best interests of the sport, should be dealt with promptly, during the show or trial if possible, after the offender has been notified of the specific charges against him, and been given an opportunity to be heard in his own defense, in accordance with Section 42 below.

SECTION 42. DISCIPLINE. The bench show, obedience trial or field trial committee of a club or association shall have the right to suspend any person from the privileges of The American Kennel Club for conduct prejudicial to the best interests of pure-bred dogs, dog shows, obedience trials, field trials or The American Kennel Club, alleged to have occurred in connection with or during the progress of its show, obedience trial or field trial, after the alleged offender has been given an opportunity to be heard.

Notice in writing must be sent promptly by registered mail by the bench show, obedience trial or field trial committee to the person suspended and a duplicate notice giving the name and address of the person suspended and full details as to the reasons for the suspension must be forwarded to The American Kennel Club within seven days.

An appeal may be taken from a decision of a bench show, obedience trial or field trial committee. Notice in writing claiming such appeal together with a deposit of five ($5.00) dollars must be sent to The American Kennel Club within thirty days after the date of suspension. The Board of Directors may itself hear said appeal or may refer it to a committee of the Board, or to a Trial Board to be heard. The deposit shall become the property of The American Kennel Club if the decision is confirmed, or shall be returned to the appellant if the decision is not confirmed.

(The Committee at a Sanctioned event does not have this power of suspension, but must investigate any allegation of such conduct and forward a complete and detailed report of any such incident to The American Kennel Club.)

277

Chapter 2   Standards for Obedience Trials

SECTION 1. PURPOSE. The purpose of Obedience Trials is to demonstrate the usefulness of the pure-bred dog as the companion and guardian of man, and not the ability of the dog to acquire facility in the performance of mere tricks. The classification which has been adopted is progressive, with the thought in mind that a dog which has earned the title of Utility Dog has demonstrated its fitness for a place in our modern scheme of living.

SECTION 2. RING CONDITIONS. If the judging takes place indoors the ring should be rectangular and should be at least 35' wide and 50' long for all obedience classes. In no case shall the ring for a Utility class be less than 35' by 50', and in no case shall the ring for a Novice or Open class be less than 30' by 40'. The floor shall have a surface or covering that provides firm footing for the largest dogs, and rubber or similar non-slip material must be laid for the take off and landing at all jumps unless the floor surface is such as not to require it. At an outdoor show or trial the rings shall be about 40' wide and 70' long. The ground shall be level, and the grass, if any, shall be cut short. An appropriate place for the handlers to go completely out of sight of their dogs must be provided by the club for the Open classes.

If inclement weather at an outdoor trial necessitates the judging of obedience under shelter, the requirements as to ring size may be waived.

SECTION 3. OBEDIENCE RINGS AT DOG SHOWS. At an outdoor dog show a separate ring or rings shall be provided for obedience, and a sign forbidding anyone to permit any dog to use the ring, except when being judged, shall be set up in each such ring by the Superintendent or Show Secretary. It shall be his duty as well as that of the Show Committee to enforce this regulation. At an indoor show where limited space does not permit the exclusive use of any ring for obedience, the same regulation will apply after the obedience rings have been set up. The ring must be thoroughly cleaned before the obedience judging starts if it has previously been used for breed judging.

SECTION 4. REWARDS. Praise and patting are allowed between exercises after the judge has said "Exercise finished," but no food may be offered in the ring or carried by the handler.

SECTION 5. USE OF LEASH. All dogs shall be kept on leash except when in the obedience ring or exercise ring. The leash used in the Novice classes shall be about six feet long. All obedience work in the regular classes, except Heel on Leash and Stand for Examination, shall be performed off leash. In the Novice and Open classes the dog may be put on leash or guided gently by the collar between exercises and to get it into proper position for the next exercise. In the Utility class the dog shall not be put on the leash, nor guided, nor controlled by the collar at any time, and the leash shall be left on the judge's table from the start of judging of each dog until it leaves the ring. Dogs shall not be picked up or carried in any obedience ring.

SECTION 6. COLLARS. Each dog in the obedience ring must wear a well fitting plain buckle or choke collar of leather, fabric or chain. Fancy collars, spiked collars or other special training collars, or collars so large that they hang down unreasonably in front of the dog, are not permitted; nor may there be anything hanging from the collar.

SECTION 7. MISBEHAVIOR. Imperfections in heeling between exercises will not be judged, but any disciplining by the handler in the ring, or any uncontrolled behavior of the dog, such as snapping, unjustified barking, fouling the ring, or running out of the ring, even between exercises, must be severely penalized by deducting points from the total score, and the judge may bar the dog from further competition at that trial.

SECTION 8. COMMANDS AND SIGNALS. Whenever a command or signal is mentioned in these Standards, a single command or signal only may be given by the handler, and any extra commands or signals must be penalized; except that whenever the standard specifies "command and/or signal" the handler may give either one or the other or both command and signal simultaneously. When a signal is permitted and given, it must be a single gesture with one arm and hand only, and the arm must be promptly returned to its normal position, except that both arms may be used simultaneously to call the dog in the Recall exercises in the Novice and Open classes. The signal for downing a dog may be given either with the arm raised or with a down swing of the arm, but any pause in holding the arm upright followed by a down swing of the arm will be considered an additional signal. Signaling correction to a dog is forbidden and must be penalized. Any unusual noise or motion may be considered to be a signal. Whistling or the use of a whistle is prohibited. The dog's name may be used once immediately before any verbal command but may not be used when a signal is employed even though the standard specifies "command and/or signal." The dog should never anticipate the handler's directions, but must wait for the specified commands or signals. Loud commands by handlers to their dogs create a poor impression of obedience and should be avoided. Shouting is not necessary even in a noisy place if the dog is properly trained to respond to a normal tone of voice.

SECTION 9. HEEL ON LEASH. In the Novice classes the handler shall enter the ring with his dog on a loose leash and shall stand still with the dog sitting straight at heel at the handler's left side until the judge asks if the handler is ready and then gives the order "Forward," at which order the handler will give the command or signal to Heel, and at the same time start walking briskly with the dog on loose leash. At the command or signal to Heel the dog shall walk close to the left side of the handler without crowding, permitting the handler freedom of motion at all times. At each order to "Halt," the handler will stop and his dog shall sit straight and smartly at heel without command or signal and not move until ordered to do so. It is permissible after each Halt before moving again for the handler to give the command or signal to Heel. Any tightening or jerking of the leash or any act, signal or command which, in the opinion of the judge gives the dog unnecessary or unfair assistance shall be penalized. The judge will give the orders "Forward," "Halt," "Right turn," "Left turn," "About turn," "Slow," "Normal," and "Fast," which last order signifies that the handler and dog must run. These orders may be given in any sequence and may be repeated if necessary. In executing the About Turn, the handler will do a Right About Turn in all cases. The judge will say, "Exercise finished" after the heeling and then "Are you ready?" before starting the Figure Eight. The judge will order the handler to execute the "Figure Eight" which signifies that the handler shall walk around and between the two stewards who shall stand about 8 feet apart, or if there is only one stewart, shall walk around and between the judge and the steward. The Figure Eight in the Novice classes shall be done on leash only. There shall be no About Turn in the Figure Eight, but the handler and dog shall go twice completely around the Figure Eight with at least one Halt during and another Halt at the end of the exercise.

SECTION 10. STAND FOR EXAMINATION. The judge will give the order for examination and the handler will stand or pose his dog, give the command and/or signal to Stay, walk in front of his dog, turn around, and stand facing his dog at the end of a loose leash. The method by which the dog is made to stand or pose is optional with the handler who may take any reasonable time in posing the dog before deciding to give the command and/or signal to Stay. The leash shall be held clear of the floor when the handler is in position. The judge will approach the dog from the front and will touch its head, body and hind quarters only, and then give the order "Back to your dog," whereupon the handler will walk around behind his dog to the heel position. The dog must remain in a standing position until the judge says "Exercise finished." The dog must show no shyness nor resentment at any time during the exercise.

SECTION 11. HEEL FREE. This shall be executed in the same manner as Heel on Leash except that the dog is off the leash. The leash shall be left on the judge's table for all work done in the Heel Free exercise. Heeling in both Novice and Open classes is done in the same manner except that in the Open classes all work is done off leash, including the Figure Eight.

SECTION 12. RECALL AND DROP ON RECALL. To execute the Recall to handler, upon order or signal from the judge "Leave your dog," the dog is given the command and/or signal to stay in the sitting position while the handler moves towards the other end of the ring, the distance to be about 40 feet. Upon order or signal from the judge "Call your dog," the handler calls or signals the dog, which in the Novice class must come straight in at a smart pace and sit straight immediately in front of the handler, and close enough so that the handler could readily touch it without moving his feet or having to stretch forward. Upon order or signal from the judge to "Finish," the dog on command or signal must go smartly to heel. In the

280

Open class, at a point designated by the judge, the dog must drop on command or signal from the handler, and then on order or signal from the judge, the handler calls or signals the dog which must rise and complete the exercise as in the Novice class. The method by which the dog goes to heel shall be optional with the handler provided it is done smartly and the dog sits straight at heel.

SECTION 13. LONG SIT. In the Long Sit in the Novice classes all the competing dogs in the class take the exercise together, except that if there are 12 or more dogs they shall be judged in groups of not less than 6 nor more than 15 dogs. Where the same judge does both classes the separate classes may be combined provided there are not more than 15 dogs in the two classes combined. The dogs that are in the ring shall be lined up in catalog order along one side of the ring. Handlers' armbands, weighted with leashes or other articles if necessary, shall be placed behind the dogs. On order from the judge the handlers shall sit their dogs, and on further order from the judge to "Leave your dogs" the handlers shall give the command and/or signal to Stay and immediately leave their dogs, go to the opposite side of the ring, and line up facing their respective dogs. After one minute from the time he has ordered the handlers to leave their dogs, the judge will order the handlers "Back to your dogs" whereupon the handlers must return promptly to their dogs, each walking around and in back of his own dog to the heel position. The dogs must not move from the sitting position until after the judge says "Exercise finished."

SECTION 14. LONG DOWN. The Long Down in the Novice classes is done in the same manner as the Long Sit except that instead of sitting the dogs the handlers, on order from the judge, will down their dogs, and except further that the judge will order the handlers back after three minutes. The dogs must stay in the down position until after the judge says "Exercise finished."

SECTION 15. OPEN CLASSES, LONG SIT AND LONG DOWN. These exercises in the Open classes are performed in the same manner as in the Novice classes except that after leaving their dogs the handlers must immediately leave the ring and go to a place designated by the judge, completely out of sight of their dogs, where they must remain until called by the judge after the time limit of three minutes in the Long Sit and five minutes in the Long Down, from the time the judge gave the order to "Leave your dogs," has expired.

SECTION 16. RETRIEVE ON THE FLAT. In retrieving the dumbbell on the flat, the handler stands with his dog sitting at heel in a place designated by the judge, and the judge gives the orders "Throw it," whereupon the handler may give the command and/or signal to Stay and throws the dumbbell; "Send your dog," whereupon the handler gives the command or signal to his dog to retrieve; "Take it," whereupon the handler may give a command or signal and takes the dumbbell from the dog; "Finish," where-

281

upon the handler gives the command or signal to heel as in the Recall. The dog shall not move forward to retrieve nor deliver to hand on return until ordered by the handler. The retrieve shall be executed at a fast trot or gallop, without unnecessary mouthing or playing with the dumbbell. The dog shall sit straight immediately in front of its handler and close enough so that the handler can readily take the dumbbell without moving his feet or having to stretch forward. The dumbbell which must be approved by the judge, shall be made of a solid piece of one of the heavy hardwoods. It may be painted or varnished but shall have no decorations or attachments. The size of the dumbbell shall be proportionate to the size of the dog. The judge shall require the dumbbell to be thrown again before the dog is sent if in his opinion, it is thrown too short a distance, or too far to one side, or against the ringside.

SECTION 17. RETRIEVE OVER HIGH JUMP. In retrieving the dumbbell over the High Jump, the exercise is executed in the same manner as the Retrieve on the Flat, except that the dog must jump the obstacle both going and coming. The High Jump shall be jumped clear and the jump shall be as nearly as possible one and one-half times the height of the dog at the withers, with a minimum height of 12 inches and a maximum height of 36 inches. This applies to all breeds except those listed below for which the jump shall be once the height of the dog at the withers or three feet, whichever is less: Bloodhounds, Bullmastiffs, Great Danes, Great Pyrenees, Mastiffs, Newfoundlands and St. Bernards. The handler has the option of standing any reasonable distance from the High Jump, but must stay in the same spot throughout the exercise.

The side posts of the High Jump shall be 4 feet high and the jump shall be 5 feet wide and shall be so constructed as to provide adjustment for each 2 inches from 12 inches to 36 inches. It is suggested that the jump have a bottom board 8 inches wide including the space from the bottom of the board to the ground or floor, together with three other 8 inch boards, one 6 inch board, and one 4 inch board. The jump shall be painted a flat white. The width in inches, and nothing else, shall be painted on each side of each board in black 2 inch figures, the figure on the bottom board representing the distance from the ground or floor to the top of the board.

SECTION 18. BROAD JUMP. In the Broad Jump the handler will stand with his dog sitting at heel in front of and within 10 feet of the jump. On order from the judge to "Leave your dog," the handler will give his dog the command and/or signal to stay, and go to a position facing the right side of the jump, about 2 feet from the jump, and within the range of the first and last hurdles. On order from the judge the handler shall give the command or signal to jump and the dog shall clear the entire width of the Broad Jump without touching and, without further command or signal, return to a sitting position immediately in front of the handler as in the Recall. The handler shall turn while the dog is in mid-air so as to be facing his dog as it returns, but shall remain in the same spot. On order from the judge, the handler will give the command or signal to Heel and the dog shall finish as in the Recall.

The Broad Jump shall consist of four hurdles, built to telescope for convenience, made of boards about 8 inches wide, the largest measuring about 5 feet in length and 7 inches high at the highest point, all painted a flat white. When set up they shall be arranged in order of size and shall be evenly spaced so as to cover a distance equal to twice the height of the High Jump as set for the particular dog, with the low side of each hurdle and the lowest hurdle nearest the dog. The four hurdles shall be used for a jump of 52″ to 72″, three for a jump of 32″ to 48″, and two for a jump of 24″ or 28″.

SECTION 19. SCENT DISCRIMINATION. In each of these three exercises the dog must select by scent alone and retrieve an article which has been handled by its handler. The articles shall be provided by the handler and these shall consist of three sets, each comprised of five identical articles, one set being made entirely of plain uncoated wood, one entirely of rigid metal which may be painted, and one of leather so designed that nothing but leather is visible except for the minimum amount of thread or metal necessary to hold the article together. The articles in each set must be legibly numbered one to five, and must be approved by the judge. The handler shall present all the articles to the judge and the judge shall designate one article from each of the three sets, and shall make a written note of the numbers of the three articles he selects. These three handler's articles shall be kept on the judge's table until picked up by the handler who shall hold in his hand only one article at a time. The handler's scent may be imparted to the article only from his hands which must remain in plain sight. The handler may pick up his articles in any order. At the start of the Scent Discrimination exercises the remaining twelve articles will be placed at random in the ring about 6 inches apart. The handler will stand about 15 feet from the articles with the dog sitting at heel position with their backs to the articles and, on order from the judge, the handler immediately will place his article on the judge's book and the judge will place it among the other articles. On order from the judge to "Send your dog," the handler and dog will turn to face the articles, and the handler shall give the command or signal to Get It. The handler may give the command to Heel before turning, and may give his scent to the dog by gently touching the dog's nose with the palm of one open hand. The dog shall go at a brisk pace to the articles, but may take any reasonable time to select the right article provided it works continuously and does not pick up any article other than its handler's. After picking up the right article the dog shall complete the exercise as in the Retrieve exercises. The same procedure is followed in each of the three Scent Discrimination exercises. Should a dog retrieve a wrong article in any of the three exercises, it shall be placed on the judge's table, and the handler's article must also be taken up from the remaining articles. The remaining exercises shall then be completed with one less article in the ring.

SECTION 20. SEEK BACK. In the Seek Back the handler will stand with his dog sitting at heel and, on order from the judge, will signal or command his dog to walk at heel, and then on specific order or signal from the judge will execute such portions of the Heel Free exercise as the judge may order. On order from the judge to "Drop It," the handler will surreptitiously drop a plain glove as he is walking with his dog at heel. The glove must be approved by the judge and must not be white nor conspicuous in color. After the handler and dog have proceeded about 30 feet following the dropping of the glove, on orders from the judge, the handler will About Turn and Halt with his dog. Then on order from the judge the handler gives the command to seek and retrieve the glove and may simultaneously point in the direction of the trail, but may not use any other signal or give his scent to the dog. The handler must remain in the place from which the dog is sent, but may turn to face in the direction of the glove as the dog is going away. The dog may retrieve either by sight or scent and must find the glove and complete the exercise as in the Retrieve.

SECTION 21. SIGNAL EXERCISE. In the Signal Exercise the heeling is done in the same manner as in the Heel Free exercise except that throughout the entire exercise the handler uses signals only and must not speak to his dog at any time. On order or signal from the judge "Forward," the handler signals his dog to walk at heel and then, on specific order or signal from the judge in each case, the handler and the dog execute a "Left turn," "Right turn," "About turn," "Halt," "Slow," "Normal," "Fast." These orders may be given in any sequence and may be repeated if necessary. Then on order or signal from the judge, and while the dog is walking at heel, the handler signals his dog to Stand in the heel position near the end of the ring, and on further order or signal from the judge "Leave your dog," the handler signals his dog to stay, goes to the far end of the ring, and turns to face his dog. Then on separate and specific signals from the judge in each case, the handler will give the signals to Drop, to Sit, and to Come and to Finish as in the Recall. During the heeling part of this exercise the handler may not give any signal except where a command or signal is permitted in the Heeling exercises.

SECTION 22. DIRECTED JUMPING. In the Directed Jumping exercise the jumps shall be placed midway the ring at right angles to the sides of the ring and 20 feet apart, the Bar Jump on one side, the High Jump on the other. The handler from a position on the center line of the ring and about 20 feet from the line of the jumps, stands with his dog sitting at heel. On order or signal "Send your dog" from the judge, he commands and/or signals his dog to go forward at a smart pace to the other end of the ring to an equal distance beyond the jumps and in the approximate center where the handler gives the command to Sit, whereupon the dog must stop and sit with its attention on the handler, but need not sit squarely. The judge will then designate which jump is to be taken first by the dog, whereupon the handler commands and/or signals his dog to return to him over the designated jump, the dog sitting in front of the handler and finishing as in the Recall. The handler may also give a command to jump at each jump, but the word used must be different from the word used to call the dog. While the dog is in mid-air the handler may turn so as to be facing the dog as it returns. The judge will say "Exercise finished" after the dog has returned to the heel position. When the dog is again in heel position for the second part of the exercise, the judge will ask "Are you ready?" before giving the order or signal "Send your dog" for the second jump. The same procedure is to be followed for the dog taking the opposite jump. It is optional with the judge which jump is taken first but both jumps must be taken to complete the exercise and the judge must not designate the jump until the dog is at the far end of the ring. The height of the jumps shall be the same as required in the Open classes. The High Jump shall be the same as that used in the Open classes, and the Bar Jump shall consist of a bar between 2 and 2½ inches in diameter, painted black and white in alternate sections of about 3 inches each. The bar shall be supported by two 4 foot upright posts about 5 feet apart. The bar shall be adjustable for each 2 inches of height from 12 inches to 36 inches and shall be so constructed that it can be knocked off without disturbing the uprights. The dog shall clear the jumps without touching them.

SECTION 23. GROUP EXAMINATION. All the competing dogs take this exercise together, except that if there are 12 or more dogs, they shall be judged in groups of not less than 6 nor more than 15 dogs. The handlers and dogs that are in the ring shall line up in catalog order, side by side down the center of the ring with the dogs at heel position. Each handler shall place his armband, weighted if necessary, behind his dog. On order from the judge to "Stand your dogs," all the handlers will stand or pose their dogs, and on order from the judge "Leave your dogs," all the handlers will give the command and/or signal to Stay, and walk forward to the side of the ring, then about turn and face their dogs. The judge will approach each dog in turn from the front and examine it, going over the dog with his hands as in dog show judging. After all dogs have been examined, and after the handlers have been away from their dogs for at least three minutes, the judge will order the handlers "Back to your dogs," and the handlers will walk around behind their dogs to the heel position, after which the judge will say, "Exercise finished." Each dog must remain standing at its position in the line from the time its handler leaves it until the end of the exercise, and must show no shyness nor resentment.

SECTION 24. TRACKING. The tracking test must be performed with the dog on leash, the length of the track to be not less than 440 yards nor more than 500 yards, the scent to be not less than one half hour nor more than two hours old and that of a stranger who will leave a leather glove or wallet to be found by the dog at the end of the track. The tracklayer will follow the track which has been staked out with flags a day or more earlier, collecting all the flags on the way with the exception of one flag at the start of the track and one flag not more than 30 yards from the start of the track to indicate the direction of the track; then deposit the article at the end of the track, and leave the course, proceeding straight ahead at least 50 feet. The tracklayer must wear leather soled shoes. The length of the leash used in tracking must be 30 to 60 feet and the dog must work at this length and shall not be guided by the handler. A dog may, at the handler's option, be given one, and only one, second chance to take the scent between the two flags, provided it has not passed the second flag.

Chapter 3 Standards for Obedience Trial Judging

SECTION 1. STANDARDIZED JUDGING. Standardized judging is of paramount importance. Judges are not permitted to inject their own variations into the exercises, but must see that each handler and dog executes the various exercises exactly as described in the Standard. A handler who is familiar with the Standard should be able to enter the ring under any judge without having to inquire as to how the particular judge wishes to have any exercise performed, and without being confronted with some unexpected requirement.

SECTION 2. RING AND EQUIPMENT. The Superintendent and the officials of the club holding the obedience trial are responsible for providing rings and equipment which meet the requirements of these Regulations. However, the judge also must check the ring and equipment provided for his use, and must report to The American Kennel Club after the trial any deficiencies that are not promptly corrected at his request.

SECTION 3. STEWARDS. The judge is in sole charge of his ring until his assignment is completed. Stewards are provided to assist him, but they may act only on the judge's instructions. Stewards shall not give information or instructions to owners and handlers except as specifically instructed by the judge, and then only in such a manner that it is clear that the instructions are those of the judge.

SECTION 4. TRAINING AND DISCIPLINING OF DOGS. The judge shall not permit any handler to train his dog nor to practice any exercise in the ring either before or after he is judged. A handler who disciplines his dog in the ring must be severely penalized by deducting points from the total score, and any abuse of a dog in the ring must be immediately reported by the judge to the Bench Show or Obedience Trial Committee for action under Chapter 1, Section 42.

SECTION 5. CATALOG ORDER. Dogs should be judged in catalog order to the extent that it is practicable to do so without holding up the judging in any ring for a dog that is entered in more than one class at the show or trial. Judges are not required to wait for dogs and it is the responsibility of each contestant to be ready with his dog at ringside when required, without waiting to be called.

SECTION 6. JUDGE'S BOOK AND SCORE SHEETS. The judge must enter the scores and sub-total score of each dog in the official judge's book immediately after the dog and handler leave the ring and before judging the next dog. Scores for the Group exercises and total scores must be entered in the official judge's book immediately after each group of dogs has been judged. No score may be changed except to correct an arithmetical error or if a score has been entered in the wrong column. All final scores must be entered in the judge's book before prizes are awarded. No person other than the judge may make any entry in the judge's book. Judges may use separate score sheets for their own purposes, but shall not give out such sheets or any other written scores, nor permit anyone else to distribute score sheets or cards prepared by the judge. Carbon copies of the sheets in the official judge's book shall be made available through the Superintendent or Show or Trial Secretary for examination by owners and handlers immediately after the prizes have been awarded in each class.

SECTION 7. ANNOUNCEMENT OF SCORES. The judge shall not disclose any score or partial score to contestants or spectators until he has completed the judging of the entire class or, in case of a split class, until he has completed the judging of his division; nor shall he permit anyone else to do so. After all the scores for the class are recorded the judge shall call for all available dogs that have won prizes or qualifying scores to be brought into the ring. Before awarding the prizes, the judge shall inform the spectators as to the maximum number of points for a perfect score, and shall then announce the score of each prize winner, and announce to the handler the score of each dog that has won a qualifying score.

SECTION 8. EXPLANATIONS AND ERRORS. The judge is not required to explain his scoring, and should not enter into any discussion with any contestant who appears to be dissatisfied. Any interested person who thinks that there may have been an arithmetical error or an error in identifying a dog may report the facts to one of the stewards or to the Superintendent or Show or Trial Secretary so that the matter may be checked.

SECTION 9. REJUDGING. If a dog has failed in a particular part of an exercise, it shall not ordinarily be rejudged nor given a second chance; but if in the judge's opinion the dog's performance was prejudiced by peculiar and unusual conditions, the judge may at his own discretion rejudge the dog on the entire exercise.

SECTION 10. TIES. In case of a tie the dogs shall be tested again by having them perform at the same time all or some part of one or more of the regular exercises in that class. In the Utility class the dogs shall perform at the same time all or some part of the Signal exercise. The original scores shall not be changed.

SECTION 11. JUDGE'S DIRECTIONS. The judge's orders and signals should be given to the handlers in a clear and understandable manner, but in such a way that the work of the dog is not disturbed. At the end of each exercise the judge shall say "Exercise finished." Each contestant must be worked and judged separately except for the Long Sit, Long Down, and Group Examination exercises, and in working off a tie.

SECTION 12. A AND B CLASSES. The same methods and standards must be used for judging and scoring the A and the B classes.

SECTION 13. NO ADDED REQUIREMENTS. No judge shall require any dog or handler to do anything, nor penalize a dog or handler for failing to do anything, that is not required by these Regulations and Standards.

SECTION 14. ADDITIONAL COMMANDS OR SIGNALS. If a handler gives an additional command or signal not permitted by the Standard, either simultaneously with or following a permitted command or signal, the dog shall be scored as though it had failed completely to perform that particular part of the exercise.

SECTION 15. STANDARD OF PERFECTION. The judge must carry a mental picture of the theoretically perfect performance in each exercise and score each dog against this visualized standard which shall combine the utmost in willingness, enjoyment and precision on the part of the dog, and gentleness and smoothness in handling. Lack of willingness or enjoyment on the part of the dog, and roughness in handling, must be penalized, as well as lack of precision. There shall be no penalty of less than ½ point or multiple of ½ point.

SECTION 16. QUALIFYING PERFORMANCE. A judge's certification in his judge's book of a qualifying score for any particular dog constitutes his certification to The American Kennel Club that the dog on this particular occasion has performed all of the required exercises at least in accordance with the minimum standards and that its performance on this occasion would justify the awarding of the obedience title associated with the particular class. A qualifying score must never be awarded to a dog whose performance has not met the minimum requirements, nor to a dog that shows fear or resentment, or that relieves itself at any time in an indoor ring, or that stops to relieve itself while performing any exercise indoors or outdoors, nor to a dog whose handler disciplines or abuses it in the ring.

SECTION 17. ORDERS AND MINIMUM PENALTIES. The orders for the exercises and the standards for judging are set forth in the following sections. The lists of faults are not intended to be complete but minimum penalties are specified for most of the more common and serious faults. There is no maximum limit on penalties. A dog which makes none of the errors listed may still fail to qualify or may be scored zero for other reasons.

SECTION 18. HEEL ON LEASH. The orders for this exercise are "Forward," "Halt," "Right turn," "Left turn," "About turn," "Slow," "Normal," "Fast," "Figure eight." These orders may be given in any order and may be repeated, if necessary, to conform to the size and shape of the ring, but the judge shall attempt to standardize the heeling pattern for all dogs in any class. The principal feature of this exercise is the ability of the dog to work with its handler as a team. A dog that is unmanageable must be scored zero. Where a handler continually tugs on the leash or adapts his pace to that of the dog, the judge must score such a dog less than 50% of the available points. Minor deductions shall be made for such things as poor sits, occasionally guiding the dog with the leash, heeling wide, and other imperfections in heeling. In judging this exercise the judge shall follow the handler at a discreet distance so that he may observe any signals or commands given by the handler to the dog.

SECTION 19. STAND FOR EXAMINATION. The orders for this exercise are "Stand your dog for examination," "Back to your dog." The principal features of this exercise are to stand in position before and during examination and to show no shyness nor resentment. A dog that sits before or during the examination or growls or snaps must be marked zero. A dog that moves away from the place where it was left before or during the examination, or a dog that shows any shyness or resentment, must receive less than 50% of the available points. Depending on the circumstances in each case, minor or substantial deductions must be made for any dog that moves its feet, or sits, or moves away at any time after the examination is completed. The examination shall consist of touching the dog's head, body and hind quarters only. The scoring of this exercise will not ordinarily start until the handler has given the command and/or signal to Stay, except for such things as rough treatment of the dog by its handler or active resistance by the dog to its handler's attempts to make it stand, which shall be penalized.

SECTION 20. HEEL FREE. The order and scoring for this exercise shall be the same as for Heel on Leash except that the Figure Eight is omitted in the Heel Free exercise in the Novice classes.

SECTION 21. RECALL. The orders for this exercise are "Leave your dog," "Call your dog," "Finish." The principal features of this exercise are the prompt response to the handler's command or signal to Come, and the Stay from the time the handler leaves the dog until he calls it. A dog that does not come on the first command or signal must be scored zero. A dog that does not stay without extra command or signal, or that moves from the place where it was left, from the time the handler leaves until it is called, or that does not come close enough so that the handler could readily touch it without moving his feet or having to stretch forward, must receive less than 50% of the points. Substantial deductions shall be made for a slow response to the Come, depending on the specific circumstances in each case; for extra commands or signals to Stay if given before the handler leaves the dog; for a dog that stands or lies down; extra commands or signals to Finish; and for failure to Sit or Finish. Minor deductions shall be made for poor Sits or Finishes.

SECTION 22. LONG SIT AND LONG DOWN. The orders for these exercises are "Sit your dogs" or "Down your dogs," "Leave your dogs," "Back to your dogs." The principal features of these exercises are to stay, and to remain in the sitting or down position, whichever is required by the particular exercise. A dog that at any time during the exercise moves a substantial distance away from the place where it was left, or that goes over to any other dog, must be marked zero. A dog that stays on the spot where it was left but that fails to remain in the sitting or down position, whichever is required by the particular exercise, for at least three quarters of the specified time in the Novice classes, or until the handler has returned to the heel position in the Open classes, and a dog that barks or whines, must receive less than 50% of

289

the available points. A substantial deduction shall be made for any dog that moves even a minor distance away from the place where it was left. In the Novice classes, a substantial deduction shall be made for any dog that fails to remain in the sitting or down position, whichever is required by the particular exercise, until the handler has returned to the heel position. Depending on the circumstances in each case, minor deductions shall be made in both Novice and Open classes for minor movements from the position in the ring, and for sitting after the handler is in the heel position but before the judge has said "Exercise finished" in the Down exercises. The dogs shall not be required to sit at the end of the Down exercises. If a dog gets up and starts to roam or follows its handler, the judge shall promptly instruct the handler or one of the stewards to take the dog out of the ring or to keep it away from the other dogs. The judge should not attempt to judge the dogs or handlers on the manner in which they are made to Sit or Down. The scoring will generally start after the judge has given the order "Leave your dogs," except for such general things as rough treatment of a dog by its handler or active resistance by a dog to its handler's attempts to make it Sit or Down. During these exercises the judge shall stand in such a position that all of the dogs are in his line of vision, and where he can see all the handlers in the ring without having to turn around.

SECTION 23. DROP ON RECALL. The orders for this exercise are the same as for the Recall, except that the dog is required to drop when coming in at a point designated by the judge, and except that an additional order or signal to "Call your dog" is given by the judge after the Drop. The Drop is a principal feature of this exercise, in addition to the prompt responses and the Stays as described under Recall above. A dog that does not stop and drop on a single command or signal must be scored zero. Minor or substantial deductions shall be made for a slow drop, depending on whether the dog is just short of perfection in this respect, or very slow in dropping, or somewhere between the two extremes. All other deductions as listed under Recall above shall also apply. The judge may designate the point at which the dog is to drop by some marker placed in advance which will be clear to the handler but not obvious to the dog, or he may give the handler a signal for the Drop, but such signal must be given in such a way as not to attract the dog's attention.

SECTION 24. RETRIEVE ON THE FLAT. The orders for this exercise are "Throw it," "Send your dog," "Take it," "Finish." The principal feature of this exercise is to retrieve promptly. Any dog that fails to go out on the first command or a dog that fails to retrieve, shall be marked zero. A dog that goes to retrieve before the command or signal is given, or that does not return with the dumbbell sufficiently close so that the handler can readily take it without stretching forward or moving his feet, must receive less than 50% of the points. Depending on the specific circumstances in each case, minor or substantial deductions shall be made for slowness, mouthing or playing with the dumbbell, dropping the dumbbell, slowness in releasing the dumbbell to the handler, failure to sit in front or to Finish. Minor deductions shall be made for poor Sits or Finishes.

SECTION 25. RETRIEVE OVER HIGH JUMP. The orders for this exercise are "Throw it," "Send your dog," "Take it," and "Finish." The principal features of this exercise are that the dog must go out over the jump, pick up the dumbbell and promptly return with it over the jump. The minimum penalties shall be the same as for the Retrieve on the Flat, and in addition a dog that fails both going and returning to go over the High Jump, must be marked zero. A dog that retrieves properly but goes over the High Jump in only one direction, must receive less than 50% of the available points. Substantial deductions must be made for a dog that climbs the jump or uses the top of the jump for aid in going over, in contrast to a dog that merely touches the jump. Minor deductions shall be made for touching the jump in going over. The judge must make certain that the jump is set at the required height for each dog, and shall measure the dog if there is any question as to the required height. He shall not seek nor base his decision on the handler's advice.

SECTION 26. BROAD JUMP. The orders for this exercise are "Leave your dog," "Send your dog," and "Finish." Any dog that refuses the jump on the first command or signal or walks over any part of the jump must be marked zero. A dog that jumps at the first command but fails to clear the full distance, or a dog that fails to wait for the handler's command or signal before jumping, shall be penalized a lesser amount depending on the circumstances in each case, and there shall be minor penalties for failure to return smartly to the handler and to sit straight in front of the handler or finish correctly. It is the judge's responsibility to see that the distance jumped is that required by the Standard for the particular dog.

SECTION 27. SCENT DISCRIMINATION. The orders for each of these three exercises are "Send your dog," "Take it," and "Finish." The principal features of these exercises are the selection of the handler's article from among the other articles by scent alone, and the prompt carrying of the right article to the handler after its selection. The minimum penalties shall be the same as for the Retrieve on the Flat and in addition a dog that fails to go out to the group of articles, or that retrieves a wrong article, or that fails to bring the right article to the handler, must be marked zero for the particular exercise. Substantial deductions shall be made for a dog that picks up a wrong article, even though it puts it down again immediately, and for roughness by the handler in imparting his scent to the dog. Minor or substantial deductions, depending on the circumstances in each case, shall be made for a dog that is slow or inattentive, or that does not work continuously. There shall be no penalty for a dog that takes a reasonably long time examining the articles, provided it is working smartly and continuously. The judge shall select one article from each of the three sets and shall make written notes of the numbers of the three articles selected. The handler may give the judge his articles in any order he may choose, but must give up each article immediately when ordered by the judge. The judge must see to it that the handler imparts his scent to the article only with his hands and that, between the time the handler picks up each article and the time he gives it to the judge, the article is held continuously in the handler's hands which must remain in plain sight. The judge must also make sure that the articles on the floor are properly separated before sending the dog out, so that there may be no confusion of scent between articles.

SECTION 28. SEEK BACK. The orders for this exercise are "Forward," followed by such other orders as the judge may give from the Heel Free exercise, "Drop it," "About Turn and Halt," "Send your dog," "Take it," and "Finish." The principal features of this exercise are that the dog, on command, must seek and retrieve the glove promptly. The minimum penalties shall be the same as for the Heel Free and Retrieve on the Flat, and in addition a dog that does not seek continuously while away from its handler, or that does not find the glove, must be marked zero.

SECTION 29. SIGNAL EXERCISE. The orders for this exercise are "Forward," "Left turn," "Right turn," "About turn," "Halt," "Slow," "Normal," "Fast," "Stand," and "Leave your dog," and in addition the judge must give the handler signals to signal his dog to Drop, to Sit, to Come, to Finish. The judge may use signals instead of any of the verbal orders, but must advise the handler of his intention in advance. The orders or signals for those parts of the exercise which are done with the dog at heel may be given in any order and may be repeated if necessary, except that the order to "Stand" shall be given when the dog and handler are walking. The signals given the handler after he has left his dog in the Stand position shall be given in the order specified above. The principal features of this exercise are the heeling of the dog and the Come on signal as described for the Heel and Recall exercises, and the prompt response to the other signals given to the dog at a distance. A dog that fails, on a single signal from the handler, to stand or remain standing where left, or to drop, or to sit and stay, or to come, or that receives a command or audible signal from the handler to do any of these parts of the exercise, shall receive less than 50% of the available points. All of the deductions listed under the Heel and Recall exercises shall also apply to this exercise.

SECTION 30. DIRECTED JUMPING. The judge's first order is "Send your dog," then after the dog has stopped at the far end of the ring, the judge shall designate which jump is to be taken by the dog, whereupon the handler commands and/or signals his dog to return to him over the designated jump, the dog sitting in front of the handler and finishing as in the Recall. After the dog returns to the handler the order "Finish" is given followed by "Exercise finished." The same sequence is then followed for the other jump. The principal features of this exercise are that the dog goes away from the handler in the direction indicated, stops when commanded, jumps as directed, and returns as in the Recall. A dog that does not leave its handler, does not go substantially in the right direction, does not stop on command, or does not jump as directed, in either half of this exercise, must receive less than 50% of the available points. Substantial deductions shall be made for anticipating the Stop or Sit, and for failure to Sit. Substantial or minor deductions shall be made for faults such as slowness in going out or returning, slow response to

292

direction, and poor sits or finishes, depending on the specific circumstances in each case.

SECTION 31. GROUP EXAMINATION. The orders for this exercise are "Stand your dogs," "Leave your dogs," and "Back to your dogs." The principal features of this exercise are that the dog must stand and stay, and must show no shyness nor resentment. A dog that moves a substantial distance away from the place where it was left, or that goes over to any other dog, or that sits or lies down before the handler returns to the heel position, or that growls or snaps at any time, must be marked zero. A dog that remains standing but that moves a minor distance away from the place where it was left, or a dog that shows any shyness or resentment, must receive less than 50% of the available points. Depending on the specific circumstances in each case, minor or substantial deductions must be made for any dog that moves its feet at any time during the exercise, or sits or lies down after the handler returns to the heel position. The judge should not attempt to judge the dogs or handlers on the manner in which the dogs are made to stand. The scoring will generally start after the judge has given the order "Leave your dogs," except for such general things as rough treatment of a dog by its handler, or active resistance by a dog to its handler's attempts to make it stand. The dogs are not required to sit at the end of this exercise. The examination shall be conducted as in dog show judging, the judge going over each dog carefully with his hands. The judge must make a written record of any deductions immediately after examining each dog, subject to further deduction of points for subsequent faults. The judge must instruct one or more stewards to watch the other dogs while he conducts the individual examinations, and to call any faults to his attention.

SECTION 32. TRACKING TESTS. For obvious reasons these tests cannot be held at a dog show, and a person, though he may be qualified to judge Obedience Trials, is not necessarily capable of judging a tracking test. He must be familiar with the various conditions that may exist when a dog is required to do nose work. Scent conditions, weather, lay of the land, etc., must be taken into consideration, and a thorough knowledge of this work is necessary. One or both of the judges must personally lay out or walk over each track after it has been laid out, a day or so before the test, so as to be completely familiar with the location of the track, landmarks and ground conditions. At least two of the major turns shall be well out in the open country where there are no fences or other boundaries to guide the dog. No major part of any track shall follow along any fence or boundary within 10 yards of such boundary. The track shall include at least two right angle turns and should include more than two such turns so that the dog may be observed working in different wind directions. No conflicting tracks shall be laid. No track shall cross any body of water. The judges shall make sure that the track is no less than 440 yards and that the tracklayer is a stranger to the dog in each case. There is no time limit provided the dog is working, but a dog that is off the track and is clearly not working should not be given any minimum time just on the chance that it might pick up the track again. The handler may not be given any assistance by the judges or anyone else. In case of unforeseen circumstances, the judges may in rare cases, at their own discretion, give a handler and his dog a second chance on a new track. A dog that is working too fast for the conditions may be restrained gently by the handler at the end of the leash, but any leading or guiding of the dog constitutes grounds for calling the handler off and marking the dog "Failed." A track for each dog entered shall be plotted on the ground not less than one day before the test, the track being marked by flags which the tracklayer can follow readily on the day of the test. A chart of each track shall be made up in duplicate, showing the approximate length in yards of each leg, and major landmarks and boundaries, if any. Two of these charts shall be marked, one by each of the judges, at the time the dog is tracking, so as to show the approximate course followed by the dog. Upon completion of the meet, the judges shall forward the marked copies of each chart to The American Kennel Club. The judges shall sign each chart forwarded, and show on each whether the dog "Passed" or "Failed," the time the tracklayer started, the time the dog started and finished tracking, a brief description of ground, wind and weather conditions, the wind direction, and a note of any steep hills or valleys. If a dog is not trailing it shall not be marked "Passed" even though it may have found the article.

Obedience Trial Sample Judging Chart

NOVICE CLASS ..... (Indicate A or B)

HEEL ON LEASH—35 points (Forward, Halt, Right Turn, Left Turn, About Turn, Slow, Normal, Fast, Figure Eight). STAND FOR EXAMINATION—30 points (Stand Your Dog for Examination, Back to Your Dog, Exercise Finished). HEEL FREE—45 points (Forward, Halt, Right Turn, Left Turn, About Turn, Slow, Normal, Fast). RECALL—30 points (Leave Your Dog, Call Your Dog, Finish). LONG SIT—30 points (one minute) (Sit Your Dogs, Leave Your Dogs, Back to Your Dogs, Exercise Finished). LONG DOWN—30 points (three minutes) (Down Your Dogs, Leave Your Dogs, Back to Your Dogs, Exercise Finished).

MAXIMUM TOTAL SCORE—200 POINTS

Dog Number							
Heel on Leash (35 Points)							
Stand for Examination (30 Points)							
Heel Free (45 Points)							
Recall (30 Points)							
Sub Totals							
Long Sit (30 Points)							
Long Down (30 Points)							
Total Score							
Less Penalty for Misbehavior							
Final Score							

NOVICE CLASS . . . . WINNERS	First Prize	Second Prize	Third Prize	Fourth Prize
	. . . . . .	. . . . . .	. . . . . .	. . . . . .

Obedience Trial Sample Judging Chart

OPEN CLASS ..... (Indicate A or B)

HEEL FREE—40 points (Forward, Halt, Right Turn, Left Turn, About Turn, Slow, Normal, Fast, Figure Eight). DROP ON RECALL—30 points (Leave Your Dog, Call Your Dog, Drop Your Dog, Call Your Dog, Finish). RETRIEVE ON FLAT—25 points (Throw It, Send Your Dog, Take It, Finish). RETRIEVE OVER HIGH JUMP—35 points (Throw It, Send Your Dog, Take It, Finish). BROAD JUMP—20 points (Leave Your Dog, Send Him, Finish). LONG SIT—25 points (three minutes) (Sit Your Dogs, Leave Your Dogs, Back to Your Dogs, Exercise Finished). LONG DOWN—25 points (five minutes) (Down Your Dogs, Leave Your Dogs, Back to Your Dogs, Exercise Finished).

MAXIMUM TOTAL SCORE—200 POINTS

Dog Number							
Heel Free (40 Points)							
Drop on Recall (30 Points)							
Retrieve on Flat (25 Points)							
Retrieve Over High Jump (35 Points)							
Broad Jump (20 Points)							
Sub Totals							
Long Sit (25 Points)							
Long Down (25 Points)							
Total Score							
Less Penalty for Misbehavior							
Final Score							

	First Prize	Second Prize	Third Prize	Fourth Prize
OPEN CLASS .... WINNERS	......	......	......	......

Obedience Trial Sample Judging Chart

UTILITY CLASS

SCENT DISCRIMINATION, ARTICLE 1—20 points (Send Your Dog, Take It, Finish). SCENT DISCRIMINATION, ARTICLE 2—20 points (Send Your Dog, Take It, Finish). SCENT DISCRIMINATION, ARTICLE 3—20 points (Send Your Dog, Take It, Finish). SEEK BACK—30 points (Forward, Drop It, Halt, Send Your Dog, Take It, Finish). SIGNAL EXERCISE—35 points (Forward, Left Turn, Right Turn, About Turn, Halt, Slow, Normal, Fast, Stand, Leave Your Dog). DIRECTED JUMPING—40 points (Send Him, Call Your Dog, Finish). GROUP EXAMINATION—35 points (Stand Your Dogs, Leave Your Dogs, Back to Your Dogs).

MAXIMUM TOTAL SCORE—200 POINTS

Dog Number								
Scent Discrimination, Article 1 (20 Points)								
Scent Discrimination, Article 2 (20 Points)								
Scent Discrimination, Article 3 (20 Points)								
Seek Back (30 Points)								
Signal Exercise (35 Points)								
Directed Jumping (40 Points)								
Sub Totals								
Group Examination (35 Points)								
Total Score								
Less Penalty for Misbehavior								
Final Score								

UTILITY CLASS WINNERS	First Prize	Second Prize	Third Prize	Fourth Prize
	. . . . . .	. . . . . .	. . . . . .	. . . . . .

BAR JUMP. The construction of the Bar Jump should be similar to that of the High Jump illustrated. In place of boards, a round wooden horizontal bar should be used which should be adjustable for raising or lowering according to the height of the dog.

DETAILS OF BROAD JUMP

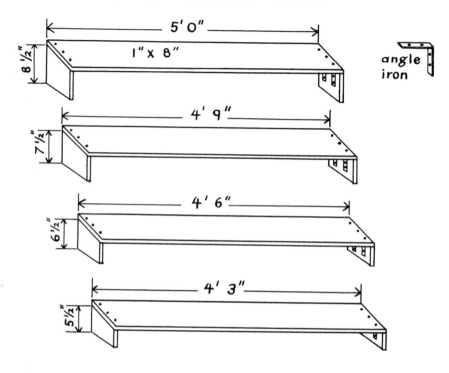

angle iron

5' 0"
8 ½"
1" x 8"

4' 9"
7 ½"

4' 6"
6 ½"

4' 3"
5 ½"

END VIEW OF
FOUR HURDLES

Highest end hurdle to be removed for small dogs

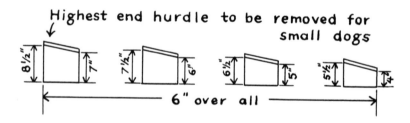

8½" 7" 7½" 6" 6½" 5" 5½" 4"

6" over all

This jump is made of four separate
hurdles spaced so as to make jump
6 feet overall. The four *sections*
built to telescope for convenience
should be painted a flat white

DETAILS OF HIGH AND BAR JUMP

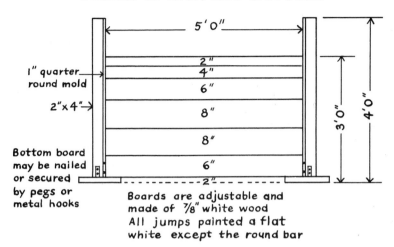

1" quarter round mold

2"x 4"

Bottom board may be nailed or secured by pegs or metal hooks

5' 0"

2"
4"
6"
8"
8"
6"
2"

3' 0"

4' 0"

Boards are adjustable and made of ⅞" white wood
All jumps painted a flat white except the round bar

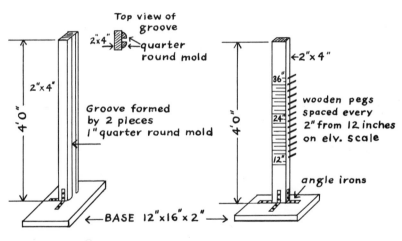

Top view of groove

2"x 4" — quarter round mold

Groove formed by 2 pieces 1" quarter round mold

2"x 4"

4' 0"

36"
24"
12"

2"x 4"

wooden pegs spaced every 2" from 12 inches on elv. scale

angle irons

4' 0"

← BASE 12"x16"x 2" →

2" round bar 6" long–Painted black and white